Second Edition

Basics *of*
Qualitative
Research

To *ANSELM*
December 1916–September 1996

Scholar and Humanist

who touched the minds and lives of
all who came into contact with him

———————

Second Edition

Basics *of* Qualitative Research

Techniques
and Procedures
for Developing
Grounded Theory

Anselm Strauss
Juliet Corbin

SAGE Publications
International Educational and Professional Publisher
Thousand Oaks London New Delhi

For information:

SAGE Publications, Inc.
2455 Teller Road
Thousand Oaks, California 91320
E-mail: order@sagepub.com

SAGE Publications Ltd.
6 Bonhill Street
London EC2A 4PU
United Kingdom

SAGE Publications India Pvt. Ltd.
M-32 Market
Greater Kailash I
New Delhi 110 048 India

Printed in the United States of America

Library of Congress Cataloging-in-Publication Data

Strauss, Anselm L.
    Basics of qualitative research: Techniques and procedures for developing grounded theory / by Anselm Strauss, Juliet Corbin. — 2nd ed.
        p.   cm.
    Includes bibliographical references and index.
    ISBN 0-8039-5939-7 (acid-free paper)
    ISBN 0-8039-5940-0 (pbk.: acid-free paper)
    1. Socal sciences—Statistical methods.   2. Grounded theory.
I. Corbin, Juliet M., 1942-   . II. Title.
    HA29.S823   1998
    300'.7'2—ddc21   98-25369

This book is printed on acid-free paper.

03   10   9   8   7   6   5

Acquiring Editor:	Peter Labella
Editorial Assistant:	Renée Piernot
Production Editor:	Astrid Virding
Editorial Assistant:	Patricia Zeman
Designer/Typesetter:	Janelle LeMaster
Cover Designer:	Candice Harman

Contents

If the artist does not perfect a new vision in his process of doing, he acts mechanically and repeats some old model fixed like a blueprint in his mind.

—John Dewey, Art as Experience, 1934, p. 50

Preface

The writing of this second edition has brought me (Corbin) both joy and sorrow. Joy, in that reader response to the first book was so positive that we were asked to write a second edition. Sorrow, in that my co-author, Anselm Strauss, died before the book was finished. This edition is a tribute to Anselm's lifelong devotion to research and his desire to share his methods with others. For Anselm, the analytic procedures and techniques contained in this book were more than just a way of doing research. They were a way of life.

Although Anselm died before this book was completed, its writing truly has been a collaborative effort. Over the years, we developed an intense and cooperative style of interaction based on differential but overlapping experiences and knowledge. Each author wrote drafts of chapters, and each reworked and added to the other's writing. In the end, the writing became so intertwined that it is difficult to tell who wrote what, nor would we want our readers to make that unnecessary and misleading distinction.

In this second edition, we have clarified on and amplified the original publication. We have added new chapters, rewritten others, and revised the remainder. However, most of the original material was retained in one form or another. For example, some of the questions addressed in the original Chapter 1 are now handled in Chapter 17, titled "Student Questions and Answers to These." Some readers might miss the format of the original book; others will welcome the change. We believe that the new edition is an improvement over the previous one and that our extended explanations will enhance understanding.

We also are very excited that although the first draft of this second edition was too long, the parts that were removed from the book will not be lost to our students but rather will be made available to them on the Internet.

We hope that the revised book will continue to influence readers. We welcome all feedback, both positive and negative. The stimulating and very useful theses and papers that students and researchers send us to read verify that we are achieving our goal—helping others to carry out their dreams.

As stated in the first edition, this book is addressed to researchers in various disciplines (social science and professional) who are interested in building theory through qualitative data analysis. However exciting their experiences may be while gathering data, there comes a time when the data must be analyzed. Researchers often are perplexed by this necessary task. They not only are dismayed by the mountains of data confronting them but also often are troubled by the following questions. How can I make sense out of all of this material? How can I have a theoretical interpretation while still grounding it in the empirical reality reflected by my materials? How can I make sure that my data and interpretations are valid and reliable? How do I break through the inevitable biases, prejudices, and stereotypical perspectives that I bring with me to the analytic situation? How do I pull all of my analyses together to create a concise theoretical formulation of the area under study?

The purpose of this book is to answer these and other questions related to doing qualitative analysis. It is written in a clear and straightforward manner. Its intent is to provide the basic knowledge and procedures needed by persons who are about to embark on their first qualitative research projects and who want to build theory at the substantive level. We also believe that we have something to offer in the way of techniques and procedures to those researchers who want to do qualitative analysis but who do not wish to build theory. Building theory is not the only goal of doing research. High-level description and what we call *conceptual ordering* also are important to the generation of knowledge and can make a valuable contribution to a discipline. Advanced researchers and those who want further examples and discussion about ways of doing and teaching qualitative analysis no doubt will find this book useful. We also suggest that advanced researchers read *Qualitative Analysis* (Strauss, 1987).

Like any set of practices, the level of analytic accomplishment will vary among users. On the other hand, the practices learned in this book might prove useful in ways originally unanticipated by either writers or readers. As remarked earlier by Strauss (1987) when referring to the analytic process, "Like any set of skills, the learning process involves hard work, persistence, and some, not always entirely, pleasurable experiences" (p. xiii). To be sure, it often is immensely exciting and enjoyable as well. Furthermore, these experiences are requisite to discovering how to use and adapt any method. The use and adaptation inevitably will be a "composite of situational contexts, and for [developing] a personal [research] biography, astuteness [in doing the work], plus theoretical and social sensitivity. On top of this, to complete any research project, one needs a bit of luck and courage" (p. xiii).

This is *not* a recipe book to be applied to research in a step-by-step fashion. Our intent is to provide a set of useful tools for analyzing qualitative data. We hope that through our examples, readers will come to realize the fluid and flexible approach to data analysis provided by this method. For those readers who would like to see how other researchers have used and modified these techniques to fit with their own research purposes and personalities, we suggest reading the book *Grounded Theory in Practice* (Strauss & Corbin, 1997).

OVERVIEW OF THE CONTENTS

This book is broken down into three major parts. Part I consists of Chapters 1 to 4. These chapters set the stage for what will follow. They provide the background information necessary to embark on this form of grounded theory research project. Chapter 1 introduces the methodology and explains something about the characteristics of users of this method. Chapter 2 explores the differences among description, conceptual ordering, and theorizing. Chapter 3 discusses the relationship between qualitative and quantitative forms of analysis. Chapter 4 presents some of the practical matters to be considered before beginning a research project; it includes sections on choosing a problem and stating the question, the need to maintain a balance between objectivity and creativity, and uses of the literature.

Part II presents the specific analytic techniques and procedures designed to be used in developing theory. This part consists of Chapters 5 to 14. Chapter 5 provides an overview of the analytic process. Chapter 6 outlines the basic operations of analysis, that is, making comparisons and asking questions. Chapter 7 introduces the idea of analytic tools, a palate of devices theorists can use to facilitate analysis and enhance discovery. Chapter 8 presents techniques for open coding, Chapter 9 discusses axial coding procedures, and Chapter 10 discusses selective coding procedures. Chapter 11 explains how we view process and describes how to code for it. Chapter 12 discusses the conditional/consequential matrix, an analytic tool for bridging the gap between micro and macro conditions/consequences. Chapter 13 reviews the sampling procedure. Chapter 14 describes how we use diagrams and memos in building theory.

Part III, which consists of Chapters 15 to 17, explores matters of concern to all researchers, that is, what comes after completing the analysis. Chapter 15 explains how to write theses and monographs and give talks about research. Chapter 16 provides criteria that can be used to evaluate the research process described in this book. Chapter 17 serves as a sort of summary of this book; it is presented in the form of questions most often asked by our students along with the answers to those questions.

On the Internet are more detailed examples of the various types of coding as well as a chapter on teaching and other suggestions for applying theory to practice, research, and teaching.

A CONCLUDING NOTE

After writing the original draft for the first edition of *Basics of Qualitative Research* and using it to teach graduate students and other researchers, it was pointed out to us that the book had value beyond the use for which it was designed, that is, teaching students how to do qualitative analysis. Persons concerned with finding new ways of thinking about phenomena also might find the book worthwhile. Professionals serving on review boards of journals or funding agencies often encounter qualitative research proposals or proposals for combination qualitative-quantitative studies. They might want to skim the entire book, to gain some understanding of the terminology that is used and the basic procedures we outline, and then focus on Chapter 16. Scholars interested in theory development, both inductive and deductive, might find certain parts of the book useful for supplementing their own methods. We are open to all of these possible uses. We only hope that those who use this book learn as much from reading it as we did from writing it.

As a final note, readers will find that throughout the book, a special system of using italics, bold print, and underlining is used. *Italics* are used for emphasis and when we want to call attention to special concepts and terminology such as *categories, properties,* and *dimensions.* **Bold print** is used when we want to emphasize a point or mark a phrase to remember. The **boldface** phrases and sentences should be useful for scanning the text because they are quickly visible. <u>Underlining is used when we especially want to emphasize a particular point.</u> Although readers might find some inconsistencies in our use of these features, please bear with us; generally, the system should work well.

I (Corbin) express my gratitude to the students and colleagues who reviewed and critiqued the drafts of this revised edition. Their encouragement and input were especially valuable after Anselm's death, when I was left with the dual tasks of grieving and completing this manuscript. I especially thank Lisa Jean More and Heiner Legewie for their comments on an early draft. I also thank Leigh Star, whose opinions I value highly, for her excellent critique and suggestions. I am grateful to Gerhard Reimann for his careful attention to detail; his comments were very important to the development of this manuscript. I especially thank my dear friend Julie Cherry, who as a novice to the methodology not only did a thorough reading and critiquing of the manuscript but also stood by to console me during the most difficult months after Anselm's death. I am forever grateful to our colleague and friend Setsuo Mizuno, whose support, encouragement, and feedback, especially during those early months after Anselm's death, kept me going. I also thank my husband Richard, who acted as my computer consultant always there to solve the mechanical problems, and Fran Strauss, who has waited patiently. Last but not least, I thank Peter Labella, the editor, who believed in me and gave me time to heal.

Part I

Basic Considerations

Discovery has been the aim of science since the dawn of the Renaissance. But how those discoveries are made has varied with the nature of the materials being studied and the times. Galileo, in the following quotation, describes his method for making discoveries:

> The method is this: direct the telescope upon the sun as if you were going to observe that body. Having focused and steadied it, expose a flat white sheet of paper about a foot from the concave lens; upon this will fall a circular image of the sun's disk, with all the spots that are on it arranged and disposed with exactly the same symmetry as in the sun. The more the paper is moved away from the tube, the larger this image will become and the better the spots will be depicted. (quoted in Drake, 1957, p. 115)

Although we are studying objects more worldly than, yet often just as elusive as, the sun and the stars, we, like Galileo, believe that we have an effective method for discovery. But before discussing the actual analytic procedures that comprise our method, we ask our readers to examine closely the chapters in this part. These first four chapters are our way of providing readers with a "telescope" with which to see. They detail some of the basic knowledge necessary for understanding this method and lay the foundation for the heavy analytic chapters to follow.

1 Introduction

Methodology: A way of thinking about and studying social reality

Methods: A set of procedures and techniques for gathering and analyzing data

Coding: The analytic processes through which data are fractured, conceptualized, and integrated to form theory

Like Coleridge and Kubla Khan, I woke up one morning dreaming, but since it wasn't a complete dream but only the germ, I thought out the words and here they are. (one of the authors)

Increasingly, we are the recipients of appreciative letters and remarks that assure us of the usefulness of our way of doing qualitative analysis. To receive these expressions is gratifying, but on further reflection it reminds us of an unforgettable story about two 19th- and early 20th-century painters, Cezanne and Monet. Legend has it that Cezanne said about Monet: "He is only an eye—but *what* an eye!" Our own interpretation of this story is that both painters offered their contemporaries and next generations of painters not merely their respective armamentariums of effective techniques but also ways of looking at the world. Monet's way was different from Cezanne's way, but it was indeed just as insightful and valuable.

Our version of qualitative analysis offers a cluster of very useful procedures—essentially guidelines, suggested techniques, *but* not commandments. We also offer a *methodology*, a way of thinking about and studying social reality. True, only God can tell infallible humans the "real" nature of reality. As American pragmatists such as Dewey (1922) and Mead (1934) taught, and as the natural scientists demonstrate daily, human grasp of reality never can be that of God's, but hopefully research moves us increasingly toward a greater understanding of how the world works. In the social science realm, readers might think of this methodology as one way of gathering knowledge about the social world. We recognize that there are many other approaches to qualitative analysis and that each is valuable. Saying this, we do not mean to underplay the value of the methodology or procedures outlined in this book. The main point we want to make is as follows. **In this book, we are offering more than a set of procedures. We are offering a way of thinking about and of viewing the world that can enrich the research of those who choose to use this methodology.** In this chapter, we describe the characteristics of a grounded theorist and define what we mean by qualitative research and grounded theory, setting the stage, so to speak, for the rest of this book.

CHARACTERISTICS OF QUALITATIVE RESEARCHERS

This section has two parts. On the one hand, it explores how users of this method have been shaped through the process. On the other hand, it describes the characteristics often associated with qualitative researchers. Yet, the two are so intertwined that it becomes difficult to separate one from the other.

Researchers and students who have used this methodology often tell us that they have been changed beneficially through the experience. The process involves both the learning, as in seminars, and the actual carrying out of the research. What are some of these changes?

Researchers tell us that they really enjoy working with data, not simply with ideas in the abstract. They relish the interplay between themselves and the data. (They may or may not love data collection principally for its own sake, but researchers enjoy what can be done with those data once they are collected.) They are unafraid to draw on their own experiences when analyzing materials because they realize that these become the foundations for making comparisons and discovering properties and dimensions. Most researchers are secure enough with their findings that they regard their theories, even after publication, as qualifiable, modifiable, and open in part to negotiation. (We say open in part to negotiation because having grounded their theories in data and validated their statements of relationship between concepts during the research process, they are confident about the conclusions they have reached.)

In the work itself, researchers using this methodology tend to be flexible, a tendency enhanced in training seminars and team research projects where members are open to helpful criticism, can enjoy the play of ideas, and can appreciate the give and take that occurs in group discussions. How this learning is carried into future interactions can be seen in the following statement made by one of our ex-students, Leigh Star:

> I'm part of a writing group which has met about once a month for a couple of years. We pass around work in process and criticize it, sometimes help with analytic rough spots. Recently, an old member of the group returned and described to us her unsuccessful attempt to start a similar group in another location. Participants in her group had followed the same procedures we had, in form, but had gotten very harsh with each other's work and focused more on competitive speeches than on genuine collaboration. Our group tried to analyze why we'd been successful and realized that it had a lot to do with the fact that four of us had been through the grounded theory [seminar]. It isn't just that we shared an analytic focus, though, because in fact we're very different. The striking thing was that we had learned to work together in a collaborative and supportive way. (quoted in Strauss, 1987, pp. 303-304)

Flexibility and openness are linked with having learned to sustain a fair amount of ambiguity. It is not that the researchers do not want to pin down things analytically, but the urge to avoid uncertainty and to get quick closure on one's research is tempered with the realization that phenomena are complex and their meanings are not easily fathomed or just taken for granted. This is quite like the processes they study. Research itself is a process about which our ex-students are likely to be self-reflective. In doing their research, they enjoy the flow of ideas, but not merely the substantive ones, as they have learned that theoretical ideas have their own precious value. Yet, they are skeptical of established theories, however enticing they might seem, unless these eventually are grounded through active interplay with the data. The self as an instrument in the data collection and analysis process is a point underscored by Rew, Bechtel, and Sapp (1993), who listed the following as attributes needed by qualitative researchers: appropriateness, authenticity, credibility, intuitiveness, receptivity, reciprocity, and sensitivity.

There are two additional important points that we want to add here. The first is that most researchers using this methodology probably hope that their work has direct or potential relevance for both nonacademic and academic audiences. This is because the methodology enjoins taking with great seriousness the words and actions of the people studied. Or, as expressed poignantly by B. Fisher, "I saw that being an intellectual didn't have to be removed from people's lives, that it could be connected directly to where people were in the world and what they thought about it" (quoted in Maines, 1991, p. 8).

Our second point is that almost inevitably, researchers trained in this method become completely absorbed in the work, which "while not always in the foreground [of our lives] is never gone" (Adele Clarke, personal communication, June 1993). That sense of absorption in, and devotion to, the work process as such provides a sense of enhanced integrity was reflected in a description written by another student, K. Jurich. We quote her at length because her words eloquently emphasize so many of our assertions about the characteristics of grounded theorists and their work. Trained in public health, she worked for 3 or 4 years on a Sioux Indian reservation, becoming engrossed with the following question: What are these people's basic conceptions of health, for their conceptions of health are so different from ours? Returning to the research seminar after several months in the field, she made the following comments soon afterward in a memo to the instructor:

> These concerns and fears [that the class would misread her non-Western, cross-cultural data] were systematically and carefully dispelled over the course of the two-hour session. I watched very carefully and listened intently to what people said and how they worked their ideas and images through the data, carefully questioning me when more information was needed and not jumping to conclusions in advance of important additions. The students seemed to search carefully for the richness in the data, picking out critical issues and playing them off against one another for more meaning, noting several possible interpretations to many situations. Not only was there inherent integrity of the data emergent, it was also maintained. I was quite overjoyed at the degree of fit between what these analysts were identifying and what I had heard and seen while doing the work. Both the integrity and precision aspects of these sessions were spared by and sustained by the pedagogical style, which is to say (for it cannot be separated from) the formulations of interactionists' epistemology and the conceptual analytic framework of grounded theory. (quoted in Strauss, 1987, pp. 302-303)

The requisite skills for becoming a grounded theorist are presented in the following box. Researchers need not necessarily begin their first studies with these characteristics fully developed. However, by carefully making use of the procedures outlined in this text and feeling their way through the process, it is possible for researchers to develop the characteristics summarized in this box.

CHARACTERISTICS OF A GROUNDED THEORIST

1. The ability to step back and critically analyze situations
2. The ability to recognize the tendency toward bias
3. The ability to think abstractly
4. The ability to be flexible and open to helpful criticism
5. Sensitivity to the words and actions of respondents
6. A sense of absorption and devotion to the work process

METHODOLOGY AND METHODS

These characteristics, however, never will develop if researchers focus solely on the procedures presented in this text and apply them in a **rote** manner. We want readers to understand what we say, to understand why they are using certain activities, and to do so flexibly and creatively. We want them to acquire a way of thinking about data and the world in which they live. We want them to question, to be able to easily move from what they see and hear and to raise that to the level of the abstract, and then to turn around again and move back to the data level. We want them to learn to think comparatively and in terms of properties and dimensions so that they can easily see what is the same and what is different. The importance of this methodology is that it provides a sense of **vision, where it is that the analyst wants to go with the research.** The techniques and procedures (method), on the other hand, furnish the **means** for bringing that vision into reality. Why provide a set of procedures and techniques if these are not meant to be approached in a step-by-step fashion? Just as painters need both techniques and vision to bring their novel images to life on canvas, analysts need techniques to help them see beyond the ordinary and to arrive at new understandings of social life. There are other research methods available to persons who want to publish competent description. However, if researchers' purpose is to create new and theoretically expressed understandings, then theory-building methods such as the one provided in this text are indicated. The value of the methodology we are about to describe lies in its ability not only to generate theory but also to ground that theory in data. Both theory and data analysis involve interpretation, but at least it is interpretation based on systematically carried out inquiry.

Qualitative methods of data gathering and analysis have gained popularity over the years. We present only one way of doing analysis, and it would be unrealistic to assume or even suggest that researchers will use every procedure described in this book. Although these authors' aim is to build theory, we realize that theory building is not the goal of every research project, nor should it be (Peshkin, 1993). Knowledge and understandings take many forms. We know that readers will treat the material in this book as items on a smorgasbord table from which they can choose, reject, and ignore according to their own "tastes"—and rightly so. Some will use our techniques to generate theory, others for the purpose of doing very useful description or conceptual ordering (classifying and elaborating). Some will blend our techniques with their own. Not only are our analytic techniques and procedures used in different ways by different researchers, but the methodology has found its way to researchers outside of sociology. As a methodology and a set of methods, our approach to research is used by persons in practitioner fields such as education, nursing, business, and social work, as well as by psychologists, architects, communications specialists, and social anthropologists. Because persons within and outside the field of sociology often are curious about how the methodology originated, it seems appropriate to briefly trace its history.

HISTORICAL BACKGROUND

The methodology, commonly known as grounded theory, originally was developed by two sociologists, Barney Glaser and Anselm Strauss (Glaser, 1978, 1992; Glaser & Strauss, 1967; Strauss, 1987). Although each man came from a different philosophical and research tradition, their respective contributions were equally important.

Strauss received his advanced degrees from the University of Chicago, which had a long history and strong tradition in qualitative research. During his studies, he was strongly influenced by interactionist and pragmatist writings. His thinking was inspired by men such as Park (1967), Thomas (1966), Dewey (1922), Meade (1934), Hughes (1971), and Blumer (1969). What this background contributed to his part in the development of this method were (a) the need to get out into the field to discover what is really going on; (b) the relevance of theory, grounded in data, to the development of a discipline and as a basis for social action; (c) the complexity and variability of phenomena and of human action; (d) the belief that persons are actors who take an active role in responding to problematic situations; (e) the realization that persons act on the basis of meaning; (f) the understanding that meaning is defined and redefined through interaction; (g) a sensitivity to the evolving and unfolding nature of events (process); and (h) an awareness of the interrelationships among conditions (structure), action (process), and consequences. Glaser came from a very different sociological tradition but with some shared features that no doubt permitted the two men to work closely together. He received his graduate education at Columbia University, and his thinking about research was influenced by Paul Lazarsfeld, known as an innovator of quantitative methods. Later, while doing qualitative analysis, Glaser especially saw the need for making comparisons between data to identify, develop, and relate concepts. The Columbia tradition also emphasized empirical research in conjunction with the development of theory. Both the Chicago and Columbia traditions were directed at producing research that could be of use to professional and lay audiences. For this reason, much of the grounded theory writing that emerged from the Glaser-Strauss collaboration, including the original monographs about dying (Glaser & Strauss, 1965, 1968), were addressed to both lay audiences and disciplinary colleagues.

The first edition of *Basics of Qualitative Research* (Strauss & Corbin, 1990) arose out of a different collaboration—that between Strauss and Corbin. Although many of the essentials of the original grounded theory method were maintained, there were some differences. These were not intentional but rather simply evolved as Strauss continued to conduct, teach, and discuss research methodology with colleagues and students. The methodology and procedures described in this book reflect Strauss's approach to doing research. The first edition of the text was written to provide a set of techniques and guidelines for beginning researchers, both in the United States and abroad, who were struggling with method and the question of how to analyze data. It was meant to be a supplement to the other texts on grounded theory, especially *Qualitative Analysis* (Strauss, 1987), and not to take their place. Before defining what these authors mean by a "grounded theory," we review a few basic facts about qualitative research in general.

QUALITATIVE RESEARCH

By the term "qualitative research," we mean any type of research that produces findings not arrived at by statistical procedures or other means of quantification. It can refer to research about persons' lives, lived experiences, behaviors, emotions, and feelings as well as about organizational functioning, social movements, cultural phenomena, and interactions between nations. Some of the data may be quantified as with census or background information about the persons or objects studied, but the bulk of the analysis is interpretative. Actually, the term "qualitative research" is confusing because it can mean different things to different people. Some researchers gather data by means of interviews and observations, techniques normally associated with qualitative methods. However, they code the data in a manner that allows them to be statistically analyzed. They are, in effect, quantifying qualitative data. In speaking about qualitative analysis, we are referring not to the quantifying of qualitative data but rather to a nonmathematical process of interpretation, carried out for the purpose of discovering concepts and relationships in raw data and then organizing these into a theoretical explanatory scheme. Data might consist of interviews and observations but also might include documents, films or videotapes, and even data that have been quantified for other purposes such as census data.

There are many valid reasons for doing qualitative research. One reason is preferences and/or experience of the researchers. Some persons are more oriented and temperamentally suited to doing this type of work. Some researchers come from disciplines (e.g., anthropology) or have philosophical orientations (e.g., phenomenology) that traditionally make use of qualitative methods. Another reason, and probably a more valid one, for choosing qualitative methods is the nature of the research problem. For example, research that attempts to understand the meaning or nature of experience of persons with problems such as chronic illness, addiction, divorce, and the act of "coming out" lends itself to getting out into the field and finding out what people are doing and thinking. Qualitative methods can be used to explore substantive areas about which little is known or about which much is known to gain novel understandings (Stern, 1980). In addition, qualitative methods can be used to obtain the intricate details about phenomena such as feelings, thought processes, and emotions that are difficult to extract or learn about through more conventional research methods.

Basically, there are three major components of qualitative research. First, there are the *data*, which can come from various sources such as interviews, observations, documents, records, and films. Second, there are the *procedures* that researchers can use to interpret and organize the data. These usually consist of *conceptualizing and reducing* data, *elaborating* categories in terms of their properties and dimensions, and *relating* through a series of prepositional statements. Conceptualizing, reducing, elaborating, and relating often are referred to as *coding* (see, e.g., Becker, 1970; Charmaz, 1983, 1995; Lofland, 1971; Miles & Huberman, 1994). Other procedures are part of the analytic process. These include nonstatistical *sampling* (see Schatzman & Strauss, 1973), the *writing of memos,* and diagramming. *Written and verbal* reports make up the third component. These may be presented as articles in scientific journals, in talks (e.g., conferences), or in books.

There are many different types or approaches to doing qualitative research (see, e.g., Cassell & Symon, 1994; Denzin & Lincoln, 1994; Gilgun, Daly, & Handel, 1992; Gubrium & Sankar, 1994; Morse & Field, 1995; Westbrook, 1994). In this book, we present just one approach, that which often is referred to as *grounded theory,* and only one version of that approach, that taught by Strauss.

GROUNDED THEORY

What do Strauss and Corbin mean when they use the term "grounded theory"? They mean theory that was derived from data, systematically gathered and analyzed through the research process. In this method, data collection, analysis, and eventual theory stand in close relationship to one another. A researcher does not begin a project with a preconceived theory in mind (unless his or her purpose is to elaborate and extend existing theory). Rather, the researcher begins with an area of study and allows the theory to emerge from the data. Theory derived from data is more likely to resemble the "reality" than is theory derived by putting together a series of concepts based on experience or solely through speculation (how one thinks things ought to work). Grounded theories, because they are drawn from data, are likely to offer insight, enhance understanding, and provide a meaningful guide to action.

Although grounding concepts in data is the main feature of this method, creativity of researchers also is an essential ingredient (Sandelowski, 1995a). In fact, Patton (1990), a qualitative evaluation researcher, made the comment, "Qualitative evaluation inquiry draws on both critical and creative thinking—both the science and the art of analysis" (p. 434). He went on to provide a list of behaviors that he found useful for promoting creative thinking, something every analyst should keep in mind. These include (a) being open to multiple possibilities; (b) generating a list of options; (c) exploring various possibilities before choosing any one; (d) making use of multiple avenues of expression such as art, music, and metaphors to stimulate thinking; (e) using nonlinear forms of thinking such as going back and forth and circumventing around a subject to get a fresh perspective; (f) diverging from one's usual ways of thinking and working, again to get a fresh perspective; (g) trusting the process and not holding back; (h) not taking shortcuts but rather putting energy and effort into the work; and (i) having fun while doing it (pp. 434-435). Analysis is the interplay between researchers and data. It is both science and art. It is science in the sense of maintaining a certain degree of rigor and by grounding analysis in data. Creativity manifests itself in the ability of researchers to aptly name categories, ask stimulating questions, make comparisons, and extract an innovative, integrated, realistic scheme from masses of unorganized raw data. It is a balance between science and creativity that we strive for in doing research. There are procedures to help provide some standardization and rigor to the process. However, these procedures were designed not to be followed dogmatically but rather to be used creatively and flexibly by researchers as they deem appropriate. The purposes of coding procedures are summarized in the following box:

CODING PROCEDURES

1. Build rather than test theory.
2. Provide researchers with analytic tools for handling masses of raw data.
3. Help analysts to consider alternative meanings of phenomena.
4. Be systematic and creative simultaneously.
5. Identify, develop, and relate the concepts that are the building blocks of theory.

As a final statement, we strongly recommend that after reading the later chapters on coding (rapidly at first if you wish), serious researchers return to **study each chapter in greater detail.** These chapters explain the basic analytic procedures and provide explanations of their logic. Each set of procedures **must be thoroughly understood before proceeding on to the next analytic step.** We want students to understand the purpose of procedures rather than to memorize the techniques themselves. We also advocate that students practice the techniques on their own and in groups so that they become comfortable with them before applying them to their own data. We realize that analyzing one's own raw data might seem daunting when compared to reading the examples given in the book. However, we believe that **if analysts understand the logic lying behind our procedures and if they develop self-confidence in their use, then they should be able to apply them flexibly and creatively to their own materials.** Doing research is hard work. It also is fun and exciting. In fact, nothing can compare to the joy that comes from discovery.

SUMMARY

This book offers both a methodology and a set of methods for building theory. The book was conceived as a text for beginning analysts, who often need guidance and structure during the early phases of their research careers. We emphasize strongly that techniques and procedures, however necessary, are only a means to an end. They are not meant to be used rigidly in a step-by-step fashion. Rather, their intent is to provide researchers with a set of tools that enable them to approach analysis with confidence and to enhance the creativity that is innate, but often undeveloped, in all of us. It is the vision of new understandings and the building of useful grounded theory that is the driving force behind this methodology.

2 Description, Conceptual Ordering, and Theorizing

Description: The use of words to convey a mental image of an event, a piece of scenery, a scene, an experience, an emotion, or a sensation; the account related from the perspective of the person doing the depicting

Conceptual ordering: Organizing (and sometimes rating) of data according to a selective and specified set of properties and their dimensions

Theory: A set of well-developed concepts related through statements of relationship, which together constitute an integrated framework that can be used to explain or predict phenomena

In Chapter 1, we introduced the notion of *theory* without defining what we mean by it. Because beginning researchers often have difficulty understanding the differences between *description* and *theory*, and because theory often is defined differently by various researchers, we take the opportunity in this chapter to present our views on these terms. Also, we touch on another mode of managing data that often is used in qualitative studies, a mode we call *conceptual ordering*. (For a similar but also somewhat different perspective on these same matters, see Wolcott, 1994.)

DESCRIPTION

People commonly describe objects, people, scenes, events, actions, emotions, moods, and aspirations in their everyday conversations. Not only do ordinary people describe, but so too, as part of their daily work, do journalists and novelists as well as technical, travel, and other nonfiction writers. Description draws on ordinary vocabulary to convey ideas about things, people, and places. For example, one might hear, "The streets were quiet early in the morning, and I looked forward to hitting the open road in my new convertible automobile." Description also makes use of similes and metaphors (Lakoff & Johnson, 1981) when ordinary words fail to make the point or more colorful word pictures are needed. Take the following sentence: "He walked with the dignity of an Arab prince, talked like a con man, and sat like a coiled snake."

Persons literally could not communicate without the ability to describe, however inept or primitive their language might be. Description is needed to convey what was (or is) going on, what the setting looks like, what the people involved are doing, and so on. The use of descriptive language can make ordinary events seem extraordinary. Great writers know this and strive to make their details so vivid that readers actually can see, taste, smell, and hear what is going on in a scene. Even mere mortals, those of us with less practiced writing skills, use description to relate to others our adventures, thoughts, and feelings as we encounter new, and sometimes routine, situations. Consider the following scene reported by a visitor to San Francisco:

> You should see the main street of Chinatown at five o'clock in the evening. It is fascinating! I could easily imagine myself in a city in China. The area is so densely populated; people are everywhere. Cars are trying to negotiate their way up and down the narrow streets, their horns constantly honking to move persons out of the

way. People are talking animatedly, mostly Chinese, and the streets are lined with colorful buildings, many replicating structural forms of the Orient.

There are many different kinds of shops with unusual produce and products. Everything smells and looks so different, I want to touch and taste it all. There are shops with all kinds of fish and strange looking mollusks. Some shops have succulent looking roasted ducks hanging upside down in the windows. There are shops with every kind of vegetable imaginable, many of which are new to me. There are jewelry stores, exotic tea shops, inviting restaurants, and merchants selling Chinese knickknacks and souvenirs. The most fascinating shops for me, however, are the ones that sell Chinese herbs. Bottles, jars, and baskets filled to the brim with objects that I can't identify. I am intoxicated by the strange smells and sights. Since names and prices are written in Chinese, all I can do is imagine, and these shops remain an exotic mystery to me. The people in Chinatown are fascinating too, such a mixture. There are young and old, Chinese and non-Chinese, the assimilated and those wearing more traditional Chinese clothing (mostly the elderly). Some women carry their children on their backs in a sort of sling made from what looks like a blanket, while others push a modern looking stroller. Other men and women have their hands loaded down with purchases as they rush along the streets, probably going home to make dinner. It was fun to watch the women and men bargain over the price of fish or vegetables, even if I couldn't understand the words they were actually saying. I bought a piece of jewelry but have never really mastered the art of negotiating, so [I] paid the asking price, which I suppose was foolish. It's just not a part of my culture to bargain over a price. I could spend days in Chinatown and still not absorb it all. What an experience! (K. C., personal communication, June 1993)

Description, such as the preceding one of Chinatown in San Francisco, might seem objective—just a report of what was seen by this person. Yet, even basic description involves purpose (otherwise why describe?) and audiences (who will see or hear the description?) and the selective eye of the viewer (Wolcott, 1994). For example, police reports are focused on criminal or investigative issues. They usually are relatively straightforward and meant to be read by superiors and other interested parties, whereas print journalists' accounts of an event, such as a riot or the uncovering of a spy ring, are likely to be written more colorfully. The latter also tend to reflect some personal or organizational stance and are meant to inform newspaper or magazine readers.

In short, the descriptive details chosen by a storyteller usually are consciously or unconsciously selective, based on what he or she saw or heard or thought to be important. Although description often is meant to convey believability and to portray images, it also is designed to persuade, convince, express, or arouse passions. Descriptive words can carry overt or covert moral judgments. This can be true not merely of sentences but also of entire books, as in exposés or in serious volumes that aim at reform. Even seemingly objective reports such as those of police or journalists might reflect deep prejudice and moral judgments without the individuals being aware of those attitudes and feelings. Aesthetic judgments also are conveyed through descriptions, for example, "The young soprano's voice was delicate and airy, although at the upper ranges she occasionally wobbled just the slightest but generally conveyed the spirit of the character; she has a great future in opera." The aesthetic and the moral sometimes are joined as in the language used by critics and audiences in rejecting Stravinsky's radically dissonant musical work, the *Sacre de Printemps*, and the first showings of Impressionist paintings, later to become the darlings of middle class museum goers and collectors.

It is important to understand that description is the basis for more abstract interpretations of data and theory development, although it might not necessarily have to. Description already embodies concepts, at least implicitly (e.g., types of shops and categories of people, as in the Chinatown description). Even at the highest levels of abstract science, there could be no scientific hypotheses and theoretical or laboratory activity without prior or accompanying descriptions. Yet, we must add that although description is important, there is a difference between making careful descriptions, say of the shifting of continents or of the many species of life that inhabit coral reefs, and making theory. In the latter, not only are events and happenings described, but the analysis is extended to involve interpretations as well (Wolcott, 1994) to explain why, when, where, what, and how events or happenings occur. These theoretical explanations often are validated through further data gathering (sometimes under varying conditions). So, although description clearly is *not* theory, it *is* basic to theorizing.

CONCEPTUAL ORDERING

Description also is basic to what we call *conceptual ordering*. This refers to the **organization of data** into discrete categories (and sometimes ratings) according to their **properties and dimensions and then using description to elucidate those categories.** Most social science analyses consist of some variety—and there are many types— of conceptual ordering. Researchers attempt to make sense out of their data by organizing them according to a classificatory scheme. In the process, items are identified from data and are defined according to their various general properties and dimensions. When presenting these dimensionalized interpretations, researchers are almost certain to present various amounts of descriptive material using a variety of communicative styles.

Already in everyday description, there is an ordering of descriptive objects. For example, in the earlier description above of Chinatown in San Francisco, the person relating the event organized the shops according to objects sold and rated them according to preference by stating that his favorite were the herbal shops. Another description might distinguish among classes of shoppers by rating persons according to the amount, type, and costs of items purchased. Another scheme might rate persons according to degrees of assimilation by using dimensions such as language spoken, clothing worn, and gestures used. The important idea to recall about dimensions and properties is that they enable researchers to differentiate items between and within classes and thus to show variation along a range. Recently, we read a description, a paragraph or so in length, comparing a vast and beautiful national park in Alaska to Yosemite in California. The author raised and answered the following question: Why is the Alaska park virtually unknown and little visited compared to the hugely popular California site? The question already rates each according to numbers of visitors and public visibility. So, why the difference between the parks? His answer was given in terms of the dimension of accessibility: The Alaskan locale is far from centers of population, whereas Yosemite can be visited by millions of tourists because it is only a few hours' drive from the highly populated Bay Area region of California.

Comparisons sometimes made among places, groups, and events are explicitly detailed, and these comparisons become the basis for an object, place, or group to be given specific ratings. Consider travel guides such as the famous Michelin tour guides that tell their readers how to find their way around France or some other country to the greatest advantage. These guides use a **rating system** (for restaurants, hotels, monuments, landscapes, cities, etc.) involving **several dimensions**—cost, service, delectability, comfort, accessibility, and aesthetic or historical value. They make suggestions that such and such a city should not be missed, whereas another city, although interesting, might be tucked away in difficult terrain.

For this mode of classifying and ordering, often not much descriptive detail is needed. After all, Michelin readers are familiar with low and high prices and with ease or difficulty of access. Yet, sometimes description is used to fill out the classifications. For instance, sometimes the Michelin tour guides will go into considerable detail about how terrific the food is in a particular restaurant or will point out that, given time constraints, some sights are not to be missed, whereas others are not so important.

The chief reason to discuss conceptual ordering here, however, is because this type of analysis is a **precursor to theorizing.** A well-developed theory is one in which the concepts are defined according to their specific properties and dimensions. What we call *conceptual ordering* also is the desired research end point of some investigators.

One example of conceptual ordering in the social sciences is in the form of some **ethnographic accounts.** Ethnographies differ in the extent of their conceptual ordering and degree of theorizing. In addition, there are variations in the amount of descriptive detail provided in papers and monographs, depending on the writer's perspective, perception of audience, and familiarity with the substantive area as well as the meaning inherent in the materials. However, for our purposes, the main point about many ethnographies is this: They reflect attempts to **depict** the perspectives and actions of the portrayed actors, **combined** with an explicit **ordering** of those into plausible nonfictional accounts. The final presentation is organized around well-developed and ordered themes, but the themes are not connected to form an integrated theoretical scheme.

A second type of conceptual ordering is to order data according to steps or stages that often are aptly described. However, often missing from such schemes are the larger theoretical schemes that explain what drives the central or organizing process, that is, the conditions that explain how, when, where, and why persons and organizations proceed from one step to another. Nor is variation built into the schemes. By not showing differences in rate, sequencing, and so on, implied (although perhaps not consciously) in such schemes is that every person and organization moves along the process in the same way and at the same rate—which, of course, is not an entirely accurate explanation of how persons or organizations operate. There always are outliers, deviations from the average or within a pattern, and one must account for these differences.

A third mode of conceptual ordering is one that relies mainly on organizing materials according to different types of actors or actions (including both persons and organizations). Headings and subheadings pertain to those types. The types usually represent well-ordered and developed concepts, but what is missing is a larger theoretical scheme that explains why these types (and not others) evolved and their relationship to the larger phenomenon under investigation. It often is implied that a listing of types constitutes a theory or theoretical explanation about events; however, a listing of types constitutes just another classification scheme unless it is placed within a larger unifying framwork.

THEORIZING

Developing *theory* is a complex activity. We use the term "theorizing" to denote this activity because developing theory is a process and often is a long one. Theorizing is work that entails not only **conceiving or intuiting** ideas (concepts) but also **formulating them** into a logical, systematic, and explanatory scheme. However illuminating or even "revolutionary" the idea of theorizing might be, development of an idea into theory still necessitates that an idea be explored

fully **and considered from many different angles or perspectives.**
It also is important to follow through with **implications** of a theory.
Those formulations and implications lead to "research activity" that
entails **making decisions** about and **acting** in relationship to many
questions throughout the research process—what, when, where,
how, who, and so on. Also, any hypotheses and propositions derived
from data must be continuously "checked out" **against incoming
data** and modified, extended, or deleted as necessary. At the heart of
theorizing lies the **interplay** of making inductions (deriving concepts, their properties, and dimensions from data) and deductions
(hypothesizing about the relationships between concepts, the relationships also are derived from data, but data that have been abstracted by the analyst from the raw data). (What should be an
obvious point, but is not, is that there are many useful ways of doing
all these things. Alas, researchers sometimes are very dogmatic about
the proper ways of collecting data, validating hypotheses, and so on.
Also, anytime that a researcher derives hypotheses from data, because it involves interpretation, we consider that to be a deductive
process.) In the end, it is hoped, the researcher has *systematically
developed* the products of analysis into a theory.

What do we mean by *theory*? For us, *theory denotes a set of well-
developed categories (e.g., themes, concepts) that are systematically interrelated through statements of relationship to form a theoretical framework
that explains some relevant social, psychological, educational, nursing, or
other phenomenon. The statements of relationship* explain who, what,
when, where, why, how, and with what consequences an event occurs.
Once concepts are related through statements of relationship into an
explanatory theoretical framework, the research findings move beyond conceptual ordering to theory. The latter is important because
"however much we can describe [a] social phenomenon with a theoretical concept, we cannot use it to explain or predict. To explain or
predict, we need a theoretical statement, a connection between two or
more concepts" (Hage, 1972, p. 34).

A theory usually is more than a set of findings; it offers an
explanation about phenomena. The phenomena that evolve from, and
are explained by, a theory are varied—work, management, leader-
ship, awareness, illness trajectories, safety, stigma, and so on. Generating theories about phenomena, rather than just generating a set of

findings, is important to the development of a field of knowledge. Further qualitative or quantitative studies about the same phenomenon can extend that knowledge. For example, one might study work in one organizational setting. Out of the study evolves the concept of "work flow." The phenomenon of work flow might be used to partially explain how work is carried out in the organization under investigation. However, the more general idea of work flow has possible application beyond this one organization. It might prove a valuable concept for explaining similar phenomena in other organizations. In doing further research, researchers will want to determine which parts of the concept apply to, or are valid in, these other organizations and what new concepts or hypotheses can be added to the original conceptualization.

In addition, theories have various properties, and when analyzed, they also can be located along certain dimensions and ordered conceptually. For example, some theories are more **abstract** than others, meaning that the concepts are highly conceptual ones. These are derived through processes of increasing conceptualization and reduction, always moving toward greater levels of abstraction (Hage, 1972). More abstract concepts have broad applicability, but they also are more removed from the raw data to which they pertain. Another dimension of theory is that of **scope**. Another term for scope is "generality." The broader the scope of a theory, the greater the number of disciplinary problems it can handle (Hage, 1972). Other terms normally associated with theory are "parsimony," "precision of prediction," and "accuracy of explanation" (Hage, 1972).

Another way of classifying theories is as follows. Some theories may be considered substantive, whereas others may be considered formal (Glaser & Strauss, 1967, pp. 32-34). A study of how gays handle disclosure/nondisclosure of their sexual identity to physicians is an example of a theory derived from one substantive area. It can be used to explain and manage problems of disclosure or nondisclosure by gays in a medical setting. More formal theories are less specific to a group and place, and as such, apply to a wider range of disciplinary concerns and problems. Formal theories usually are derived from studying phenomena under a variety of conditions such as researching disclosure/nondisclosure under conditions of people acting as spies, engaged in illicit relationships, carrying out illegal activities such as theft, belonging to secret societies and groups, or picking up someone in a bar or on a street corner.

There are other ways of thinking about and evaluating theories (Strauss, 1995), but we are not concerned with those here; the main point is that theories are constructed, vary in nature, and are not all the same. Regardless of how theories are **constructed,** each one is unique.

In social science, it is true that some theories are very systematically formulated but have very little anchoring in actual research. Some sociologists, such as Parsons (1937, 1951), wrote predominantly what we call "speculative theories." Our criticism of this type of theory is that although it is systematic and abstractly formulated, it is not empirically grounded in research (Blumer, 1969; Glaser & Strauss, 1967). Granted, there are different conceptualizations about the nature and role of "theory" in social science (Daly, 1997) and many disagreements about how theorizing actually should be done or even whether it should be done at all (Hammersley, 1995). There are several other misconceptions about theory and theorizing in qualitative research that are touched on briefly here. One is that a theoretical framework such as feminism, structuralism, or interactionism is a theory. It is not; it is a stance, more of a philosophy than a well-developed and related set of explanatory concepts about how the world works. The value of these frameworks is that they can provide insight or a perspective on phenomena and also help to generate theoretical questions. On the other hand, they also can focus an individual on one perspective or set of ideas so that he or she is not able to see what else might be in the data. A second misconception is that simply applying a concept or theory to one's data constitutes theorizing. It does not; it is an assumed application of a concept or theory. Theorizing denotes building theory or extending and broadening one. A third misconception is that qualitative research never "validates" theory. Some qualitative studies do and some do not, but even those that do validate theory do not do so in the sense of testing as in quantitative research. Rather, it is a process of comparing concepts and their relationships against data during the research act to determine how well they stand up to such scrutiny. Properly done, the methodology explained in this text is an example of the latter. (For a very good discussion on how to develop new theory from old theory, see Strauss, 1970.)

SUMMARY

Before beginning the process of developing theory, a researcher must have some understanding of what constitutes theory. The first step toward understanding is to be able to differentiate among *description, conceptual ordering,* and *theorizing.* A second step is realizing that these forms of data analysis actually build on one another, with the theory incorporating aspects of both. In brief, *describing* is depicting, telling a story, sometimes a very graphic and detailed one, without stepping back to interpret events or explain why certain events occurred and not others. *Conceptual ordering* is classifying events and objects along various explicitly stated dimensions, without necessarily relating the classifications to each other to form an overarching explanatory scheme. *Theorizing* is the act of **constructing** (we emphasize this verb as well) from data an explanatory scheme that systematically integrates various concepts through statements of relationship. A theory does more than provide understanding or paint a vivid picture. It enables users to explain and predict events, thereby providing guides to action.

3 The Interplay Between Qualitative and Quantitative in Theorizing

Building on Chapter 2, one might think of theorizing as a process involving a continual flow of work. That thought leads logically to a comparable methodological position concerning relationships between qualitative and quantitative procedures designed to generate theory. Lest our readers be disappointed, we want to clarify that this is not a chapter **about how** to combine qualitative and quantitative data; we leave that to others with more experience in this process (see, e.g., Fielding & Fielding, 1984). Nor are we stating that all research calls for or should make use of a combination of both. Rather, this chapter is meant to present some "food for thought" and to offer an alternative way of thinking about the relationship between two seemingly incongruent research paradigms. Briefly, we maintain that the aim of theorizing is to develop useful theories. So, *any* technology, whether qualitative or quantitative, is only a means for accomplishing that aim. We do not believe in the primacy of either mode of doing research (see also Dzurec & Abraham, 1993; Porter, 1989; Power, 1996). An instrument is an instrument, not an end in itself. The issue is not primacy but rather when and how each mode might be useful to theorizing (McKeganney, 1995).

Unfortunately, as some of our readers know all too well from their own experiences, dogmatic positions often are taken in favor of either qualitative or quantitative research. (These positions pertain to both conceptual ordering and theorizing.) Extreme stances on this issue mirror each other. Many quantitative researchers are apt to dismiss qualitative studies completely as giving no valid findings—indeed, as being little better than journalistic accounts. They assert that qualitative researchers ignore representative sampling, with their findings based only on a single case or a few cases. (See different perspective on this argument in Kvale, 1994; Sandelowski, 1995b.) Equally obdurate are some qualitative researchers who firmly reject statistical and other quantitative methods as yielding shallow or completely misleading information. They believe that to understand cultural values and social behavior requires interviewing or intensive field observation, with these being the only methods of data collection sensitive enough to capture the nuances of human living.

However, there are intermediary positions. Combining methods may be done for supplementary, complementary, informational, developmental, and other reasons. (See, e.g., Greene, Caracelli, & Graham, 1989, for an excellent discussion on this topic. See also Cuevas, Dinero, & Feit, 1996.) Combining methods is not new. Two eminent founders of sociological survey methods, Lazersfeld and Wagner (1958), promulgated a long-enduring attitude for survey researchers, namely that exploratory interviews should precede the formulation and final development of questionnaire instruments. Only with this use of qualitative materials, basic to (although only supplementary to) statistical procedures and analyses, could questionnaires tap "reality." A parallel stance, but with a different emphasis, is taken by other qualitative researchers. Counting, measuring, and even statistical procedures can usefully supplement, extend, or test their ways of doing research (Murdaugh, 1987). Although some researchers make one mode primary and the other supplementary (see explanation by Morse, 1991), other researchers basically view the research paradigms as complementary. Each adds something essential to the ultimate findings, even to the final theory if that is the aim of the particular research project (Breitmayer, Ayers, & Knafl, 1993). Also with statistics, as with qualitative data collection and analysis, one never can be certain whether one has captured the essence of the situation (Gephart, 1988).

Even these intermediate positions represent a misleadingly simple view of the realities of actually carrying out research, especially when one begins to view theorizing **as comprising a complex flow of work.** In addition, researchers want to know more specifically when and how to use each mode.

Before addressing those issues, let us return to our basic point about research being a **"flow of work"** that evolves over the entire course of any investigative project. **Each of the types of work (e.g., data collection, analysis, interpretation) entails choices and decisions concerning the usefulness of various alternative procedures, whether these are qualitative or quantitative,** but also more specifically, when making choices, *which* qualitative and *which* quantitative ones would be most appropriate.

Think, as an exercise in imagination, of the many decisions involved in data collecting. Should we interview? What type or types of interview? How many interviews should we aim for, and on what grounds? Where will we go to find the interviewees? Given the difficulties encountered in a research situation, how will we have to alter our original notions of what to search for in our interviewing? Or, how might we have to change the initial sample population? On the other hand, one might ask, would it make more sense to use questionnaires to collect our data? Should these data be collected with thought given to the type of statistical procedures that can be performed including the analytic ones? If data-gathering instruments seem best or seem more feasible, then which instruments would be most appropriate to obtain the type of information we are seeking? Also, what are the validity and reliability of these measures? What about combinations of any and all of these methods, qualitative *or* quantitative? How will the various changes in conditions during the research process actually affect our data collecting—all the way from obtaining access to our respondents, to securing their cooperation, to obtaining truthful and maximally useful information. How do we keep the flow of data going? There is, to underscore the main point of this example, no end to the options, choices, and decisions that we face. To think otherwise, to impose as *the* standard criterion only one type of interview, to insist wholly or predominantly on field observation, or to adopt as proper only scaling measures enormously restricts our efforts. Such a decision discounts the complexities of the world out there and our ability to understand them.

True, different research projects are affected by different conditions. Some face considerable limitations on, say, the data collection techniques or on the populations available to researchers because of bureaucratic regulations, costs, shortages of time, or language barriers. Some aspects of a project might be done under particularly difficult conditions so that unexpected contingencies are more likely to affect the initial plans. Nevertheless, all research studies involve the major, and often overlapping, steps comprised of different types of work including data collection, analysis, some degree or type of verifying, and ultimately the presenting or publishing of results. At the risk of repetition, we emphasize that choices and decisions abound and are different for various aspects of the overall research process. It is nearly impossible to prepare ahead of time for every possible contingency that might arise during the research process in the biological and social sciences. In fact, in many ways, research may be conceived of as a circular process, one that involves a lot of going back and forth and around before finally reaching one's goal.

This being so, it follows that researchers can, and do, put together **combinations** of procedures. There is no one standard set of methods equally useful for every research step, and it is not always useful to join the same specific techniques for all steps of all research projects. So, unless researchers are extremely constrained by either external pressures or internal mandates, they are pragmatists, connecting various available techniques to obtain desired results (Creswell, 1994).

Contemporary studies of physical and biological scientists are unearthing how researchers put together useful pastiches of instruments and procedures as well as concepts, models, and particular theories drawn from their own and other disciplines. (This is shown in the research of Clarke, 1990; Fujimura, 1988; Star, 1989.) Also, there are several crossover disciplines in sociology (and probably in other disciplines) where there is back-and-forth interplay between qualitative and quantitative methods, for example, in "qualitative demography" and in those areas of social science that analyze the implications of computers for society (Star & Ruhleder, 1996). Researchers in the human and social sciences are operational pragmatists. The more flexibly scientists work or are allowed to work, the more creative their research is apt to be.

Implications of those points for the relationship of qualitative and quantitative procedures are straightforward. Unless unduly constrained, routinized, or ideologically blinded, useful research can be accomplished with various combinations of both qualitative and quantitative procedures. This is so for each and every phase of the research, whether researchers are collecting data, formulating hypotheses, seeking to verify them, or giving illustrations when writing publications.

Getting to the heart of the matter, our advice to readers concerning this matter is to think in terms of the **interplay between qualitative and quantitative methods.** Comforting but overly simple positions, such as "They supplement each other" and "They complement each other," will not provide sufficient guides in your work if you are aiming at building theory. True, some interview materials are capable of being supplemented by statistical analysis, and conversely, statistical data also are likely to be analyzed qualitatively in part. Yet, the more operational point is that data collection and analysis can be done in both modes, and in various combinations, during all phases of the research process.

Just as important is that there *can* be back-and-forth interplay between combinations of both types of procedures, with qualitative data affecting quantitative analyses and vice versa. Following is just one apt example of psychiatric ideologies held by personnel in mental hospitals (Strauss, Schatzman, Bucher, Ehrlich, & Sabshin, 1964). Basic data were obtained by three sociologists through field observations on a multitude of wards in two hospitals and through interviews held with physicians, nurses, and nurses' aides. In addition, a psychologist was hired to develop research instruments that would differentiate the physicians according to which of the three then predominant psychiatric ideologies they were most likely to use in their practices. In this study, the questionnaires were constructed after collecting about 6 months of field data, through observations and informal interviews, and after performing preliminary analyses of these data. Hence, the qualitative aspects of the research directly influenced both the questionnaire construction and the later associated statistical analysis.

Unfortunately, there was no flow back from the instrument analysis to the fieldwork. In fact, one field-worker (Leonard Schatzman) wryly remarked several years later that he had been reproached by one psychiatrist who had scored high on the psychotherapeutic scale but seemingly acted like a typical somatically oriented practitioner when giving shock therapy to an elderly patient. Queried about this, the psychiatrist chided the sociologist, saying, "You researchers are so dumb. You ask on your questionnaire about what we believe, but not [about] what we *do!*" The sociologist was taken aback, realizing only then that, indeed, the fieldwork was focused on action, whereas the questionnaire was designed to capture basic psychiatric beliefs. Alas, at the time, it did not occur to the sociologists to build further questions into the questionnaire that would highlight discrepancies between belief and action, nor did they think to explore differences for observed behavior between those idealistic positions and what they termed the actual "operational philosophies" demanded by the exigencies of daily life on the hospital wards. The research project certainly could have profited from thinking in terms of genuine interplay between quantitative and qualitative procedures—and perhaps even several exchanges between them.

Ideally speaking, and as outlined in many books on method, research is planned, designed, and fairly neatly "carried out." (Most research proposals assume this sequence as well.) But as any experienced researcher will tell you if pressed to think about the matter, research really is a rather "messy affair." This does not mean that the results are dubious or useless; rather, it means that research rarely proceeds completely as planned.

You may ask, what then makes a research situation different, if indeed it is, when theory, rather than findings or conceptual ordering, is the aim? In general the answer is that it is not different. It is only that some procedures, especially the analytic ones, are more extensive and elaborate. In terms of this book's discussions, analysis does not necessarily end with conceptual ordering, and thus with open and axial coding, but rather may go on to include integrative selective coding. The point of this discussion is that researchers must think of quantitative procedures as representing not the enemy but rather a potential ally to theory building when its use seems appropriate. Just when and how might quantitative procedures fit? The following is but one brief example.

A group of researchers might identify a cluster of conditions that seem to bear on a phenomenon, say a tendency toward juvenile delinquency. However, their qualitative data will not tell them the degree to which these conditions lead to delinquency, how they interact with each other, which conditions have a stronger relationship to the phenomenon than do others, and so on. By doing a quantitative study at this point, the researchers could use that information to build further hypotheses. These hypotheses could be examined and refined through more pointed theoretical sampling using qualitative procedures.

One point has been omitted in this discussion so far. This is that a researcher's own preference, familiarity, and ease with a research mode inevitably will influence choices. Although the purpose of the research and the nature of questions asked often will determine the mode, a researcher ultimately has to work with those modes with which he or she feels most comfortable. That is why, with large projects, it is good to work as a team with representatives from each style of research. Once queried by a qualitative researcher (Strauss) as to why one should learn statistical techniques for use in social research, a highly respected statistical theorist (Leo Goodman) answered by pointing out that once they were learned, the knowledge of these techniques sensitized you to new aspects of data and, indeed, toward collecting the data themselves. The same is true of our qualitative work. Each mode of research must be given its due recognition and valued for its unique contribution.

We want to make it clear that when we speak about combining methods, we are not talking specifically about triangulation in the traditional sense (Denzin, 1970), although we recognize this as a valuable research tool and advocate its use where and when appropriate. Rather, we want to make the point that to build dense, well-developed, integrated, and comprehensive theory, a researcher should make use of any or every method at his or her disposal, keeping in mind that a true **interplay of methods** is necessary. **Most important,** because our approach to theory building is one of **emergence,** we believe that unless the researcher is building on or continuing with his or her own previous studies, the researcher will not be able to enter into the project with a set of preestablished concepts or with a well-structured design. Rather, the design, like the concepts, must be allowed to **emerge** during the research process. As concepts and relationships emerge from data through qualitative analysis, the researcher can use that information to decide where and how to go about gathering additional data that will further evolution of the theory. The decisions made at any of these critical research junctures will be varied. Sometimes, it might be necessary to make use of quantitative measures; other times, qualitative data gathering and analysis might be more appropriate. We admit that this open approach to design can pose some problems when trying to obtain permission from human subjects committees or when writing proposals for grants. To satisfy the demands of others, a research project might have to be presented as a series of smaller investigations, each one building on the results of previous studies before being integrated into a whole that is theory. Whatever approach one takes, the driving force always should be the evolving theory. The methods represent the means to achieving that end.

SUMMARY

Qualitative and quantitative forms of research both have roles to play in theorizing. The issue is not whether to use one form or another but rather how these might work together to foster the development of theory. Although most researchers tend to use qualitative and quantitative methods in supplementary or complementary forms, what we are advocating is a true interplay between the two. The qualitative should direct the quantitative and the quantitative feedback into the qualitative in a circular, but at the same time evolving, process with each method contributing to the theory in ways that only each can. However, one must remember that because **emergence** is the foundation of our approach to theory building, a researcher cannot enter an investigation with a list of preconceived concepts, a guiding theoretical framework, or a well thought out design. Concepts and design must be allowed to emerge from the data. Once relevant concepts and hypotheses have emerged from and validated against data, the researcher might turn to quantitative measures and analysis if this will enhance the research process. Remember, the idea behind varying methods is to carry out the most parsimonious and advantageous means for arriving at theory. Such a task calls for sensitivity to the nuances in data, tolerance for ambiguity, flexibility in design, and a large dose of creativity.

4 Practical Considerations

DEFINITIONS OF TERMS

Research problem: The general or substantive area of focus for the research

Research question: The specific query to be addressed by this research that sets the parameters of the project and suggests the methods to be used for data gathering and analysis

Objectivity: The ability to achieve a certain degree of distance from the research materials and to represent them fairly; the ability to listen to the words of respondents and to give them a voice independent of that of the researcher

Sensitivity: The ability to respond to the subtle nuances of, and cues to, meanings in data

Technical literature: Reports of research studies and theoretical or philosophical papers characteristic of professional and disciplinary writing that can serve as background materials against which one compares findings from actual data

Nontechnical literature: Biographies, diaries, documents, manuscripts, records, reports, catalogs, and other materials that can be used as primary data, to supplement interviews and field observations, or to stimulate thinking about properties and dimensions of concepts emerging from data

Whereas Chapters 1, 2, and 3 prepared the way for what is to follow, this chapter is a transitional one, moving the discussion from a theoretical level to a more practical level. It combines Chapters 2, 3, and 4 from the first edition of the book to form a discussion on topics that are important to consider when getting started. The topics provide a foundation for later data collection and analysis. This chapter consists of three main sections: (a) choosing a problem and stating the research question, (b) maintaining a balance between objectivity and sensitivity, and (c) using the literature. Because this is a book about analysis and not about doing fieldwork, the latter subject is not discussed here. (Some texts that readers might refer to include Adler & Adler, 1987; Punch, 1986; Schatzman & Strauss, 1973; Stringer, 1996; Wolcott, 1995.)

CHOOSING A PROBLEM AND STATING THE RESEARCH QUESTION

One of the most difficult parts of doing research is deciding on a topic. The two major questions that seem most troublesome are the following. How do I find a researchable problem? How do I narrow it down sufficiently to make it workable? These questions might seem especially difficult if the researcher is a novice at doing qualitative research because at first glance, the process of making choices and commitments seems less well structured and more ambiguous than in quantitative inquiries. The purpose of this chapter is to clarify some of the basic principles that pertain to making those initial choices.

Sources of Research Problems

The **sources** of research problems in qualitative inquiries often are not much different from those in other forms of research. First, there are the **suggested or assigned research problems.** One way in which to arrive at a problem is to ask for suggestions from a professor doing research in an area of interest. Such an individual often will have ongoing research projects and will welcome having a graduate student do a small part of a project. This way of finding a problem tends to increase the possibility of getting involved in a doable and relevant research problem. This is because the more experienced researcher already knows what needs to be done in a particular substantive area. On the other hand, a choice arrived at in this manner might not be the most interesting to the student. It is important to remember that whatever problem is selected, the researcher will have to live with it for quite a while, so the final choice should be something that engages his or her interest.

A **variant** on the assigned or suggested source is to **follow up on a professional or collegial remark** that an inquiry into such and such would be useful and interesting. This often is a more palatable source of a research problem, especially if the researcher has some inclination toward that substantive area. For example, the interest of a woman who is athletic might be sparked by a remark such as "How do women who go to gyms feel about their bodies?" This broad and open statement can lead to all sorts of questions including the following. Do women who go to gymnasiums feel differently about their bodies than do women who do not? Do women weightlifters feel differently about their bodies than do women runners or men weightlifters? How are women's body images defined, and how does going to a gym enter into those definitions? What is the process through which women come to know their bodies and their limitations? What happens when they exceed those limitations?

Another **variation** on the assigned problem **is whether or not funds are available for research on certain topics.** In fact, faculty sponsors might steer students in directions where funds are available. This is quite a legitimate suggestion because often those are problem areas of special need.

A second source of problems is the **technical and nontechnical literature** (Silverman, 1993). This can be a stimulus to research in several ways. Sometimes, it points to a relatively unexplored area or suggests a topic in need of further development. Other times, there are contradictions or ambiguities among the accumulated studies and writings. The discrepancies suggest the need for a study that will help to resolve those uncertainties. Alternatively, a researcher's reading on a subject might suggest that a new approach is needed to solve an old problem, even though it has been well studied in the past. Something about the problem area and the phenomenon associated with it remains illusive, and that something, if discovered, might be used to reconstruct understanding. Also, while reading the literature, a researcher might be struck by a finding that is dissonant with his or her own experience that can lead to a study resolving that dissonance. Finally, reading might simply stimulate curiosity about a subject. The moment that one asks the question "But, what if . . . ?" and finds that there is no answer, one has a problem area.

A third source of problems is **personal and professional experience.** A person may undergo a divorce and wonder how other women or men experienced their own divorces. Or, someone may come across a problem in his or her profession or workplace for which there is no known answer. Professional experience frequently leads to the judgment that some feature of the profession or its practice is less than effective, efficient, human, or equitable. So, it is believed that a good research study might help to correct that situation. Some professionals return to school to work for advanced degrees because they are motivated by a reform ambition. The research problems that they choose are grounded in that motivation. Choosing a research problem through the professional or personal experience route might seem more hazardous than choosing one through the suggested or literature routes. This is not necessarily the case. The touchstone of one's own experience might be a more valuable indicator of a potentially successful research endeavor than another more abstract source.

A fourth source is **the research itself.** A researcher might enter the field having a general notion about what he or she might want to study but no specific problem area. A good way in which to begin is to do some initial interviews and observations. If the researcher is carefully listening to or observing the speech and actions of respondents, then analysis should lead him or her to discover the issues that are important or problematic in the respondents' lives. **This acid test of paying attention to respondents' concerns is the key to where the focus of a research project should be.** Admittedly, there is no one and only relevant focus, but the particular one arrived at through respectful examination of respondents' concerns reduces the risks of being irrelevant or merely trivial. Consider the following example.

A student from Botswana, who was taking a class in fieldwork, grew desperate when studying "older Americans" in a senior resident home. To begin with, the ideas she had when she entered the field did not seem to fit what she was hearing and observing. But if that were so, then what were the "real" issues? What she initially carried into this research situation were assumptions probably derived from three different sources. She was young and had some incorrect and even stereotypical conceptions about older people. Also, she was from a foreign country and thought in terms of her own culture. Then again, she was a beginning researcher and had not yet learned how to pick up cues from the respondents themselves about their concerns and to let this information guide her choice of research problem. In the instance of this particular student, there was an additional difficulty that she faced. She was working voluntarily for a social work agency that had its own agenda that included an evaluation of its work with these elders. So, the agency was urging her to obtain particular information that she discovered had little or nothing to do with the elders' lives or interests. Yet, she was responsible to the agency. Finally, by dint of listening closely to the elders, she formulated a significant research problem.

Certainly, anyone who is curious or concerned about the world around himself or herself and who is willing to take risks should not, after some deliberation, have too much trouble finding a problem area to study. The next step is asking the proper research question.

The Research Question

The way in which one asks the research question is important because it determines, to a large extent, the research methods that are used to answer it. Herein lies a dilemma. Does one choose qualitative analysis because the problem area and question stemming from it suggest that this form of research will be most productive? Does one decide to use a qualitative method and then frame the question to fit the method? Is it conscious or unconscious theoretical perspectives that color approaches (Pierce, 1995). These issues are difficult to respond to because their answers are not cut-and-dried. Although the basic premise is that the research question should dictate the method, many persons are oriented toward quantitative research. So, even when the problem area suggests that a qualitative study might be a more fruitful approach, these researchers frame their questions in a quantitative manner. Other researchers, because of personal orientations, training, or convictions, tend to see problems from a qualitative perspective. The questions they ask about any problem areas are couched in qualitative terms because they simply do not see problems in any other way. There is no reason for us to belabor this point; we only want to emphasize that some problem areas clearly suggest one form of research over another and that an investigator should be true to the problem at hand. For instance, if someone wants to know whether one drug is more effective than another, then a double-blind clinical trial is the appropriate approach. However, if a researcher is interested in knowing what it is like to be a participant in a drug study or in knowing some of the problems inherent in adhering to a very rigid drug protocol, then he or she might sensibly engage in qualitative research. Clearly, preference and training play a part in these decisions, but these should not blind investigators to other methodological options (Hathaway, 1995). Furthermore, even when one decides to use a qualitative approach, there remains the question of which particular method the investigator should use (Morse & Field, 1995).

Another important aspect of the research question is setting the boundaries on what will be studied. It is impossible for any investigator to cover all aspects of a problem. The research question helps to narrow the problem down to a workable size.

Asking the Research Question

What do questions look like in qualitative studies? How do they differ from those of quantitative studies, and why? The main purpose of this form of qualitative research is to develop theory. To do this, it is necessary to frame a research question in a manner that will provide the flexibility and freedom to explore a phenomenon in depth. Also underlying this approach to qualitative research is the assumption that all of the concepts pertaining to a given phenomenon have not yet been identified, at least not in this population or place. Or, if so, then the relationships between the concepts are poorly understood or conceptually undeveloped. Or, perhaps there is the assumption that nobody ever has asked this particular research question in quite the same way, so it is as yet impossible to determine which variables pertain to this area and which do not. This reasoning creates the need for asking a type of question that will enable researchers to find answers to issues that seem important but remain unanswered.

Although the initial question starts out broadly, it becomes progressively narrowed and more focused during the research process as concepts and their relationships are discovered. So, the research question begins as an open and broad one, but not so open, of course, as to allow for the entire universe of possibilities. On the other hand, it is not so narrow and focused that it excludes discovery. Qualitative research does not entail making statements about relationships between a dependent variable and an independent variable, as is common in quantitative studies, because its purpose is not to test hypotheses. The research question in a qualitative study is a statement that identifies the phenomenon to be studied. It tells the readers what the researcher specifically wants to know about this subject. Following is an example of how one might write a qualitative research question. "How do women manage pregnancies complicated by a chronic illness?" This question (at least in such global form), although too broad and unstructured for a quantitative study, is a perfectly good one for a qualitative research study. The question tells the readers that the study will investigate women during pregnancies and that the pregnancies will be complicated by a chronic illness. Furthermore, the study will be looking at management of the pregnancies from the women's perspective, that is, what they do and think, not what the doctors or significant others do and think. Of course, in a qualitative inquiry, it also is important to investigate what the doctors and significant others do and say because these actions/interactions might influence how women manage their pregnancies and be an important source of data. However, the focus of the study remains on the women, and keeping that in mind prevents the researcher from becoming distracted by unrelated and unproductive issues and from going off on paths that can lead away from the problem.

Also, an investigation can be focused on organizations, industries, interactions, and the like, not only on persons. For instance, an example of an interaction question might be the following: "What happens when a patient complains of being in pain but the nurse does not believe him or her?" In this case, the focus of the observations, chart reviews, and interviews, as well as the analysis, will be on the interaction between nurse and patient.

A researcher who is studying organizations, such as a laboratory that makes use of illegal drugs when doing some of its experiments, might ask a question such as the following: "What are the procedures or policies (written and implied) for handling the illegal drugs in this organization?" The focus of data collection and analysis will be on the broader organizational processes of monitoring and accounting for the amounts and types of drugs used. Data will be gathered not only through interviews but also by studying written policies and then observing how these are carried out. Not all organizational policies will be studied; rather, only those related to the handling of illegal drugs will be studied.

A person interested in biographical studies or case histories might write a question that looks like the following: "What difference does it make to patients' responses to pain that they have had long histories (at least 2 years) with pain management and treatments?" Not only will the focus be on present ways of experiencing and managing pain, but this also will be examined in light of oral histories that shed light on past experiences with pain and its treatment.

MAINTAINING A BALANCE BETWEEN OBJECTIVITY AND SENSITIVITY

In this methodology, data collection and analysis occur in alternating sequences. Analysis begins with the first interview and observation, which leads to the next interview or observation, followed by more analysis, more interviews or fieldwork, and so on. It is the analysis that drives the data collection. Therefore, there is a constant interplay between the researcher and the research act. Because this interplay requires immersion in the data, by the end of the inquiry, the researcher is shaped by the data, just as the data are shaped by the researcher. (This does not imply that the researcher has "gone native"; rather, he or she is sensitive to the issues and problems of the persons or places being investigated.) The problem that arises during this mutual shaping process is how one can immerse oneself in the data and still maintain a balance between objectivity and sensitivity. Objectivity is necessary to arrive at an impartial and accurate interpretation of events. Sensitivity is required to perceive the subtle nuances and meanings in data and to recognize the connections between concepts. Both objectivity and sensitivity are necessary for making discoveries. As the famous biologist Selye (1956) once wrote, "It is not to see something first, but to establish solid connections between the previously known and hitherto unknown that constitutes the essence of specific discovery" (p. 6).

Maintaining an Objective Stance

It is difficult to say which is the more problematic—maintaining objectivity or developing sensitivity. During the analytic process, we are asking researchers to set aside their knowledge and experience to form new interpretations about phenomena. Yet, in our everyday lives, we rely on knowledge and experience to provide the means for helping to understand the world in which we live and to find solutions to problems we encounter. Fortunately, over the years, researchers have learned that a state of complete objectivity is impossible and that in every piece of research—quantitative or qualitative—there is an element of subjectivity. What is important is to recognize that subjectivity is an issue and that researchers should take appropriate measures to minimize its intrusion into their analyses.

In qualitative research, objectivity does not mean controlling the variables. Rather, it means openness, a willingness to listen and to "give voice" to respondents, be they individuals or organizations. It means hearing what others have to say, seeing what others do, and representing these as accurately as possible. It means having an understanding, while recognizing that researchers' understandings often are based on the values, culture, training, and experiences that they bring to the research situations and that these might be quite different from those of their respondents (Bresler, 1995; Cheek, 1996). Over the years, we have wrestled with the problem of objectivity and have developed some techniques to increase our awareness and to help us control intrusion of bias into analysis while retaining sensitivity to what is being said in the data.

The first technique is to think comparatively. (This is explained further in Chapter 7.) By comparing incident to incident in the data, we are better able to stay grounded in them. However, comparing one piece of data to another does not entirely remove the potential of intrusion of bias into interpretations. Thus, we also might turn to the literature or experience to find examples of similar phenomena. **This does not mean that we use the literature or experience as data per se.** Rather, what we do is use the examples to stimulate our thinking about properties or dimensions that we can then use to examine the data in front of us. For example, when confronted with a round sphere of unknown use, we might compare it to a baseball for similarities and differences. We are not calling the unknown object a baseball but rather are saying that a baseball is hard and round, is about the size of an orange, and travels well through the air when thrown or hit. Now we can take those properties and examine the piece of data in front of us for similarities and differences. Although we still might not be able to name it, at least we will know that it is not a baseball. Furthermore, we can begin to describe the unknown object in terms of size, degree of firmness, shape, and ability to travel through the air, and then we can even give it a name. The comparative example does not give us data. Rather, it stimulates our thinking or sensitizes us so that we recognize instances of properties in the actual data. In other words, making comparisons forces analysts to examine data at a dimensional level. We emphasize that the logic behind the use of comparisons is to stimulate thinking at a property and dimensional level to gain some perspective when examining a piece of data.

Another technique for gaining distance is to obtain multiple viewpoints of an event, that is, to attempt to determine how the various actors in a situation view it. Still another is to gather data on the same event or phenomenon in different ways such as interviews, observations, and written reports. It also is important to interview and/or observe multiple and varied representatives of persons, places, events, and times. (The process of varying data-gathering techniques and approaches is referred to as triangulation [Begley, 1996; Sandelowski, 1996].) We are not arguing in this chapter so much for triangulation per se as for the need to obtain the varied meanings and interpretations of events, actions/interactions, and objects so that we can build these variations into our theory. We also want to know how situations are negotiated and how consensus or disensus of meanings are arrived at and maintained. For example, physicians (say a surgeon and a medical cancer specialist) often have different approaches to patient management, and it sometimes takes considerable discussion and negotiation before they can arrive at a mutual plan for intervention. Different shifts in an organization often do different types of work or do the same work in alternative ways. Therefore, the more persons, places, and events that are interviewed or observed, the more one is able to check out his or her interpretations against alternative explanations of events while also discovering properties and dimensional ranges of relevant concepts. Readers who are familiar with interviewing know that although some respondents are polite and will tell the researcher what they think he or she wants to hear, there always are those who are willing to tell the investigator just how wrong his or her interpretations are. Therefore, another analytic strategy is to occasionally check out assumptions, and later hypotheses, with respondents and against incoming data; that is, simply explain to respondents what you think you are finding in the data and ask them whether your interpretation matches their experiences with that phenomenon—and if not, then why.

Also, it is important to periodically step back and ask, "What is going on here?" and "Does what I think I see fit the reality of the data?" The data themselves do not lie. How this difficult lesson was learned by one of us (Corbin) is described in the following. While doing a study on how women with a chronic illness manage their pregnancies, it quickly became evident that their actions were aimed at doing what was necessary to have healthy babies. Furthermore, it was noticed that the risks varied over the course of the pregnancies; sometimes the risks were higher, and other times they were lower. One would expect, then, that women's management strategies would match the level of risks. What the researcher discovered, much to her frustration, was that action did not always match risk level. Try as she would, she could not force the hypothesis on the data. Why not? What the researcher finally discovered was that she was categorizing the pregnant women according to her own perception of the risks, which was not necessarily always the women's perception. In other words, because of her training as a nurse, the researcher bought into the medical model of risks, whereas the women often did not. Rather, they had their own interpretations of what the risks were, and although these included or were based on medical perceptions, they were *not* limited to these. In fact, sometimes the women's perceptions of what constituted risks were quite different from those of the physicians. Once the researcher returned to the data and recategorized the women according to how *they* defined the risks, their management actions made sense.

Still another strategy for obtaining objectivity is maintaining an attitude of skepticism. All theoretical explanations, categories, hypotheses, and questions about the data arrived at through analysis should be regarded as provisional. These should be validated against data in subsequent interviews or observations. This validation process is especially important for researchers who use categories derived from the research literature (variables identified in previous studies) because categories always are context specific. Concepts might fit with the studies from which they were derived. They might even have some relevance or explanatory power for the present problem under investigation; however, their properties and how they are expressed might be quite different with a different set of data. The reason for this is that forms of concepts (i.e., their properties and dimensional ranges) tend to vary with conditions.

The final piece of advice is to follow the research procedures. Although researchers may pick and choose among some of the analytic techniques that we offer, the procedures of making comparisons, asking questions, and sampling based on evolving theoretical concepts are essential features of the methodology. They differentiate it from other methods and provide the means for developing theory. The idea is not rigid adherence to procedures but rather **fluid and skillful application.** Coding cannot be done haphazardly or at the whim of the analyst. There is a reason for alternating data collection with analysis. Not only does this allow for sampling on the basis of emerging concepts, but it also enables validation of concepts and hypotheses as these are being developed. Those found not to "fit" can then be discarded, revised, or modified during the research process.

Developing Sensitivity to the Meanings in Data

Having sensitivity means having insight into, and being able to give meaning to, the events and happenings in data. It means being able to see beneath the obvious to discover the new. This quality of the researcher occurs as he or she works with data, making comparisons, asking questions, and going out and collecting more data.

Through these alternating processes of data collection and analysis, meanings that often are illusive at first become clearer. Immersion in the analysis leads to those sudden insights, "aha" experiences so familiar to those of us who do qualitative research.

But insights do not just occur haphazardly; rather, they happen to prepared minds during interplay with the data. Whether we want to admit it or not, we cannot completely divorce ourselves from who we are or from what we know. The theories that we carry within our heads inform our research in multiple ways, even if we use them quite un-self-consciously (Sandelowski, 1993). Knowledge coupled with objectivity, as explained earlier, does prepare an analyst to understand. To quote Dey (1993), "In short, there is a difference between an open mind and an empty head. To analyze data, we need to use accumulated knowledge, not dispense with it. The issue is not whether to use existing knowledge, but how" (p. 63). As we come across an event of interest in our data, we ask, "What is this?" Later, as we move along in our analysis, it is our knowledge and experience (professional, gender, cultural, etc.) that enables us to recognize incidents as being conceptually similar or dissimilar and to give them conceptual names. It is by using what we bring to the data in a systematic and aware way that we become sensitive to meaning without **forcing** our explanations on data.

As professionals, most of us are familiar with the literature in the field. Literature can be used as an analytic tool if we are careful to think about it in theoretical terms. Used in this way, the literature can provide a rich source of events to stimulate thinking about properties and for asking conceptual questions. It can furnish initial ideas to be used for theoretical sampling (see Chapter 13).

Professional experience is another potential source of sensitivity. Although it can easily block perception, it also can enable the researcher to move into an area more quickly because he or she does not have to spend time gaining familiarity with surroundings or events. Two things are important to remember. The first is to always <u>compare what one thinks one sees to what one sees at the property or dimensional level because this enables the analyst to use experience without putting the experience itself into the data.</u> The second is that <u>it is not the researcher's perception or perspective that matters but rather how research participants see events or happenings.</u> For example, one of the authors (Corbin) might know that a certain piece of equipment in a hospital is used to take x-rays. But others might view it as an outdated machine, as a physical threat, or as meaning more work to do. It is these other interpretations that the researcher is seeking. What helps is that the researcher has a comparative base against which she can measure the **range of meanings given by others and a beginning list of properties and dimensions that she can use to gain greater understanding of their explanations.**

Personal experience can increase sensitivity if used correctly. Although one might never experience a divorce, having undergone the death of a loved one does help a researcher to understand the meaning of grief and loss. Again, it provides a comparative base for asking questions about grief and loss in divorce. Once one has some general properties, one can use them to begin to define the meanings of grief and loss in divorce. One always should look for opposites as well. For instance, one might be happy that a person is dead because that person was abusive (although it might not be socially acceptable to say so), just like it might be liberating to be divorced.

It is amazing how insight sparks more insight and how discovery builds. Sometimes analysts come upon a piece of data and are stuck, unable to discern its meaning. What we have discovered is that researchers often carry their analytic problems around in their heads as they go about their daily activities. Then, perhaps while reading the newspaper, talking with colleagues on the telephone or via e-mail, or awakening from dreams, insights occur and the analysts are able to make sense out of the previously unexplainable data. Technically, these insights emerged from the data, even though understanding was stimulated through other experiences. In the end, the essential process to keep in mind is maintaining a workable balance between objectivity and sensitivity.

USING LITERATURE

The researcher brings to the inquiry a considerable background in professional and disciplinary literature. This background may be acquired while studying for examinations or simply through efforts to "keep up" with the field. During the research itself, the analyst often discovers biographies, manuscripts, reports, or other materials that seem pertinent to the area under investigation. The question is how these can be used to enhance, rather than constrain, theory development. Of course, the discipline, school, and perspective of the researcher will greatly influence how much literature he or she comes with and how it is used. To begin with, let us assure our readers that there is no need to review all of the literature in the field beforehand, as is frequently done by analysts using other research approaches. It is impossible to know prior to the investigation what the salient problems will be or what theoretical concepts will emerge. Also, the researcher does not want to be so steeped in the literature that he or she is constrained and even stifled by it. It is not unusual for students to become enamored with a previous study (or studies) either before or during their own investigations, so much so that they are nearly paralyzed in an analytic sense. It is not until they are able to let go and put trust in their abilities to generate knowledge that they finally are able to make discoveries of their own.

Making Use of the Nontechnical Literature

Although the following list is by no means exhaustive, it does describe how we use the technical literature.

1. Concepts derived from the literature can provide a source for making comparisons to data at the dimensional level. If a concept emerges from the data that seems similar or opposite to one recalled from the literature, then the concepts can be compared in terms of their properties and dimensions (see Chapters 8 and 9). This enables an analyst to differentiate and give specificity to the emergent concept.

2. Familiarity with relevant literature can enhance sensitivity to subtle nuances in data, just as it can block creativity. Although a researcher does not want to enter the field with an entire list of concepts, some concepts might turn up over and over again in the literature and *also* appear in the data and, thus, might seem significant. The important questions for the researcher to ask include the folllowing. Are these concepts truly emergent, or am I seeing these concepts

in the data because I am so familiar with them? If they are truly emergent and relevant, then how are they the same as, and how are they different from, those in the literature?

3. There is a special sense in which published descriptive materials can be used to enhance sensitivity. These writings often give very accurate descriptions of reality, with very little interpretation other than, perhaps, organizing sections of materials according to a few themes. It is almost like reading field notes collected by another researcher for the same or another purpose. Reading them can make an analyst sensitive as to what to look for in data and help him or her to generate questions to ask respondents. Any themes or concepts borrowed from other studies might have relevance to the problem under investigation. However, the researcher must be very careful to look for examples of incidents in his or her data and to delineate the forms that the concepts take in the present study.

4. Knowledge of philosophical writings and existing theories can be useful under certain circumstances. There is no doubt that the theoretical perspective of a researcher influences the stance that he or she takes toward the study. For instance, a person who perceives himself or herself as a symbolic interactionist might investigate interaction, structure, and the relationships between these. A phenomenologist might study the meaning of various types of experiences. A Marxist might consider investigating power and exploitation inherent in a situation. If the researcher is interested in extending an already existing theory, then he or she might enter the field with some of the concepts and relationships in mind and look for how their properties and dimensions vary under a different set of conditions. For example, the investigator might wish to begin with the concept of "awareness." This concept pertains to the interactional strategies used to manage levels of knowledge about death (the keeping or revealing of secrets) and evolved from a study on dying (Glaser & Strauss, 1965). The researcher wishing to extend this theory could study how spies, those engaged in marital infidelities, and "in the closet" gays and lesbians manage to hide or reveal their secrets. New categories and further information about existing awareness categories no doubt would emerge.

5. The literature can be used as a secondary source of data. Research publications often include quoted materials from interviews and field notes, and these quotations can be used as secondary sources of data for a researcher's own purposes. The publications also might include descriptive materials concerning events, actions, setting, and actors' perspectives that can be used as data and analyzed using the methods described in the subsequent chapters of this book. In fact, one form of qualitative research is the analysis of theoretical or philosophical statements and writings per se.

6. Before beginning a project, a researcher can turn to the literature to formulate questions that act as a stepping off point during initial observations and interviews. After the first interview(s) or observation(s), the researcher will turn to questions and concepts that emerge from analysis of the data. Initial questions derived from the literature also can be used to satisfy human subjects committees by providing them with a list of conceptual areas that will be investigated. Although new areas will emerge, at least the initial questions demonstrate overall intent of the research.

7. The technical literature also can be used to stimulate questions during the analysis process. For example, when there is a discrepancy between a researcher's data and the findings reported in the literature, that difference should stimulate the researcher to ask the following questions. What is going on? Am I overlooking something important? Are conditions different in this study? If so, then how are they different, and how does this affect what I am seeing?

8. Areas for theoretical sampling (see Chapter 13) can be suggested by the literature, especially in the first stage of the research. The literature can provide insights into where (place, time, papers, etc.) a researcher might go to investigate certain relevant concepts. In other words, it can direct the researcher to situations that he or she might not otherwise have considered.

9. When an investigator has finished his or her data collection and analysis and is in the writing stage, the literature can be used to confirm findings *and*, just the reverse, findings can be used to illustrate

where the literature is incorrect, is overly simplistic, or only partially explains phenomena. Bringing the literature into the writing not only demonstrates scholarliness but also allows for extending, validating, and refining knowledge in the field. What the researcher should avoid is being insecure about his or her discoveries. Running to the published literature to validate or negate everything that one is finding hinders progress and stifles creativity.

How to Use the Nontechnical Literature

Nontechnical literature consists of letters, biographies, diaries, reports, videotapes, newspapers, catalogs (scientific and otherwise), and a variety of other materials. The nontechnical literature can be used for all of the purposes listed in the preceding subsection. In addition, it has the following uses.

1. It can be used as primary data, especially in historical or biographical studies. Because it often is difficult to authenticate and determine the veracity of some historical documents, letters, and biographies, it is very important to cross-check data by examining a wide variety of documents and supplementing these, if possible, with interviews and observations.

2. It can be used to supplement interviews and observations. For example, much can be learned about an organization, its structure, and how it functions (which might not be immediately visible in observations or interviews) by studying its reports, correspondence, and internal memos.

SUMMARY

This chapter covered three major areas: (a) choosing a problem and stating the research question, (b) maintaining a balance between objectivity and sensitivity, and (c) using the literature. Each of these areas must be considered before beginning the research inquiry.

Choosing a problem and stating the research question. The original research question and the manner in which it is phrased lead the researcher to examine data from a specific perspective and to use certain data-gathering techniques and modes of data analysis. The question(s) sets the tone for the research project and helps the researcher to stay focused, even when there are masses of data. The original question in a qualitative study often is broad and open-ended. It tends to become more refined and specific as the research progresses and as the issues and problems of the area under investigation emerge. The original research questions may be suggested by a professor or colleague, derived from the literature, or derived from the researcher's experience. Whatever the source of the problem, it is important that the researcher have enthusiasm for the subject because he or she will have to live with it for some time.

Maintaining a balance between objectivity and sensitivity. The interplay between research and researcher means that the researcher is an instrument of analysis in qualitative studies. Therefore, it is important to maintain a balance between the qualities of objectivity and sensitivity when doing analysis. Objectivity enables the researcher to have confidence that his or her findings are a reasonable, impartial representation of a problem under investigation, whereas sensitivity enables creativity and the discovery of new theory from data.

Using the literature. The literature tends to be useful in somewhat different and specific ways. Ingenious researchers, besides using the usual technical literature, sometimes will use various other types of published and unpublished materials to supplement their interviews and field observations. Although reports and biographies often come to mind, catalogs (especially scientific ones) also are sources of data. Nontechnical literature can provide questions, initial concepts, and ideas for theoretical sampling. It also can be used as data (both primary and supplemental) or for making comparisons, and it can act as the foundation for developing general theory. The important point for the researcher to remember is that the literature can hinder creativity if it is allowed to stand between the researcher and the data. But if it is used as an analytic tool, then it can foster conceptualization.

Part II
Coding Procedures

At the beginning of my journey, I was naive. I didn't yet know that the answers vanish as one continues to travel, that there is only further complexity, that there are still more interrelationships and more questions. (Kaplan, 1996, p. 7)

Although Kaplan was writing about travel, his words are just as applicable to research. What we discover by doing research is just how complex the world is. When we answer some questions, we raise others. And no matter how well thought out we think our project is at the beginning, there always are those unanticipated twists and turns along the way that lead us to rethink our positions and question our methods and to let us know that we are not as smart as we think we are.

It is our analytic eyes that lead us to see, imperfect as that seeing might be. In this part, we offer some guideliness and techniques for helping researchers through the analytic process. We offer suggestions for both raising and answering questions. We discuss the art of making comparisons, for an art it is. We explore the various types of coding and explain what analysts are trying to accomplish through each type. It is our hope that our explanations will provide an understanding of the logic that lies behind procedures, enabling analysts to use them flexibly and innovatively.

Although we do not create data, we create theory out of data. If we do it correctly, then we are not speaking for our participants but rather are enabling them to speak in voices that are clearly understood and representative. Our theories, however incomplete, provide a common language (set of concepts) through which research participants, professionals, and others can come together to discuss ideas and find solutions to problems. Yes, we are naive if we think that we can "know it all." But even a small amount of understanding can make a difference.

5 Analysis Through Microscopic Examination of Data

DEFINITION OF TERM

Microanalysis: The detailed line-by-line analysis necessary at the beginning of a study to generate initial categories (with their properties and dimensions) and to suggest relationships among categories; a combination of open and axial coding

This chapter demonstrates how we approach analysis, thus giving our readers a feel for the actual process. We believe that a detailed type of analysis, such as that exemplified here, is necessary at the beginning of a project to generate initial categories (with their properties and dimensions) and to discover the relationships among concepts. Although microanalysis sometimes is referred to as "line-by-line" analysis, the same process also can be applied to a word, a sentence, or a paragraph.

Notice several features of microanalysis as you read this chapter. First, it comes with features of both open and axial coding, which are described in more detail in Chapters 8 to 12. Second, it demonstrates that analysis *is not* a structured, static, or rigid process. Rather, it is a free-flowing and creative one in which analysts move quickly back and forth between types of coding, using analytic techniques and procedures freely and in response to the analytic task before analysts. **This chapter illustrates what coding actually is.** It contrasts considerably with the step-by-step sequence of operations presented in subsequent chapters. The latter are designed to take the coding process apart and break it down artificially to explain the logic and procedural steps involved. This chapter shows how we put it all together. It might seem odd that we place it first. We have a very good reason for that. We want to provide readers with a sense of what they should be doing before they become bogged down by the details. We hope that readers will keep our examples in mind as they read on. Clearly, this chapter illustrates that **techniques and procedures are tools only.** They are there to assist with analysis *but* never should drive the analysis in and of themselves.

Microanalysis, therefore, includes open and axial coding and makes use of the many analytic techniques presented in subsequent chapters as well as in previous ones. Microanalysis involves very careful, often minute **examination and interpretation of data.** When we say "data," we mean interviews, observational field notes, videos, journals, memos, manuals, catalogs, and other forms of written or pictorial materials (Silverman, 1993). We take data apart and work with the pictures, words, phrases, sentences, paragraphs, and other segments of material.

Included in this microscopic examination are two major aspects of analysis: (a) the data, be they participants' recounting of actual events and actions as they are remembered or texts, observations, videos, and the like gathered by the researcher; and (b) the observers' and actors' interpretations of those events, objects, happenings, and actions. There also is a third element: the interplay that takes place between data and researcher in both gathering and analyzing data. This interplay, by its very nature, is not entirely objective as some researchers might wish us to believe. Interplay, by its very nature, means that a researcher is actively reacting to and working with data. We believe that although a researcher can try to be as objective as possible, in a practical sense, this is not entirely possible. Thus, it is preferable to self-consciously bring disciplinary and research experience into the analysis but to do so in ways that enhance the creative aspects of analysis rather than drive analysis. Experience and knowledge are what sensitizes the researcher to significant problems and issues in the data and allows him or her to see alternative explanations and to recognize properties and dimensions of emergent concepts. **However, we are not saying that experience is used as data. Rather, we are saying that it can be drawn on for the purpose of sensitizing the researcher to the properties and dimensions in data, always with considerable self-awareness of what the researcher is doing.**

CLASS EXAMPLES

The examples of microanalysis presented in this chapter were taken from class sessions. When **teaching** analysis, especially open coding, we usually begin with a demonstration of line-by-line analysis. We do this so that students have some vision of what the analytic process looks like before beginning to learn the individual procedures. It also conveys some of the fun that researchers experience when doing qualitative analysis.

Doing microanalysis is an eye-opener for students because it illustrates concretely that **qualitative analysis involves a radically different way of thinking about data.** It is distinct from any other research tradition in which they may have been trained. Learning this new mode of thinking sometimes creates difficulties for students. They must learn to listen, letting the data speak to them. They must learn to relax, adopting a more flexible, less preplanned, and less controlled approach to research.

A class on microanalysis looks somewhat like the following. First, we ask the class to scan a section of an interview. Then, we follow up with questions such as "How would you interpret what the interviewee is saying?" and "What is in this material?" Generally, the students easily name many themes, for their personal and disciplinary experiences have made them sensitive to a range of issues and "problems." We write each of these on the blackboard and eventually point out their considerable range. But we also note that connections among the issues, problems, or themes, as actually stated, are only implicit and certainly not systematically worked out.

Then, we ask the class to scan a short paragraph taken from an interview quoted in an article usually written by a qualitative researcher (although sometimes we examine a speaker's words quoted by a newspaper journalist). Next, we say that we are about to do a line-by-line analysis together. This will consist of carefully discussing how the person quoted has used single words, phrases, and sentences.

Our discussion/examination usually begins with the very first word of the quotation. "What does this word seem to mean, or what could it mean?" In addition, "Think about this **just by itself** as though you had not read the remainder of the paragraph, even if actually that is impossible. The idea is to get you focused minutely on just the data in front of your eyes." Usually, the discussion of this first quoted word takes many minutes, perhaps as much as an hour, depending on the richness of the discussion and the range of the word's possible meanings explored in it. As we said in the first edition of this book,

> Usually, when anyone sees words, he or she will assign meaning to them, derived from common usage or experience. We often believe that because we would act and feel in a particular manner, that this, of course, is what the respondent means by those words. That belief is not necessarily accurate. Take a word—any word—and ask people what it means to them. The word "red" is a good example. One person may say, "bulls, lipstick, and blood." Another might respond, "passion." Perhaps for you it means a favorite dress, a rose, a glamorous sports car, or none of the above. As an exercise, we suggest that you list all of the thoughts that come to mind when you think about the word "red." Amazing, isn't it? Red is far more than a color. It has sentiment, feeling, texture, sensation, smell, and action all built into it. These associations are derived from the meanings we have come to associate with this word over the years, whether for personal or cultural reasons. (Strauss & Corbin, 1990, p. 81)

During the discussion, students invariably are amazed at how many different meanings they are able to give to an object or event. This exercise/research technique indeed has many important functions, but perhaps the most critical is that each person interprets differently and that any one of the interpretations could potentially be correct. Before detailing the functions of microanalysis, we reproduce part of a class session. Although the class worked on the entire paragraph for about 3 hours, only a few points taken from the first couple of sentences are reproduced here.

Class Session

Fieldnote quotation:

When I heard the diagnosis, it was scary. I panicked. Everything was doing well early in this pregnancy, and I felt good—no morning sickness, and I had a lot of energy. Then all of a sudden, I was told I had diabetes. What a shock since this is my first baby. My main concern is for the baby. I worry about the baby. I want this baby so much. I am really scared 'cause I waited so long to have this baby and I don't want anything to go wrong.

Discussion and Commentary

Teacher: Let's focus on the first word, "when." What could "when" mean?

Student: It represents time to me. A point in time. Some time, indeterminately, in the past.

Teacher: Well, it could stand for some time in the future. Like, "When the telephone rings, I will answer because I anticipate he will be calling."

Student: "When" also stands for a *condition*. [It indicates that] something is happening. [It is a] question [that] forces you to look [for answers].

Teacher: Suppose the word isn't "when" but [rather] "whenever." What then?

Student: Then it means to me there's a repeated time. A pattern of something happening.

Teacher: So, that's a different kind of *condition* for something that follows because of some event or events. . . . Suppose that instead of "when," the speaker said "at the time"?

Student: Oh, then it might mean telling a story with the "when" further back in time, maybe.

Teacher: Okay, so far, we have been minutely focused on that single word and some variant alternatives. Now, what about possible *properties* of "when"?

Student: It could be sudden or not sudden. . . . Or unexpected [or not]. . . . Or the accompanying events noticed only by you and not by others or noticed by others too. . . . Or they might be unimportant or very important.

Teacher: We could dream up lots of properties of this "when" and its accompanying events. There's no end to them, and only some of them might be relevant to your investigation and in the data, though that has to be discovered. But notice how my *questions* force you to look at *properties and dimensions*. [See Chapter 7 for an explanation of properties and dimensions.] . . . Now, let's think about the phrase "I heard the diagnosis." What about that first word, "I"?

Student: Could have been we who heard—was told the diagnosis —or they, like parents. This would have made a difference.

Teacher: And *under what conditions* maybe would it be told to a kinsman, or parent, or to the patient? And what might be the different consequences of this? . . . Now, what about the verb "heard"?

Student: Oh, a diagnosis might be written or shown to the patient [also], like on an x-ray if she were diagnosed for TB [tuberculosis] or had a shattered hip.

Teacher: Presumably, there'd be different conditions in which each of those would occur as well as perhaps different *consequences* [for] them. TB is interesting because often the diagnosis is accompanied by the listener's skepticism; therefore, the physician shows the x-ray. Of course, the patient is unlikely to be able to interpret it, so he or she has to take the diagnosis on faith—or reject it if not trusting—so we are talking about the issue of legitimacy of the diagnosis. That gets us methodologically into the question of the possibly different relevant *properties* of diagnoses. What might some be?

Student: A partial list of properties named by the students: "difficult to make, obscure versus well known, symbolic like cancer or not particularly symbolic, important [to oneself, to others, to the physician, or to all], expected or not, awful or actually reassuring when worst is expected or preceded by days of anxious waiting, easily believable."

Teacher: Then, there are some interesting *theoretical questions* about the announcements of diagnoses and the *structural issues* behind the answer to each. *Who* [and why]? Your well-known family physician, a strange specialist, a resident in the hospital, or [if you are a child] your mother? *How* [and why this way]? Think of the difference between a sudden abrupt announcement on an emergency ward, by an attending resident, to a mother that "your child has died" as against how coroners pace their announcement of death after knocking on the door of a spouse. Another question might be *When*? Right away, after a judicious interval, etc., or whenever the father had arrived so that both could be told about their child's death? In hospitals, if someone dies at night, the nurse usually doesn't announce on the phone but is just likely to signal that things have gotten worse and waits for the spouse or kin to arrive so that a physician can make the announcement. "When" here also includes a parent or spouse announcing the death to other kinsmen—later, sometimes hours later, and questions about how they do that and whether face-to-face or on the telephone, etc. . . . Can those kinds of questions also stimulate questions to be asked in interviews too? Yes, they certainly can stimulate *descriptive questions*. . . . Now, in the next phrase in that sentence, notice "everything was going well." That could possibly turn out to be an *in vivo concept*, a phrase used repeatedly by pregnant women and so representing events probably important to them—and so it should be to us as researchers. So, we take note of it, just in case it should turn out to be relevant to our work. . . . What could this phrase, as such, mean analytically?

Student: Well, it strikes me as indicating temporality, a course of something. . . . And the course is anticipated; there's a normal course [as well as one that goes off course] . . . , which means they are evaluating whether it's normal or not.

Teacher: Yes, but that means there must be criteria [properties], which in fact she names later in the sentence. . . . But note also that it's she who locates herself dimensionally on this course. Analytically, we can ask why she [using commonsense criteria] and not the physician or a nurse is doing the locating. What we are talking about here is a locational process and the locational agents. If you think comparatively, you can quickly see that in other situations, for different structural reasons, there will be different locational agents. Like the economists will tell you that you are entering a recession; you might never recognize you were otherwise. . . . Now a related phrase here is her "early in this pregnancy." Leaving aside the "this"—for here she is surely comparing it with other one or ones—think about "early in." How does she know this?

Student: Every mother knows there's 9 months in the course of a pregnancy and so can locate herself—cultural, commonsense knowledge.

Teacher: Again thinking *comparatively*—and to startle you a little with an extreme but analytically stimulating comparison—think of what happened in Germany when Hitler attained high office. People interpret this event in very different ways, though with hindsight we can see that Germany was by then deep into its evolution of Nazism. Who were the locational agents? How did they know where in the course Germany was? How did they achieve legitimacy for others—or not? What were the consequences for oneself [say you were a Jew] of correctly or incorrectly reading this evolutionary course? Such questions that are raised by these kinds of comparative cases [and even extreme ones are useful early in the research] can stimulate your thinking about the properties of women such as the interviewee who is thinking about and reacting to her pregnancy in the sense of applying the same questions about "locating" to her situation [not the idea about Nazism]. . . . Notice also that these kinds of comparisons, even when not as extreme as this one about Hitler, can stimulate you to ask questions about your own assumptions and interpretations of the pregnancy data. These kinds of questions jolt you of your standard, taken-for-granted ideas about pregnancies and their nature and force you to consider the implications of your assumptions in making the analysis.

Student: It seems to me that there is a crisscrossing of two temporal courses. There's the mother's course of a hopefully successful pregnancy, and there's the baby's course, dependent biologically certainly on the mother's physiology but involving a different set of concerns. [The rest of the quoted paragraph certainly suggests that.] Socially, they involve different actions too, like preparing for the baby's entry into the family and acting "right" during the pregnancy for the baby's foreseen welfare.

Teacher: You are pointing to different phenomena, and you could coin two different *concepts* to stand for these—also a concept to represent what you call "crisscrossing." I would call it "intersecting" or "linking," as in axial coding. You are also pointing to sequence and phases of actions and events, another aspect of the temporality noted earlier. There is also *process* [see Chapter 11] or movement through phases of action.

Major Points About Microanalysis

What this type of examination—of single words, of phrases, of sentences—does for students and also mature researchers can be invaluable. For beginning students, it makes them aware of **how much is packed** into small bits of data. It also makes them aware that it is up to them to **mine that data;** the nuggets do not become disinterred by themselves. It also brings home to students that this type of analysis represents a style or approach to data *quite* different from anything they have done before.

Quickly summarizing the analytic discussion of the quoted paragraph, we now enumerate several important additional functions of microscopic examination of data. You can easily see these in the discussion itself.

1. Overall, this procedure is a very **focused** one. The focusing forces **researchers to consider the range of plausibility, to avoid taking one stand or stance toward the data. Notice we say that it is the researcher who is being jolted out of his or her usual modes of thinking. It is not the data that are being forced. The data are not being forced; they are being allowed to speak.**

2. Microscopic analysis obliges the researcher to examine the specifics of data. As one student said, "I tend to look at data in a very general way, but this makes me look at details." The instructor responded, "Yes, but not just details in a descriptive sense but also in the **analytic sense,**" that is, making comparisons along the level of properties and dimensions and in ways that allow the analyst to break the data apart and reconstruct them to form an interpretive scheme.

3. Doing microanalysis compels the analyst to **listen** closely to **what** the interviewees are saying *and* **how** they are saying it. This means that we are attempting to understand how they are interpreting certain events. This prevents us from jumping precipitously to our own theoretical conclusions, **taking into account the interviewees' interpretations.** It helps us to avoid laying our first interpretations on data, forcing us to consider alternative explanations. Also, if we are fortunate, then participants will give us **in vivo concepts** that will further stimulate our analyses.

4. We are moved through microanalysis by asking **questions, lots of them,** some general but others more **specific.** Some of these questions may be descriptive, helping us to ask better interview questions during the subsequent interviews. More important, we are stimulated to ask abstract **theoretical questions** (probing questions that stimulate discovery of properties, dimensions, conditions, and consequences such as who, when, what, how, and why). These theoretical questions are especially important during the earliest phases of our research project to flush out concepts and their relationships.

5. It is very important to understand that, from an analytic standpoint, **it is the data that are relevant,** not the **specifics** of a case or an individual or a collective. Systematic use of the analytic techniques and procedures presented in the chapters on open and axial coding (see Chapters 8 and 9) help to give **analytic distance.** There is a radical difference between this type of close "listening" to data (i.e., abstraction from data) and the opposite, which is application or laying on top of data theories and concepts.

6. In doing our analyses, we **conceptualize and classify** events, acts, and outcomes. The categories that emerge, along with their relationships, are the foundations for our developing theory. This abstracting, reducing, and relating is what makes the difference between **theoretical and descriptive coding (or theory building and doing description).** Doing line-by-line coding through which categories, their properties, and relationships emerge automatically takes us beyond description and puts us into a **conceptual mode of analysis.**

7. Classifying indicates grouping concepts according to their salient properties, that is, for similarities and differences. We are asking not only what is going on in a descriptive sense but also how this incident compares dimensionally along relevant properties with the others already identified.

8. As you will see in Chapter 6, our concepts (classifications) are "categories" that, when developed, show variation according to their various properties and dimensions.

9. The imaginative use of *making theoretical comparisons* (different from what is sometimes referred to as *constant comparisons*) is an essential subsidiary instrument for raising questions and discovering properties and dimensions that might be in the data by increasing researcher sensitivity. Theoretical comparisons are a vital part of our method of building theory and are one of the important techniques we use when doing microscopic analysis.

10. Comparisons are additionally important because they enable identification of *variations* in the patterns to be found in the data. It is not just one form of a category or pattern in which we are interested but also how that pattern varies dimensionally, which is discerned through comparison of properties and dimensions under different conditions. Sometimes, those differences are immediately visible in our data. Other times, we have to theoretically sample, that is, purposefully observe or interview while looking for instances of similarity or difference. But where we go to sample theoretically is deduced by the researcher. For example, one concept that might emerge from the data on medically complicated pregnancies is the notion of risks that seem to vary over time and with type and degree of complicating factors. To know where, when, and how to theoretically sample (i.e., where to look for how perceptions of risks vary dimensionally under various conditions), the researcher has to draw on knowledge of situations (based on experience, talking to others, or overhearing something) known to produce risks during pregnancies such as having uncontrolled diabetes. Then, the researcher would want to do some interviewing and/or observing of diabetic pregnant women to determine what they say about their pregnancies, risks, and how they go about managing their pregnancies and diabetes. By theoretically sampling women with diabetes and other medical conditions at different stages of their pregnancies and comparing concepts along properties and dimensions, the researcher will either verify, modify, clarify, expand, or discard hypotheses regarding perceptions of risks and how these affect management of complicated pregnancies. Although the notion of risks arose from the data, the researcher would not know where to go for additional comparative data without drawing on experiences, asking questions, or looking into possible readings.

11. *Provisional hypotheses* (statements about how concepts relate) also are likely to arise during line-by-line analysis. Under such and such a condition, such and such will happen or this and that outcome will occur. At first, these hypotheses will be stated very crudely. Later, they will be stated more precisely.

12. Finally, doing microanalysis enables researchers to examine what assumptions about data they are **taking for granted.** Comparing one's own assumptions against the data in such directed ways cannot help but bring those assumptions to the surface. False assumptions will not stand up when rigorously compared against the data incident by incident. The data talk for themselves. The making of constant and theoretical comparisons also forces the research to confront **respondents' assumptions** and to provisionally make hypotheses about the implications of those assumptions.

To graphically illustrate this latter point, we use the following example.

Interviewer: Now, when you say all girls got a little bit of "ho" in them, what do you mean by that?

Interviewee: A "ho" will sell her body, right? A ho sells her body. But a girl is less obvious with it. I could talk to a girl. I could never take her out. I could never buy her anything, y'know, never spend a dime on her. She ain't gonna want to give me nothing. She ain't gonna want to do nothing for me. So, what I do for her, she do for me. So if I, say if I, I got my own money, I could get myself money. I don't need no money. It's like, so, I'll buy her something. She, she doesn't feel, first, offhand, that she owes me anything, but like I say, I be like, so, why don't we have sex? Or something like that. And she be like, no. Then I'll buy her something else. And then she'll be like, man, he's buying me all this and I ain't doing nothing for him. He got his own money. He got his own, his own. He don't, he got his own clothes. He could buy, he got his own money to buy his own clothes. So whatever I bought her, she'll think to herself, well, he got could buy it for his self. So she'd be, like, what else is there for me to give him? Or I say, I got everything, what else you got to offer? You don't have nothing to offer. And then that'd make a girl think, man, I got something to offer. It be like, and then a guy play the game, like play along, like, what? And she'll say, y'know, she'll say, well, I could give you some sex, you know. And you be like, and it'd be like, oh, for real? You really want to do that? (field note, courtesy of Steve Eyer, University of California, San Francisco, Department of Adolescent Medicine)

Commentary

At the class session, students read the quotation and discussed it. These data were from a study of black adolescent males in San Francisco by one of the students, Steve Eyer, a young but experienced researcher with training in anthropology and psychology. He commented that he could not get the idea of exchange theory out of his head; this statement by the respondent was so patently about exchanging gifts for sex and maneuvering by the boy. In fact, this process was extremely frequent among the adolescent boys whom he had interviewed. He just had difficulty in *not* seeing exchange theory in these interviews; he could not seem to shake that idea.

1. Another student immediately and correctly remarked that this reflected the adolescent boy's ideology—*a folk theory* about exchange. But this theory should not be the researcher's view because the data showed other things as well. "Besides," commented the instructor, "you see exchange theory because you are steeped in this perspective because of your training in psychology. Maybe it is relevant, but maybe not. Such a theory must earn its way into *your* interpretation in conjunction with careful examination of **your data.**"

2. The instructor also said, "Even if you, as a researcher, entertained the idea that exchange was reflected in the quotation, you should ask questions about exchange and that the data [themselves] suggested some of these questions. What's the actual interaction during this exchange? What is exchanged? Who begins the exchange? What's the other's immediate response? Between how many people? Is it visible to others? How long does this exchange take? Is the exchange considered equally and by each? What are the criteria for what's being proffered? And so on."

3. Then, the instructor continued, "What else is reflected in the quotation *besides or other than exchange?*" Then, the class attempted to answer that question analytically. Some of the ideas the students brought out included that there is manipulation and negotiation, that there are cultural mores regarding male-female relationships and sex, that there is the notion of intimacy and how it develops through interaction, and that one might even make the leap to the "dominance of consumerism" in American society and how it transcends every-thing—even virginity.

Through this discussion, Eyer (and the other students in the class) was able to realize that we all carry with us certain sets of **recognized** and **unrecognized assumptions** and that somehow we have to break through these, or at least learn to work with them, if we are to make any advances in knowledge. Eyer was able to leave the session with new insights, different ways of looking at the data that took him beyond his original idea of exchange theory.

Where Does Microanalysis Fit Into the Analytic Process?

Having said all this, there is one question that readers are likely to be asking themselves at this time: When does one do this microana-lysis—at the beginning of the research, all the time, or occasionally? We know that doing microanalysis takes an enormous amount of time and energy. The general answers are as follows.

1. It certainly is necessary to do this detailed type of analysis at the beginning of a research project to discover categories (with their properties and dimensions) and to uncover the relationships among concepts. Once categories are established, analysis becomes more focused on filling out those categories and verifying relationships.

2. This does *not* mean that a researcher steadily codes every bit of data, word by word or phrase by phrase, in every document. That would take forever, and the analyst would end up with more data than he or she ever could use or that are necessary, for that matter. Rather, the researcher learns to **scan** an interview or any other data (e.g., field data, videos, documents), looking for potentially interesting or rele-

vant analytic materials. When a paragraph or segment is singled out, the line-by-line procedure may be used on parts or all of it. At later stages of the research inquiry, this procedure is of much less use but occasionally may be used.

3. When? When some bit of new data seems puzzling, or when old data are revisited and we feel that they have been inadequately analyzed or that there is more to be mined in this particular segment of data, or when new categories emerge, or when it is discovered that old ones are not very well developed.

Invariably, this close examination of data is likely to be of help to the researcher, no matter how experienced and skilled he or she is. In fact, strictly speaking, without this **microscopic analysis,** it would be extremely difficult to systematically discover relevant dimensions, to relate categories and subcategories, and to track down the more subtle aspects of causality.

SUMMARY

Doing microanalysis is an important step in theory development. It is through careful scrutiny of data, line by line, that researchers are able to uncover new concepts and novel relationships and to systematically develop categories in terms of their properties and dimensions. This chapter demonstrated the free-flowing and creative aspects of analysis and the interplay that occurs between the analyst and data during the analytic process. However, one cannot do microanalysis without an understanding of some of the specific techniques and procedures that can be used for opening up text and discovering its meanings and variations. The subsequent chapters present a series of analytic tools in the form of procedures and techniques. Although each is discussed separately and in a somewhat structured way to facilitate understanding, it is the ability to put them together in flexible and creative ways through microanalysis that enables the analyst to rise above the commonplace and develop truly innovative but grounded theory.

6 Basic Operations

Asking Questions and Making Comparisons

Asking questions: An analytic device used to open up the line of inquiry and direct theoretical sampling (see Chapter 13)

Making theoretical comparisons: An analytic tool used to stimulate thinking about properties and dimensions of categories

Theoretical sampling: Sampling on the basis of emerging concepts, with the aim being to explore the dimensional range or varied conditions along which the properties of concepts vary

Two operations are absolutely essential for the development of theory using our method of analysis. The first is *asking questions*. Every type of inquiry rests on the asking of effective questions. In our methodology, the main questions are directed at advancing our understanding of the theoretical issues. The second operation is *making comparisons*. Asking questions and making comparisons have various functions. In this chapter, we address some of these in a general manner. In Chapters 7 to 12, we further explain how to make use of these operations during coding.

THE USE OF QUESTIONING

Every researcher is concerned about how to ask "good" questions, ones that will take the research to a productive conclusion. Throughout this book, a number of suggestions are directed at that concern. However, even readers who are impatient about getting quickly to those operational details should profit from a more general discussion about questions and their role in research inquiry.

Our old but still serviceable dictionary defines **"inquiry"** as "a request for information, a systematic investigation" (Merriam-Webster, 1984, p. 624). Using questions for the purpose of gathering information and doing inquiries (or investigations) go together. Note that although questions and inquiries are expressed here as nouns, they actually involve *actions* such as asking, doing, locating, and searching.

Logician and philosopher John Dewey expressed some of the subtlety of this linkage of actions:

> Inquiry and questioning, up to a certain point, are synonymous terms. We inquire when we question, and we inquire when we seek for whatever will provide an answer to the question asked. Thus, it is of the very nature of the indeterminate situation which evokes inquiry to be *questionable*. . . . Indeterminate situations . . . are disturbed, troublesome, ambiguous, confused, full of conflicting tendencies, [and] obscure. (Dewey, 1938, p. 105, emphasis added)

Dewey, then, is pointing to indeterminate (or problematic) situations, but actually these are only so because someone **defines** them as such; however, experienced researchers know that particular acts of defining may lead somewhere or nowhere. Also, Dewey is pointing to problematic situations as stimulating inquiry or investigation, but what must be emphasized is that it is not the situation as such that is the directing force but rather the questions the investigator is asking about the situation. Also, Dewey is pointing to the interplay of problem/inquiry and answer stimulating the asking of more questions.

In addition, there are multiple levels of questions—abstract and theoretical, substantive and mundane. In an effort to answer some questions, very complex activities might be required, whereas other questions might be answered quickly and easily. Different types of methodological technologies also might be requisite to answering certain questions.

The preceding paragraphs barely begin to suggest the complexity of thought and action required to raise and answer questions. Scientists often borrow questions and answers in the form of techniques, procedures, and technologies—even from other disciplines or specializations—to proceed with their own investigations. Some questions (in both social science and natural science) stimulate further questions, which in turn stimulate further questions, in a chaining of extended investigations.

Furthermore, some questions turn out to be wonderfully productive, leading us to answers or, more interesting, raising more problems than they solve. The discovery of electricity, for example, linked generations of productive theoretical and practical questions and answers. Unfortunately, as all researchers know, some questions turn out to lead nowhere. Others are so ideologically driven that they answer themselves, although incorrectly, shutting off further inquiry. "Good" questions sometimes depend on luck, but more often they are prompted by relevant knowledge, a sense of "something is missing here," and (more important) sensitivity to what the data really are saying. Yet, even questions properly phrased but incorrectly answered can be amazingly consequential after investigators become dubious about those answers.

Among the further subtleties of the question and answer relationship, two are especially relevant for readers of this book. The first is that different questions and issues arise at different points of the inquiry. At the beginning, for instance, the researcher might be much concerned, even puzzled, about where the proper focus of the inquiry should be, that is, what the central phenomenon (problem) in this area of research is all about. After this is determined, there will be many more specific questions about the phenomenon and how it relates to events and happenings that are observed. Much later, an absorbing issue might be how to integrate all of one's thoughts about the data into a coherent theoretical formulation. Even when that becomes clear, a lot of details might require further clarification, with specific questions and answers evolving around those details.

A second very important point was touched on earlier. Some questions are directed at substantive matters, for example, "What are the most common types of drugs that teenagers are likely to take?"

Other are directed at more theoretical issues, for example, "How do images of a future biography affect whether or not teens take drugs?" Here, the question has to do with **how** and **if** two categories—"future biographical imaging" and "drug taking"—relate. This question demands a theoretically oriented inquiry; that is, the researcher moves from merely listing, as with types of drugs, to closely examining incoming data to look for cues that indicate how teens view themselves and how those perceptions of self might alter or affect when drugs are taken as well as how much and what types.

It is necessary to emphasize that only some of the questions we ask during the research process are, in fact, "theoretical" (pertaining to the development of theory, as in "How do these two concepts relate?"). Many questions are practical in nature, for example, "How do I get access to this organization?" or "How can I best use this computer program to facilitate my analysis?"

Whereas all of the questions we ask and their answers are linked in some manner with the course of a research project, questions often are transformed as a result of social changes that produce new phenomena. These social changes, once identified and defined, stimulate further inquiries. Yet, continuity is given to long lines of research by the appearance of new variations of older phenomena. For instance, German sociologist Max Weber brilliantly analyzed the functioning of governmental bureaucracy in imperial Germany (Weber, 1958). His writing stimulated countless studies of bureaucracies as they have developed in the United States and elsewhere. When researchers come across phenomena in a site that differ from their perceptions of what should be, or when new conceptions seem more appropriate than usual theoretical explanations, good questions may be stimulated by looking back at older analyses of those phenomena. An example here is the twin concepts of "negotiation" and "negotiated order" (Strauss et al., 1964; Strauss, 1978).

Central to any research investigation, then, is the asking of questions along with the pursuit of their answers. How does one know what a good question is? This question is difficult to answer because so much depends on the particular investigation and the research and professional experience of the inquirer. A good question is one that leads the researcher to answers that serve the developing theoretical formulation. Many questions can be asked, and just as many can lead the researcher down a subsidiary path, one that might be interesting but not in service of the evolving theory. In fact, some questions can lead the researcher astray, off in directions that have little or no bearing on the present investigation. Although we are reluctant to provide a listing of types of questions because beginners tend to take the specifics rather than the essence of what we are saying, we offer a few suggestions.

1. First, there are *sensitizing* questions. These tune the researcher into what the data might be indicating. Questions of this type might look something like the following. What is going on here (e.g., issues, problems, concerns)? Who are the actors involved? How do they define the situation? What is its meaning to them? What are the various actors doing? Are their definitions and meanings the same or different. When, how, and with what consequences are they acting, and how are these the same or different for various actors and various situations?

2. Second, there are *theoretical* questions. These are questions that help the researcher to see process, variation, and the like and to make connections among concepts. They might look like the following. What is the relationship of one concept to another (i.e., how do they compare and relate at the property and dimensional levels)? (See later section on the making of theoretical comparisons.) What would happen if . . .? How do events and actions change over time? What are the larger structural issues here, and how do these events play into or affect what I am seeing or hearing?

3. Third, there are the questions that are of a more *practical* and *structural* nature. They are the questions that provide direction for sampling and that help with development of the structure of the evolving theory. These questions include, among many others, the following. Which concepts are well developed and which are not? Where, when and how do I go next to gather the data for my evolving theory? What types of permission do I need? How long will it take? Is my developing theory logical? Where are the breaks in logic? Have I reached the saturation point?

4. Fourth, there are the *guiding* questions. These are the questions
that guide the interviews, observations, and analyses of these and
other documents. These questions will change over time, are based on
the evolving theory, and are specific to the particular research; therefore, it is difficult to provide examples. They begin open-ended and
tend to become more specific and refined as the research moves along.
A question at the beginning of a series of interviews might look like
this: Have you ever taken drugs, and if so, then what was the experience like for you? In later interviews, the same general question still
will be relevant; however, the researcher also will want to ask questions that give further information about specific concepts and their
properties and dimensions. Later questions might resemble the following one, which puts two concepts together: How does the fact that
drugs are "easily available" influence the frequency, amount, and type
of "drug using" in which you engage? (See the section on the use of
questioning in Chapter 7 for more examples.)

THE MAKING OF COMPARISONS

Comparative analysis is a staple feature of social science research.
It usually is built into a project's design, whether explicitly or implicitly. For instance, a sociologist compares gender behavior with respect
to sexual activity, a criminologist compares the rates of homicide
among ethnic groups, or an anthropologist comments on the differences between ritual and other cultural behaviors, as evinced in the
society he or she has studied and those reported on about other
societies. Of course, such comparative studies often are very valuable.
Our method of analysis also uses comparisons, but their nature
and use are different to some degree. The making of comparisons is
an essential feature of our methodology, as even a quick reading of
this book makes evident. We not only speak of comparing incident to
incident to classify them, but we also make use of what we call
theoretical comparisons to stimulate our thinking about properties and
dimensions and to direct our theoretical sampling. In this section, we
again discuss more general aspects of making comparisons, leaving
the details to emerge in our chapters on analysis.

Comparing incident to incident (as in Glaser & Strauss, 1967) to classify data is self-explanatory. Each incident is compared to other incidents at the property or dimensional level (see Chapter 8) for similarities and differences and is grouped or placed into a category. However, there are times during coding when we come across an incident and are stumped for indications of its significance or meaning. We do not know how to name or classify it because we cannot identify or grasp its properties or dimensions. Either they are not in the data, or they are there but we are not sensitive enough to recognize these. At these times, we turn to what we call *theoretical comparisons*. The making of theoretical comparisons requires further explanation. People constantly are thinking comparatively and making use of metaphors and similes when they speak (which is a type of comparison making or letting of one object stand for another). We use these techniques to clarify and increase understanding. For instance, we might say, "Yesterday, work was like a zoo. Everyone wanted something from me at once, and people were running around with no sense of purpose or direction." When we speak in this manner ("work was like a zoo"), it is not the specifics that we are trying to convey but rather a mood or tone. It is the properties of the situation that convey these, and the properties transcend the specific situation. Words such as "demanding," "hectic," and "directionless" all are properties of the situation and convey our meaning about the tone and experiences of the day. We are not saying that we were at a zoo but rather that some of the properties that we might think of as pertaining to daily life at a zoo also applied to our day at work. We give another, more specific example. While out grocery shopping, we come across two bins of oranges, each priced differently. To comprehend why they are **priced** differently (a cost property), we might compare them along certain other properties such as color, size, shape, smell, firmness, juiciness, sweetness (if samples are provided), and so on. Hopefully, by examining the two groups of oranges according to these dimensions or specific properties, we will come to understand why there is a price difference and then choose the most cost-effective oranges, which might not necessarily be determined by price alone. If the cheaper ones are dry and small, then they might not be a bargain. However, commonsense comparisons are not always as systematic as those that are used in research, nor do they address theoretical issues such as how the two bins of oranges relate to each other or how they came to be of different sizes, shapes, and/or degrees of sweetness, which in turn gets us into issues such as care, soils, and temperatures and then into lobbying, price controls, and so on. The first pursuit is classification, and the second leads us to theory.

To summarize briefly, comparisons at the property and dimensional levels provide persons with a way of knowing or understanding the world around them. People do not invent the world anew each day. Rather, they draw on what they know to try and understand what they do not know. It is not that they call a sofa a bed or call a tree a flower. Rather, they take the properties of one object and compare them to those of the other. And in that way, they discover what is similar and different about each object and thus define the objects. People learn that a bed can be used as a sofa and vice versa, but at the same time they get to know or understand the functions or characteristics of each specific object more fully as well as the conditions under which one might be used as the other.

We use theoretical comparisons in analysis for the same purposes as we do in everyday life. When we are confused or stuck about the meaning of an incident or event in our data, or when we want to think about an event or object in different ways (range of possible meanings), we turn to theoretical comparisons. Using comparisons brings out properties, which in turn can be used to examine the incident or object in the data. The specific incidents, objects, or actions that we use when making our theoretical comparisons can be derived from the literature and experience. It is not that we use experience or literature as data but rather that we use the properties and dimensions derived from the comparative incidents to examine the data in front of us. Just as we do not reinvent the world around us each day, in analysis we draw on what we know to help us understand what we do not know. **Theoretical comparisons are tools (a list of properties) for looking at something somewhat objectively rather than naming or classifying without a thorough examination of the object at the property and dimensional levels.** If the properties are evident within the data, then we do not need to rely on these tools. However, because details are not always evident to the "naked" eye, and because we (as humans) are so fallible in our interpretations despite all attempts to "deconstruct" an event, incident, or interview, there are times when this is not so easy and we have to stand back and ask, "What is this?" In asking this question, we begin, even if unconsciously, to draw on properties from what we do know to make comparisons.

The incidents that we use to derive our theoretical comparisons may be quite similar in nature to, or quite different from, the incident in the data (see Chapter 7). This is possible because we always work with concepts rather than specifics of data or cases. It is not the specific incident per se but rather what the incident symbolizes or represents. For example, suppose that in an interview, a nurse states, "When working alone at night, I prefer to work with another experienced nurse. When I work with an inexperienced nurse, I end up carrying most of the workload." To gain some understanding of what she means by this statement, we turn to thinking comparatively about the terms "experienced" and "inexperienced" and not so much about the fact that this nurse does not like to work with some people. We might say, "Let us look at inexperienced seamstresses or drivers instead of nurses to see what we might learn." Because it is the concepts "inexperienced" and "experienced" that interested us rather than the particulars of seamstress or driver, what our comparative group consists of does not matter. We are just looking for a list of properties that we can use to examine the incident in the data. **These properties will not be applied to the data; rather, they give us a means for examining the data.** An inexperienced seamstress or driver might have the properties of being cautious, apprehensive, frequently seeking direction, afraid to deviate from the pattern, prone to making errors, unsure of himself or herself, afraid to act in a crisis, and so on. Now, with some idea of what the properties of being inexperienced might be, we can look to the data to see whether any of these are in the data and thus help us to determine more specifically what the nurse meant when she made her remark. We are more sensitive to what to look for in the data because we have some idea of what it means to be inexperienced. Again, we are not saying that these properties are in the data or that they describe what the nurse meant. The difference now is that we are thinking at the property and dimensional levels. This is important because to define the meaning of experienced versus inexperienced, we must be able to state the properties of each. (However, we always keep in mind that perhaps experienced and inexperienced are not the issues but that rather there is something else. But we can eliminate this, or at least hold it in abeyance, if we find no properties or dimensions in this or other instances of data.) In further interviews or observations, we can ask questions or make observations that will give us more specific and defining information. For instance, we can observe both experienced and inexperienced nurses, watching how they function and how they handle problems under various conditions such as routine and crisis situations, thereby doing *theoretical sampling* or sampling on the basis of concepts and by varying the situations to maximize differences. (See Chapter 13 for more information about theoretical sampling.)

In our chapters on open and axial coding (Chapters 8 and 9), readers will note that we make theoretical comparisons when we are in doubt or confused; however, the nature of the activity might look different, depending on the analytic problem we are trying to solve. Sometimes, we use comparisons that are quite similar. Other times, we use what we call **far-out comparisons.** In so doing, we are following the example of sociologist E. C. Hughes, who enjoyed making striking and sometimes shocking comparisons such as between the work of psychiatrists and prostitutes; both belong to professions, have clients, get paid for their work, and "take care not to become too personally involved with clients who come to them with their intimate problems" (Hughes, 1971, p. 316). But comparisons can be made, even early in the research project, between classes of objects, incidents, or acts. The object, then, is to become sensitive to the number and types of properties that might pertain to phenomena that otherwise might not be noticed or noticed only much later.

We would like to provide another example of how making theoretical comparisons helps us to understand by enlarging our thinking about properties and dimensions. Notice how making comparisons helps us to break away from standard ways of thinking and stimulates the asking of questions about the data as we go along. The concept we examine here is "gardens." What we want is to enlarge our understanding of this phenomenon. Suppose that we are studying the **nature** of small gardens in the English countryside. We notice that some are full of flowers, seemingly grown pell-mell and without order and located in front of English middle class houses. We want to find the answers to questions such as why they look like this and not that, what they are used for, how they got to look like they do, and who appreciates them. A short list of their properties might look something like small, seemingly without order, colorful, and random, with the corresponding dimensions (size, degree, and time) left implicit. Now, suppose that we compare them to the famous gardens visited by tourists that still grace 17th- and 18th-century French palaces and mansions. Their characteristics would include their formality—some people say "stiffness" or "static"—as well as the predominant symmetry of their foliage, the gravel paths that constrain walkers to confine their strolling to them and nowhere else, their graceful fountains and statuary, and their sense of aristocracy and age. Think next of rose gardens that specialize in many varieties of just that one species of flower (a very symbolic and popular one) arranged so that people can both find and look at them—but not pick them. Then, there are village gardens, as in Botswana, which a Botswana student has described as "communal," affording lots of "sociability," and which we added are designed primarily to produce food. Turning back to our focus on the English home gardens, we ask questions about them based on the properties elicited from examining those other types of gardens. **We do not say that the English gardens necessarily share those properties; rather, we say that they use the properties as tools to examine the English ones.** Through such a comparative process, we learn to think and ask questions about the gardens much more quickly than if it had not occurred to us to make such comparisons. We might ask why there are no statues or vegetables in these gardens, why they are individual rather than communal gardens, and why they are designed for looking at rather than for picking—or whether they are for both looking and picking. Our example is not meant to emphasize the procedural aspects of making comparisons but rather is a major function of how this speeds up and facilitates analysis.

The making of theoretical comparisons has another function that can be sensed in our example: It moves the researcher more quickly away from describing the specifics of a case such as that this particular garden is very pretty to thinking more abstractly about what the various gardens share in common and what is different about them. One difficulty that plagues beginners of qualitative analysis is that they get focused on pinning down the exact "facts." So, they expend a great deal of energy in examining and arguing detail after detail rather than thinking abstractly and more generally, thus moving from the particular to the general. The issue, we say, is not how many teeth this particular horse has but rather what looking at its teeth (number, size, shape, care, pinkness of gums, etc.) and comparing them to the teeth of the other horses tells us about this horse's state of health and presumed ability to win the race. We want to know on which horse to place our bets.

If you hate or love any one of the preceding types of gardens, then the comparisons are likely to force you to confront reasons (biases) for your reactions. Making these types of comparisons forces analysts to question their assumptions and to ask how these might be affecting their study. At the very least, this type of examination prompts the breaking through of stereotypical views of gardens such as that they are only for growing vegetables and should be orderly as well as that they are only for the rich versus poor, urban versus country, apartment versus house, and so on.

We might add that such comparisons can be made for any phenomena. Suppose, for example, that you want to study the computer industry. This industry, which previously was dominated by one corporation (IBM), has wondrously burgeoned over the past decade, with its increasing numbers of companies, customers, outlets, and connections with a similarly expanding software industry. A quick review of a few other industries will sharpen your eye for what appears—and fails to appear—in the data or will soon collect on the computer industry. Think of the lumber industry. It has a long history, is linked with regional sites, and is in frequent conflict with environmentalists and other groups often located in the same region. Or, think of the oil industry, which is international in scope and of vital interest to various national states. Understandably, both the oil and lumber industries produce powerful lobbying. In addition, they have vast and diversified consumerships that are linked with a great many other industries and, of course, are very much in the public eye. Or, consider certain industries that have substantial, and sometimes huge, governmental subsidies such as the farming industry in the United States. With these lists of properties, we turn to our data about computers to see whether any of these properties (e.g., relationship to other industries, lobbying, conflict of interests) can be found in our data. These might show up in our analyses as conditions that affect the actions of people in and toward the industries as well as the actions of the industries' representatives. The mental stimulation derived from such comparisons broadens our horizons (i.e., sensitizes us to what is in our data) and enables us to delineate the properties and dimensions that define meaning of phenomena and give specificity to our theory.

SUMMARY

As a way of summarizing this chapter, we present a list of the functions of questions and making of theoretical comparisons.

ASKING QUESTIONS AND MAKING THEORETICAL COMPARISONS

1. Help analysts obtain a grasp on the meaning of events or happenings that might seem otherwise obscure.
2. Help sensitize researchers to possible properties and dimensions that are in the data but remain undiscovered.
3. Suggest further interview questions or observations based on evolving theoretical analysis.
4. Help analysts move more quickly from the level of description to one of abstraction.
5. Counter the tendency to focus too greatly on a single case by immediately bringing analysis up to a more abstract level.
6. Force researchers to examine basic assumptions, their biases, and their perspectives.
7. Force a closer examination of the evolving theory, sometimes resulting in the qualification or altering of the initial framework.
8. Make it more likely that analysts will discover both variation and general patterns.
9. Ensure the likelihood of a more fluid and creative stance toward data analysis.
10. Facilitate the linking and densifying of categories.

As a final note, we emphasize again that when we ask questions and make theoretical comparisons, we are *not* using the answers to our questions or the properties and dimensions that we identify as data but rather are using them as tools to help us gain a better understanding of the data in front of us.

7 Analytic Tools

Analytic tools: Devices and techniques used by analysts to facilitate the coding process

In Chapter 6, we introduced the basic operations of making comparisons and asking questions. These are the major procedures of this method and should be used consistently and systematically during analysis. In this chapter, we present a set of analytic tools. These are different from the basic procedures, but in their own way they are equally as important as the analytic process. These are devices or techniques that can be used by analysts to assist them with making comparisons and asking questions. All craftspersons, be they artists or carpenters, need tools to help them with their work. The tools are used as extensions of the body and enable the users to carry out their work. Imagine a house painter trying to paint without a brush or roller. Or, imagine a musician trying to play a piece of music without an instrument. He or she might hum the tune, but it would not be quite the same. Tools are used at the discretion of the user and matched to the task at hand. The same holds for the "analytic tools." Their purpose is to increase sensitivity, help the user recognize "bias" to some degree, and help him or her overcome "analytic blocks." The analytic techniques that we describe here are examples of some that we use during analysis. Other researchers make use of other analytic tools for similar, and often differing, purposes such as to order and organize data. (See, e.g., Dey, 1993, who uses a variety of techniques; Feldman, 1995, who draws on ethnomethodology, semiotics, dramaturgy, and deconstruction for techniques; Miles & Huberman, 1994, especially their use of matrices; and Weitzman & Miles, 1995, for their examples of the use of computers.) What this indicates is that even experienced researchers need ways of probing into and organizing data. Even they develop analytic blocks or barriers during analysis and need techniques to move the process along. How we actually use our tools during analysis was illustrated somewhat in the chapter on microanalysis (Chapter 5).

As already stated, the analytic tools are very useful for sensitizing us to relevant properties and dimensions of a category. Recall that earlier we stated that the purpose of our analysis is to build theory. Our way of building theory is *not* just to work with a single case, then proceed to the next one and treat it as a separate case, and so on. Rather, we want to know what **this case** teaches us about other cases. We want to move from the **specific** to the **more general.** Therefore, we use a case to open up our minds to the range of possible meanings, properties, dimensions, and relationships inherent in any bit of data. Therefore, when we move on to the next case and those that follow, we are more sensitive both to those possibilities and to **what else** the new cases might teach us. In other words, if we are analyzing flowers in gardens and identify that the flowers in this garden have a certain color, size, and shape, then we will want to examine the flowers in the next garden and compare them along those same, and possibly other, dimensions. Thus, we can see how they are the same and how they are different from the previous flowers we examined. This allows us to define a phenomenon very precisely.

The specific case provides guidelines (properties and dimensions) for looking at all cases, enabling researchers to move from description to conceptualization and from the more specific to the general or abstract. When we say that we are coding **theoretically,** we mean that we are coding on the basis of concepts and how they vary according to their properties and dimensions. We are not just sticking to one case. Rather, **by** asking theoretical questions about this case and

by thinking comparatively according to properties and dimensions of categories, we are opening up our minds to the range of possibilities, which in turn might apply to, and become evident, when we sample other cases. As we examine other cases and compare incident against incident, we are more likely to recognize both sameness and variation in categories and to see how what applied in one case also might be relevant in the next case and where the two cases differ. Again, we remind our readers of the provisional nature of our analysis early in the research process and the necessity of validating our categories (which is, in fact, our naming or interpreting what is going on) by constantly making comparisons against **incoming cases**. The following box provides a summary of the purposes of the analytic tools.

Purpose of Analytic Tools

1. Steer a researcher's thinking away from the confines of both the technical literature and personal experience.
2. Avoid standard ways of thinking about phenomena.
3. Stimulate the inductive process.
4. Focus on what is in the data, and do not take anything for granted.
5. Allow for clarification or debunking of assumptions made by those being studied.
6. Listen to what people are saying and doing.
7. Avoid rushing past "diamonds in the rough" when examining data.
8. Force the asking of questions and the giving of provisional answers.
9. Allow fruitful labeling of concepts, although provisionally.
10. Discover properties and dimensions of categories.

THE USE OF QUESTIONING

The first analytic tool we discuss is the use of questioning. We want to ask good questions, ones that will enhance the development of our evolving theory. Although asking questions was given considerable attention in the chapter on basic operations (Chapter 6), the type of questioning we are referring to here is more specific and includes questions such as the following: Who? When? Why? Where? What?

How? How much? With what results? These questions will gain added significance in later chapters on axial and selective coding (Chapters 9 and 10). These questions are especially useful to analysts when they are blocked in their analyses and cannot seem to see anything but the standard ways of explaining phenomena. In a book on writing by Lamont (1994), the use of questions was suggested as a way of getting a writing project off the ground. She suggested that asking questions helps a writer get past that initial block of not knowing where to start. Although Lamont was talking about writing and not analyzing data, it is the concept of being blocked to which we are responding and along which we are making comparisons. Being blocked can happen to both analysts and writers. An important point to keep in mind is that we are using questions not to generate data but rather to generate ideas or ways of looking at the data.

To illustrate what we mean, let us jump ahead of ourselves and use one of the concepts that emerges from an exercise on labeling concepts in Chapter 8 on open coding. The concept has to do with illegal drug taking. Readers may look ahead and read this chapter if they so desire. However, because most persons have at least some common knowledge about illegal drugs and their use, reading ahead might not be necessary. The concept is **"obliging supply network."** Questions that we might ask about this concept include the following. **Who** is doing the supplying? **Who** is doing the buying? We might see whether we can find the answers in the data—other students, friends, a special boyfriend or girlfriend, students from another school, outsiders, gang members, hardcore drug dealers? The asking of these types of question not only enables us to learn more about what is going on here but also raises other issues that we might want to look for when we continue with our interviews and analysis of this document. For example, drug use could vary considerably, depending on who was doing the supplying and who was doing the buying and why. A boy might feel pressured into trying a drug if his girlfriend or a member of his football team puts pressure on him to try. On the other hand, perhaps a teen is curious about drugs but does not want his girlfriend or football teammates to know; in that case, he might prefer to buy from someone outside the school unknown to friends and acquaintances. Now that we have raised these issues, we can begin to theoretically sample, either in this data set or through further data collection, differences in whether drugs are used and the amount of drug use by crosscutting the concept of "drug use" with the concept of "supplier." (Notice that we are working with the property of amount of drug use.) The next question is **where**. Where is this obliging supply network most likely to be operating—at parties, during school breaks on campus, when students go off campus for lunch, around the campus after school, at local teen hangouts? This question helps us to think about "site" and provides places to go to theoretically sample the concept of "supplying." The next question is **what**. What drugs are being supplied? Or, to make the question more complicated, what drugs are being supplied at which places? Now we are crosscutting "types of drugs" with "supplier." We now turn to the question of **how**. How does one go about tapping into this supply network? Or, how does one go about letting others know that one is in the business of supplying? Are there verbal or nonverbal codes that kids use to indicate their desire to purchase or sell? Is there a testing out process to determine whether one is a legitimate user or seller and not a cop? What about visibility of exchange—drugs for money? How is that done to keep it hidden? What happens to kids if they cannot pay for their drugs or if they get caught selling or using? If drugs supposedly are available everywhere, then why is it that not everyone knows that or that not everyone uses drugs? Still another question is **how much**. How much of a supply is there of what types of drugs? Is the supply unlimited, that is, any drug at any time of day? Are there enough drugs at parties for everyone to get stoned, or is the purpose more to create group cohesiveness so that just a puff or two for every person is sufficient?

One could go on and on with this type of questioning. No one is saying that the answers are available in the data or that the questions constitute data. Rather, the questions become stimuli for thinking about where to go to theoretically sample or what further questions one should ask of interviewees and what other observations one should make. What becomes obvious is that, by asking questions, we realize that there is much more for us to learn about the concept of "obliging supply network." It no longer is just a label, a title of an event or a happening, but rather is a whole new set of ideas that can tell us a great deal more about teens and drugs if we follow through with data gathering based on these questions.

Another type of question that is useful is **temporal** questions such as frequency, duration, rate, and timing. Another type is **spatial** questions such as how much space, where, whether circumscribed or not, and open or closed. Questions of this nature give us even more insight. Where do teens who sell and buy hide their drugs while on campus? Where do they sell them? How often? How long does a sale take? Is it visible or invisible to others? One could ask **technological** questions such as the following. Is special equipment needed to sell or use drugs? If so, then where does this come from, and who sells it? Or, one could ask **informational** questions such as who knows who is using, selling, and where to buy. In addition, one could ask questions about **rules, cultural values or morals, and standards** (purity in the case of drugs). All of these questions would stimulate our thinking about teens and drugs and would make us more sensitive to what to look for in these and future data.

ANALYSIS OF A WORD, PHRASE, OR SENTENCE

Next, we demonstrate how, when we get stuck in an "analytic rut," we often can pull ourselves out through analysis of a word, phrase, or sentence. This technique is especially valuable because it enables the analyst to raise questions about possible meanings, whether assumed or intended. It also can help bring into awareness an analyst's assumptions about what is being said or observed while demonstrating to him or her that there are other possible meanings and interpretations. This exercise is invaluable as an opening gambit even for experienced researchers as a way of checking themselves against their preconceptions.

Usually, when a person sees or hears a word, he or she will assign a meaning to it (interpretation), derived from common cultural usage or experience. It is what we, the analysts, perceive the respondent intended by this action or what the incident indicated. Regardless of how much we try to maintain an analytic distance, our interpretations may or may not be accurate. Take the word "drug." For a person who needs a certain medication to survive, the term might mean "life giving." For another person, it might mean those over-the-counter pills one takes for a headache. For an addict, it might mean "relief."

For the addict's significant others, it might mean "pain." Some persons might say that the use of all drugs is "destructive" all of the time, whereas others might say that it depends on who uses them, why, and when. Of course, the context in which the concept is used should indicate meaning. However, it is not always evident, and sometimes what a respondent tells us is not necessarily what he or she means. We might have to look for hidden or obscure meanings that might not be immediately evident to us in the data.

Doing analysis of a word, phrase, or sentence consists of scanning the document, or at least a couple of pages of it, and then returning to focus on a word or phrase that strikes the analyst as being significant and analytically interesting. Then, the analyst begins to list all of the possible meanings of the word that come to mind. With this list in mind, the analyst can turn to the document and look for incidents or words that will point to meaning. For instance, take a phrase mentioned by a teen when talking about drug taking, namely that teens use drugs as a "challenge to the adult stance." The word "challenge" can have many different meanings. Because our interviewee did not specify what she meant when she said that, we can only speculate on what she intended. "Challenge" could mean a sense of independence, a way of rebelling, a way of learning something about oneself or about drug use, a way of escaping from parental authority, or a way of defining who the person is. All of these are possible interpretations. It is up to the analyst to discern which interpretations are most accurate by looking to the data and doing a comparative analysis. Do other teens express the same idea when giving reasons for why they use drugs? Or, do they offer alternative explanations? We might find that none of these meanings holds up to scrutiny when we make comparisons against data. But at least when looking at the data, the analyst has some ideas of what to look for rather than simply staring into space with nothing emerging because the analyst has no idea what he or she is looking for.

FURTHER ANALYSIS THROUGH COMPARISONS

As discussed in the chapter on basic operations (Chapter 6), making comparisons is essential for identifying categories and for their development. In that chapter, we discussed two types of comparisons. The first pertains to the comparing of incident to incident or of object to object, looking for similarities and differences among their properties to classify them. For example, by comparing two flowers for size, shape, color, and other characteristics, we learn that one flower has the characteristics of what we know as a rose and that another has those of a violet.

The second type of comparison is the making of theoretical comparisons. This involves **comparing categories** (abstract concepts) to similar or different concepts to bring out possible properties and dimensions when these are not evident to the analyst. (They might be there, but perhaps the analyst is blocked and cannot identify them.) Two types of theoretical comparisons are discussed in what follows, namely the flip-flop technique and the systematic comparison of two or more concepts, which can be broken down further to the making of "close-in" comparisons and the making of "far-out" comparisons. **Again, no one is saying that these properties pertain to this piece of data or can be found in future data or are in of themselves data, only that these are possibilities and that we must look to the data to see what is there with more sensitivity and with greater awareness. Theoretical comparisons also provide ideas for theoretical sampling to discover variation.**

The Flip-Flop Technique

The first comparative technique is the flip-flop technique. This indicates that a concept is turned "inside out" or "upside down" to obtain a different perspective on the event, object, or action/inter-action. In other words, we look at opposites or extremes to bring out significant properties. For example, another concept pertaining to teens and drug taking is "access," which has the characteristic of being "easy." To better understand what is implied by "easy access," we can ask the opposite. What would happen to teens and drug taking if access were "difficult," that is, if one had to travel a long distance to obtain drugs, ask around a lot, or pass a certain test before obtaining a drug? Would "difficult access" make a difference in amount or type of teen drug use? Once we think through what "difficult access" might mean, we can then return to our interview with more questions to ask about what "easy access" might mean in terms of amount, type, and frequency of drug use. To continue with this example, if one thinks about "difficult access," one might conclude that there could be fewer places to buy drugs, that drugs could be less available at parties, and that drugs could be more expensive. Returning to the concept of "easy access," one might look for properties such as **degree** to which drugs are accessible, **how much** drugs cost, and **places** to purchase drugs. This raises other important questions. If "easy access" makes it easier for teens to use drugs, then why is it that not all teens use drugs? What makes some teens take advantage of the easy accessibility, while others do not? Are some more adventurous, more rebellious, more curious, and more vulnerable to peer pressure? These questions lead to further sampling along conceptual lines during data collection. Another approach would be to turn teen drug use around and look at teen "non-drug use" to see what insights that might provide. The researcher could then interview teens who do not use drugs and compare their interviews to those of teens who do—always, of course, thinking not about specific interviews per se but rather in terms of incidents of concepts and their properties and dimensions.

Systematic Comparison of Two or More Phenomena

Another comparative technique is the making of a **systematic comparison.** This means comparing an incident in the data to one recalled from experience or from the literature. The purpose of this comparison is to sensitize the researcher to properties and dimensions in the data that might have been overlooked because the researcher did not know what he or she was looking for. The comparative or "other" category stimulates the analyst to think in terms of properties and dimensions. Recall that we stated earlier that when making theoretical comparisons, we are comparing concepts and not individuals or cases. **We are interested not in how many individuals exhibit this concept but rather in how often this concept emerges and what it looks like (i.e., its properties) under varying conditions.** The comparative concept might be close in (i.e., similar in nature to the concept the researcher wants to explore) or far out (i.e., dissimilar to the concept under exploration). An example of a close-in comparison would be comparing the concept of "limited experimenting" with drugs to that of "occasional user" of alcohol, with the qualifiers "limited" and "occasional" being dimensions of the property of frequency and with alcohol and drug use both having the potential to be addictive substances. We might ask the following. What does it mean to be an "occasional user" of alcohol? What are some of the properties of occasional use? Once these questions have been raised and answered about alcohol abuse, the analyst might then look at "limited experimenting" with drugs to see whether any properties might be in the data such as how often they are used, how much is used, and the intensity of the effect. An example of a far-out comparison would be comparing "limited experimenting" with drugs to the concept of "professional violinist." First, one would list the properties of "professional violinist" (e.g., frequency of practice, intensity of playing, demands of time and travel, degree of interest in playing along with interest in other activities). Then, one would see whether any of these properties might apply to drug use. Although the latter exercise might seem far-fetched, in reality it provides considerable analytic mileage. One can think of frequency of drug use, intensity of the experience, amount of time put into obtaining and using drugs, degree of interest in this activity, degree of interest in other activities when using drugs, and so on. All of these issues raise questions about drug use and give further insight into what the profile of a "limited experimenter" might look like. **Although the actual properties emerge from the data, the techniques help analysts to recognize the properties, to get past the analytic blinders that often obstruct our view of what is in the data.**

One makes theoretical comparisons based on what one knows, either from experience or from the literature. For example, one might read an excellent research report on alcoholics and then list all of the properties of alcoholics brought out in the article along with their dimensions. Then, one might ask whether any of those properties have any relevance to drug taking. In so doing, the analyst would look at the data for indications of these properties and dimensions (i.e., whether they are repeated) along with any emerging variations in how the concept differs along the dimensional continuum. Once sensitive to what he or she is looking for, the analyst begins to build a list of properties and dimensions from the actual data, validated and extended through further analysis and data collection. **In the end, the researcher's theoretical explanations are fuller, more specific, and** denser because properties and dimensions that previously might not have been visible to the researcher become evident once he or she is sensitive to them. Of course, they emerge from data, but they emerge to a sensitive mind rather than to a blocked mind.

Waving the Red Flag

The last technique that we discuss in this chapter is waving the red flag. Analysts, as well as research participants, bring to the investigation biases, beliefs, and assumptions. This is not necessarily a negative trait; after all, persons are the products of their cultures, the times in which they live, their genders, their experiences, and their training. The important thing is to recognize when either our own or the respondents' biases, assumptions, or beliefs are **intruding into the analysis.** Recognizing this intrusion often is difficult because when persons share a common culture, meanings often are taken for granted. Researchers sometimes become so engrossed in their investigations that they do not even realize they have come to accept the assumptions or beliefs of their respondents. They "go native," so to speak. Yet, to do justice to our participants and give them a proper "voice," we must be able to stand back and examine the data at least somewhat objectively. **We emphasize that it is not possible to be completely free of bias.** However, there are certain gross indicators that bias might be intruding into the analysis, and when certain situations arise, we must stand back and ask ourselves, "What is going on here?"

One of the indicators of bias intruding is the face value acceptance of the words or explanations given by respondents or the complete rejection of these without questioning what is being said. Whenever we hear the terms "always" and "never," these should wave a red flag in our minds. So should phrases such as "It couldn't possibly be that way" and "Everyone knows that this is the way it is." Remember that we are thinking dimensional ranges, and "always," "never," "everyone," and "no other way" each represents only one point along that continuum. We also want to understand the other dimensional variations such as "sometimes" and "occasionally" and the conditions that lead to these. For example, a student in one of our classes was studying the use of interpreters in clinics treating Asian women. The student explained that a male interpreter may be called on to interpret for a female client when no female is available. The use of men in these cases is problematic because some issues such as those involving sex or gynecological problems are considered too sensitive to be discussed in mixed-gender company. From an analytic standpoint, the concepts of "taboo" and "never" stand out, immediately waving a red flag in our minds. It would be very easy for persons familiar with Asian cultures to accept this stance and not raise any further questions about the matter. Yet, the concept of "taboo" brings up some very interesting questions. What happens in life-threatening situations, when a woman's life is immediately at stake? Would the woman and/or the interpreter let her die because no one is willing to talk about what is happening? Or, are there subtle ways of getting around taboos by making inferences, by providing subtle clues, or by using nonverbal communication? Would a sensitive clinician who is familiar with this population pick up on what is not being said and follow up on it? Would the woman find an excuse to come back at another time? To simply accept what we are told and to never question or explore issues more completely forecloses on opportunities to develop more encompassing and varied interpretations.

The analytic moral is to not take situations or sayings for granted. It is important to question everything, especially those situations in which we find ourselves or our respondents "going native" or accepting the common viewpoint or perspective. Also, when we hear a term such as "sometimes," we want to explore the conditions that bring about "some times" and determine whether there are other situations that also produce "never" or "always." We want to look for contradictory or opposite cases so that we might find examples of how concepts vary when conditions are changed. Even if "never" is the situation, we want to know why this is so and what conditions enable this to be so. We should remember that people are very resourceful. Over the years, they seem to find strategies for managing or getting around many different types of situations.

Certain words, such as "never" and "always," are signals to take a closer look at the data. We must ask questions such as the following. What is going on here? What is meant by "never" or "always"? Never, under what conditions? How is a state of "never" maintained (i.e., by what interactional strategies)? Or, by what strategies are persons able to circumvent it? What happens if a state of "never" is not maintained? That is, what if some unaware person breaks the interactional rules or taboos? Finally, we need to ask under what conditions the rules are likely to be broken and kept and what happens after that.

This concludes our chapter on analytic tools. Tools and procedures have no relevance without an understanding of the purpose for which they were designed. We move to that discussion in the subsequent chapters.

SUMMARY

In this chapter, we presented a set of analytic tools or techniques to facilitate analysis. We expect that analysts will use them like any good craftsmen, flexibly and as extensions of their own abilities. As analysts, we want to build creative, grounded, and dense theory. To do so requires sensitivity to what the data are saying and the ability to recognize when our own biases, or those of our participants, are intruding into our analysis. Although some analysts claim to be able to "bracket" their beliefs and perspectives toward data, we have found that doing so is easier said than done. We know that we never can be completely free of our biases, for so many are unconscious and part of our cultural inheritances. We find it more helpful to acknowledge that these influence our thinking and then look for ways in which to break through or move beyond them. Keeping a journal of the research experience is a useful way in which to keep track of what one is thinking during data gathering and analysis. This technique is used successfully by many researchers. In addition, analysts can make use of tools such as the ones provided in this chapter. Although certainly no guarantee, they do stimulate thinking, provide for alternative interpretations, and generate the free flow of ideas.

8 Open Coding

In the chapter on microanalysis (Chapter 5), we demonstrated that coding is a dynamic and fluid process. In this chapter, we want readers to keep that image in mind as we break the coding process down into a series of activities. Breaking the analytic process down is an artificial but necessary task because analysts must understand the logic that lies behind analysis. That is what analysts are trying to accomplish through the use of techniques and procedures. Without this comprehension, procedures and techniques are likely to be used in a rote manner, with no real sense of when, where, and how they are to be used; when they can be omitted; or how they may be modified. This chapter begins with a discussion of concepts and the act of conceptualizing. It goes on to explain how categories are discovered in data and developed in terms of their properties and dimensions (also derived from data). It ends with an overview of the different approaches to open coding.

SCIENCE AND CONCEPTS

Science could not exist without *concepts*. Why are they so essential? By the very act of naming phenomena, we fix continuing attention on them. Once our attention is fixed, we can begin to examine them comparatively and to *ask questions* about them. Such questions not only enable us to **systematically specify** what we see, but when they take the form of *hypotheses* or *propositions*, they suggest how phenomena might possibly be **related** to each other. In the end, communication among investigators, including the vital interplay of discussion and argument necessary to enhance the development of science, is made possible by the **specification of concepts and their relationships**. These points are discussed in greater detail in Blumer (1969, pp. 153-182).

The discovery of *concepts* is the focus of this chapter. Why, then, is this chapter titled "Open Coding"? Because to uncover, name, and develop concepts, we must open up the text and expose the thoughts, ideas, and meanings contained therein. Without this first analytic step, the rest of the analysis and the communication that follows could not occur. Broadly speaking, during open coding, data are broken down into discrete parts, closely examined, and compared for similarities and differences. Events, happenings, objects, and actions/interactions that are found to be conceptually similar in nature or related in meaning are grouped under more abstract concepts termed "categories." Closely examining data for both differences and similarities allows for fine discrimination and differentiation among categories. In later analytic steps, such as axial and selective coding, data are reassembled through statements about the nature of relationships among the various categories and their subcategories. These statements of relationship are commonly referred to as "hypotheses." The theoretical structure that ensues enables us to form new explanations about the nature of phenomena.

This chapter builds on the previous chapters, especially Chapters 5 to 7. However, it focuses more on the discrete analytic tasks rather than on procedures and techniques as such. The analytic tasks include naming concepts, defining categories, and developing categories in terms of their properties and dimensions.

CONCEPTUALIZING

The first step in theory building is *conceptualizing*. A concept is a **labeled phenomenon**. It is an abstract representation of an event, object, or action/interaction that a researcher identifies as being significant in the data. The purpose behind naming phenomena is to enable researchers to group similar events, happenings, and objects under a common heading or classification. Although events or happenings might be discrete elements, the fact that they share common characteristics or related meanings enables them to be grouped.

Conceptualizing Leading to Classifying

Examples of concepts include a tornado, a flight, and a government agency. Each of these stands for a given phenomenon. When concepts are used in interaction, they often provoke a common cultural imagery. This is because concepts share certain properties. For example, the word "flight" has the same connotation whether we are speaking about a bird, a kite, or a plane. Although the objects might differ in form and size, each has the specific property of being able to fly. When we think about any of these objects, we imagine something soaring in the air. Therefore, a labeled thing is something that can be located, placed in a class of similar objects, or *classified*. Anything under a given classification has one or more "recognizable" (actually defined) properties (characteristics) such as size, shape, contour, mass, or (in this case) the ability to soar through the air. What is less apparent

when we classify objects is that a classification implies, either explicitly or implicitly, *action* that is taken with regard to the classified object.
A flight consists of taking off and landing as well as moving through
the air, either through self-propulsion (as with birds) or through
assistance of persons and/or wind (as with planes and kites).

Objects Classified in Multiple Ways

Let us now look at a more extended example of classifying. Once
we placed on the seminar table a small plastic box containing paper
clips. We asked, "What is this object and what is it used for?" Naturally, everyone answered correctly. Then, we asked further, "What else
is it?" There were blank stares from the students. So, we continued,
"What else **could** it be? What else could it be used for?" The students
quickly warmed to this imaginary game—a paperweight, a weapon,
an element in a design, a toy, or an example of an efficient industrial
product. They added that it also was an example of *multiple possible
classifications*. Thus,

> Any particular object can be named and thus located in countless
> ways. The naming sets it within a context of quite differently related
> classes. The nature or essence of an object does not reside mysteri-
> ously within the object itself but is dependent upon how it is defined.
> (Strauss, 1969, p. 20)

But also,

> The direction of activity depends upon the particular ways that
> objects are classified. . . . It is the definition of what the object "is"
> that allows action to occur with reference to what it is taken to be.
> Mark Twain tells how, as an apprentice pilot, he mistook a wind reef
> (not dangerous) for a bluff reef (deadly dangerous) and, to the
> hilarity of his boss, who "properly" read the signs, performed
> miraculous feats of foolishness to avoid the murderous pseudo-
> bluff. (pp. 21-22)

For our analytic purposes, it also is important to understand that
classified objects, events, acts, and actions/interactions have attributes and that how one defines and interprets those attributes (or the

meanings given to them) determines the various ways in which concepts are classified. For example, the paper clip box has sufficient weight for it to be used as a paperweight. It also has sharp edges, so it might function as a weapon. A ripe orange has some degree of juice as well as size, color, shape, weight, and perhaps cost when sold in the market.

Conceptualizing or Abstracting

Let us now look at the act of *conceptualizing*. In conceptualizing, we are abstracting. Data are broken down into discrete incidents, ideas, events, and acts and are then given a name that represents or stands for these. The name may be one placed on the objects by the analyst because of the imagery or meaning they evoke when examined comparatively and in context, or the name may be taken from the words of respondents themselves. The latter often are referred to as "in vivo codes" (Glaser & Strauss, 1967). As we continue with our data analysis, if we come across another object, event, act, or happening that we identify through *comparative analysis* as sharing some common characteristics with an object or a happening, then we give it the same name, that is, place it into the same code. (Another way of saying this is that particular properties of an object or event evoke a similar imagery in our minds, and because of that, we group them together. For instance, when we see a bird, a plane, or a kite, we might be struck by their common ability to remain in, and move through, the air; therefore, we classify these as examples of flight.) Thus, when we classify like with like and separate out that which we perceive as dissimilar, we are responding to characteristics, or properties inherent in the objects that strike us as relevant. The images that are provoked in our minds may or may not be different from common cultural perspectives or notions about things. If our imagery differs from the usual or standard ways of thinking about things and we are able to see objects, events, or happenings in new ways, then we can create novel theoretical explanations. That is why we, as theorists, are called on to do such detailed analyses of data. We want to see new possibilities in phenomena and classify them in ways that others might not have thought of before (or, if considered previously, were not systematically developed in terms of their properties and dimensions).

Illustration of Conceptualizing

In this second edition of *Basics of Qualitative Research*, we have chosen to use actual field notes to illustrate the analytic process. We do so because we believe that unaltered field notes more closely resemble the materials with which researchers are working. Excerpts from the same interview are used both in this chapter and in Chapter 9. This particular interview was done with a woman in her early 20s and is about drug use by teens. Notice that the respondent needed prodding in the form of direct questioning to verbalize her thoughts. With some respondents, one might be able to say "Tell me about teens and drugs," and the respondents would talk for hours. This was not the situation here. However, it is important to point out that the interviewer did not have a list of preset questions to ask. Rather, she asked the questions based on responses given to the previous queries. These field notes were obtained as part of a larger study by us looking at biographically relevant incidents in individuals' lives.

What we would like to illustrate in this first section of this chapter is the technique of *naming* or *labeling*. Contrary to what many persons think, conceptualizing is an art and involves some creativity, but it is an art that can be learned. Because our purpose is to illustrate the **act of naming and not how we actually analyze data,** only the first few pages of the interview are used. Not every possible phrase or idea is conceptualized. Also, the names that we use are arbitrary; other researchers might use other labels, depending on their foci, training, and interpretations. **Also note—and this is very important—that the conceptual name or label should be suggested by the context in which an event is located.** By "context," we mean the conditional background or situation in which the event is embedded. For example, we are talking about teen, rather than adult, drug use, and part of being a teen often is having an exploratory nature, a need or desire to challenge adult values and sometimes rebel against them; we get quite a different situation from that of adult hard-core drug use.

(Note: Conceptual names are in bold print.)

Interviewer: Tell me about teens and drug use.

Respondent: I think teens use drugs as a release from their parents ["**rebellious act**"]. Well, I don't know. I can only talk for myself. For me, it was an experience ["**experience**"] [in vivo code]. You hear a lot about drugs ["**drug talk**"]. You hear they are bad for you ["**negative connotation**" to the "**drug talk**"]. There is a lot of them around ["**available supply**"]. You just get into them because they're accessible ["**easy access**"] and because it's kind of a new thing ["**novel experience**"]. It's cool! You know, it's something that is bad for you, taboo, a "no" ["**negative connotation**"]. Everyone is against it ["**adult negative stance**"]. If you are a teenager, the first thing you are going to do is try them ["**challenge the adult negative stance**"].

Interviewer: Do teens experiment a lot with drugs?

Respondent: Most just try a few ["**limited experimenting**"]. It depends on where you are [and] how accessible they are ["**degree of accessibility**"]. Most don't really get into it hard-core [good in vivo concept] ["**hard-core use**" vs. "**limited experimenting**"]. A lot of teens are into pot, hash, a little organic stuff ["**soft core drug types**"]. It depends on what phase of life you're at ["**personal developmental stage**"]. It's kind of progressive ["**progressive using**"]. You start off with the basic drugs like pot ["**basic drugs**"] [in vivo code]. Then you go on to try more intense drugs like hallucinogens ["**intense drugs**"] [in vivo code].

Interviewer: Are drugs easily accessible?

Respondent: You can get them anywhere ["**easy access**"]. You just talk to people ["**networking**"]. You go to parties, and they are passed around. You can get them at school. You ask people, and they direct you as to who might be able to supply you ["**obliging supply network**"].

Interviewer: Is there any stigma attached to using drugs?

Respondent: Not among your peers ["**peer acceptance**"]. If you're in a group of teenagers and everyone is doing it, if you don't use, you are frowned upon ["**peer pressure**"]. You want to be able to say you've experienced it like the other people around you ["**shared peer experience**"]. It's not a stigma among your own group ["**being an insider**"]. Obviously, outsiders like older people will look down upon you ["**outsider intolerance**"]. But within your own group of friends, it definitely is not a stigma ["**peer acceptance**"].

Interviewer: You say you did drugs for the experience. Do kids talk about the experience?

Respondent: It's a more of sharing the experience rather than talking about the experience ["**taking part in**" vs. "**dialoguing about**"]. You talk about doing drugs more than what it's like

when you take drugs ["**drug talk**"]. It depends upon what level
you are into it ["**hard core**" vs. "**limited experimenting**"], I
guess. Most kids are doing it because it is a trend in high school
["**part of social scene**"]. They are not doing it because of the
experience in some higher sense ["**not self-discovery**"]. They are
doing it because they are following the crowd ["**peer mimicry**"
vs. "**self-discovery**"].

Interviewer: Did I hear you say teens were attracted to drugs
because there was some element of risk, daring, [and] testing
associated with them?

Respondent: It's like living in the fast lane ["**tempting fate**"]. You
see all the people in Hollywood. Most teens idolize those people
who have fame and are living a fast-paced life ["**idol mimicry**"].
Often, these people are on drugs.

Interviewer: Were you attracted to drugs because of the Hollywood scene?

Respondent: To some degree, I was. I thought it was pretty cool
["**in thing**"]. It was part of a dangerous fast-paced life ["**tempting
fate**"]. To some degree, I too was following the crowd ["**peer
mimicry**"]. I wanted to be like everyone else. But I also did it
because I was sick of hearing people talk about the evils of drugs
and not knowing anything about what they really did to you
["**challenging the adult stance**"]. I saw people all around me
taking them with no long-lasting effects. They weren't evil or
addicted ["**fact discrepancy**"]. I got sick of the adults lecturing
about drugs when they had never tried them so that they could
present them fairly ["**presenting a one-sided view**"]. All they
talked about were the negative effects ["**negative connotations**"]. Yet, most of the people around you were not having those
negative effects ["**fact discrepancy**"].

Interviewer: What did doing drugs do for you?

Respondent: It gave me a different perspective on drug taking
["**experiential knowing**"]. It opened my mind ["**broadening
experience**"]. I think the preaching that they do totally blows the
issue out of proportion ["**addiction overblow**"]. Not everyone
who tries drugs will become addicted ["**refuting the argument**"].
I learned, yes, you can take them, and it is just like anything else;
you can walk away from them ["**self-control**"]. There is more to
addiction than just trying a drug ["**addiction as a complex process**"]. Not everyone that drinks is an alcoholic ["**critical defining**"]. If you were to drink all the time, it is just as bad as doing

drugs all the time ["**comparative analysis**"]. A lot of drugs are not as devastating to your body as alcohol. Pot, for example—yes, it affects you, but you are in a lot more control of yourself than if you are drunk or even have a couple of drinks ["**control as a criterion**"].

Interviewer: Getting back to your experience . . .

Respondent: I started with pot ["**initiating experience**"]. Pot, you don't get stoned the first time you try it ["**delayed experiencing**"]. Most people have to take it two to three times before they feel remotely high ["**body adaptation**"]. I did it five to six times ["**repeated tries**"] before I felt high ["**being stoned**"]. I tried it at a party ["**social act**"]. Kids break it out, [and] no one even questions it ["**peer acceptance**"]. It is just understood that it will be passed around and everyone will try it ["**peer pressure**"]. I was pretty young, 13 I guess. It turned out I was pretty allergic to pot ["**negative reaction**"]. It was never anything I took to ["**negative reinforcement**"].

Digging Deeper Into Analysis

At this point, we would like to stop the act of labeling. We have some concepts now, but as a result of our putting names on events, objects, and happenings, did we discover anything new or do we have any greater understanding of what the concepts stand for or mean? The answer to this question is **not really**. To discover anything new in data and to gain greater understanding, we must do more of the detailed and discriminate type of analysis that we call "microanalysis." This form of analysis uses the procedures of comparative analysis, the asking of questions, and makes use of the analytic tools to break the data apart and dig beneath the surface. We want to discern the **range of potential meanings** contained within the words used by respondents and develop them more fully in terms of their properties and dimensions. The act of labeling may do some of this. Any time one classifies, selects, or places a conceptual name on something, there is some degree of interpretation of meaning as derived from context; that is, there is some identification of property (or properties) that, in turn, stimulates the analyst to name an event and, in so doing, to classify it and define its use. (For example, if we see an object that has four legs, a flat surface, a back, and some padding, then we might label it a "chair" and try sitting on it to see what happens. Other persons seeing the same object might call it a "piece of art" or a "stand," depending on their interpretations.) However, just naming objects does not **always** explain what is going on in any deeper or complete sense. **It is important to note that we do not go through an entire document, put labels on events, and then go back and do a deeper analysis. The labels that we come up with are, in fact, the result of our in-depth detailed analysis of data.** Therefore, we would like to take these same data and use them to demonstrate how we might open up the text. In this short analytic section, we do a microanalysis of data, which is much more reflective of how we do our early coding. We introduce the readers to some new terms such as "memos." This should not cause concern. What is important is for the readers to get the sense of what is going on. Memos are explained later in Chapter 14. Also take note of how we use the procedures and techniques introduced in previous chapters to open up the text. We present only a short example here.

Memos: The researcher's record of analysis, thoughts, interpretations, questions, and directions for further data collection

We begin our analysis with the first paragraph by doing a line-by-line analysis.

1. **Interviewer:** Tell me about teens and drug use.
2. **Respondent:** I think teens use drugs as a release from their parents.

Memo. The first thing that strikes me in this sentence is the word "use." This is a strange term because, when taken out of the context of drug taking, the word means that an object or a person is being employed for some purpose. It implies a willful and directed act. In **making a comparison,** when I think about a computer, I think about employing it to accomplish a task. I think of it as being at my disposal. I am in control of when, where, and how it is used. I employ it because it makes writing easier for me. It is a help, an object outside of me that I use under certain conditions. Now, when I go back and think about "using" drugs, the word might mean simply to "take" or "ingest." But it also might imply some of these other ideas too, for example, being used for some reason, having control over what one does, making things easier, or being used under certain conditions but not others. This opens up a broader interpretation of the term "drug use" because the connotation now is that it might mean more than just ingestion; it also might encompass issues such as self-control over use, a purposeful and directed act that serves an end and that has a desired effect, plus there are times and places when it is used or not used. Although none of this is evident yet in the data, I have something to keep in mind while I continue my analysis.

Memo. I think it would help me to think more about the word "use" if I **make another comparison closer in, this time with alcohol.** If one were to say "I use alcohol," then what could that mean? It could mean sometimes, such as on special occasions, or all of the time, such as every day. I could use a little or a lot. I could use different types of alcohol, such as beer and vodka. It could mean that I ingest it or that I use it to cook with, to keep around to offer to company, or to bring as gifts when I am invited out to dinner. Then, there is how long I have been using it—a long time or a short time. I might use it at home, at parties, or at bars. Perhaps it gives me confidence, helps me to relax after a hard day's work, or helps me to fall asleep when I am tense. Maybe I use it to forget or escape my daily worries. **What this tells me is that alcohol use has certain properties such as frequency, duration, degree, type, purpose, way of using, and place of use.** I could locate myself dimensionally along each of these properties. These properties also might have applicability to **drug use.** Therefore, when I go on with analysis of this interview and in subsequent interviews, I look for how often, how long, how much, for what purposes, when, where, and what types of drugs are used and by whom. In this way, I can begin to get some idea of how drug use varies across teens and to see whether any patterns of drug use emerge.

Memo. The next interesting word in this sentence is "release." The first thing that comes to mind is **"rebellion."** But the word could mean other things too, such as get away from, escape, let go of, be different from, or not be under parental control. But in this case, it does not appear that it is the parent who is releasing the teen; rather, it appears that the teen is letting go of the parent. This is an interesting thought. When I think about "release" from jail, I think about being free, able to go and do **what** I want, **when** I want, and **how** I want. I served my time, paid a debt, gained or even earned my independence. I am in control of my destiny now; I no longer have to live by the jail's schedule. But what if I said I **escaped** from jail rather than being released. I still would be free, but now there is the fear of getting caught and having to go back. So, what are the similarities of and differences between being released from jail and our teen being "released" from her parent. One similarity is the ideas of freedom and control, the ability to make one's own life choices and do something on one's own initiative. One difference is that with jail, the higher authority is doing the releasing, whereas here it appears that the teen is taking the initiative or engaging in an act that distances her from the parent. This raises all sorts of questions such as the following. To teens, what does the term "parent" stand for? Is it authority, a lack of independence, or the inability to make one's own choices? Does release, then, imply a sort of gaining of independence, stepping out on one's own and making one's own choices? In a more profound sense, what implications does drug use have for identity issues in teens? Is the use of drugs or a comparable activity a stepping stone toward greater independence of thought and choice? What other activities besides drug taking might have the same outcome (after all, not all teens use drugs)? Also, why use drugs and not one of these other activities? Is it because drugs are accessible, or are there other connotations to their use that make them attractive to teens? These are questions that I might want to keep in mind to see whether they come up in further interviews and data analysis.

Memo. Now, as an analyst, **I must go back and look at my original conceptualization of "release."** It initially was labeled as a "rebellious act." After thinking through many different possible meanings of the word, there is the question: Would I still label it the same way? When I think about "rebellious act," I translate that into defiance. Perhaps there is some defiance implied, and to defy their parents might be one reason why some teens take drugs. But after thinking through the "release" more thoroughly, I think that rebellion is just one part of what is going on. There is something much deeper going on, at least in this teen. Release also can mean letting go, going forward, moving from dependence to independence both of thought and of action. It is one step on the path to growing up, although perhaps not the best choice or path. I think that through these analytic exercises, I now have a much more comprehensive insight into what the word "release" might mean. Even if one chooses to call this a "rebellious act," one has to ask the following questions. What does rebellion mean here? What are its properties? Against whom and what are teens rebelling? As I continue with my analysis, I will look for situations, events, and examples that will help me to better understand the meaning of the term "release."

DISCOVERING CATEGORIES

Once we have opened up text and have some concepts, where do we go next? In the course of doing analysis, an analyst might derive dozens of concepts. (It is not unusual for a beginning student to arrive at a teaching session with three to four pages of concepts.) Eventually, the analyst realizes that certain concepts can be grouped under a more abstract higher order concept, based on its ability to explain what is going on. For example, if a person observes 10 objects in the sky and labels them as "birds," then observes 5 different objects and defines them as "planes," and then observes 7 more objects and calls them "kites," sooner or later, he or she might ask what these objects share in common and come up with the concept of "flight." This term not only allows the objects to be classified but also explains what they are doing (in terms of action). Grouping concepts into categories is important because it enables the analyst to reduce the number of units with which he or she is working. In addition, categories have analytic power because they have the potential to explain and predict. For example, when we talk about the concept of flight, we can ask the following. What makes birds, kites, and planes fly? What attributes do they have that enable them to lift off the ground, remain in the air, and come down without crashing? How long, how high, and how far can they fly? With this information, we can begin to explain what properties birds, planes, and kites have in common that enable them to fly and what might happen to that ability, say, if one of those properties were to change, such as a bird developing a broken wing.

Categories and Phenomena

Categories are concepts, derived from data, that stand for phenomena. One example is our category of "flight." Phenomena are <u>important analytic ideas that emerge from our data.</u> They answer the question <u>"What is going on here?"</u> They depict the problems, issues, concerns, and matters that are important to those being studied. The name chosen for a category usually is the one that seems the most logical descriptor for what is going on. The name should be graphic enough to quickly remind the researcher of its referent. Because categories represent phenomena, they might be named differently, depending on the perspective of the analyst, focus of the research, and (most important) **the research context.** For example, whereas one analyst might label birds, planes, and kites as "flight," another might label them as "instruments of war" because the context is entirely different. In the latter case, the birds might be used as carrier pigeons delivering messages to troops behind enemy lines, the kites as signals of an impending attack, and the planes as troop and supply carriers bringing in much needed relief. Also, to return to our example of teens and drug use, if we look at the first paragraph that we analyzed, there are several different concepts (e.g., easy access, novel experience, rebellious act). However, if we stand back and ask what is going on, then we might say that teens are "experimenting" with drugs and the interviewee is providing us with some of the reasons why. In other words, all of the other concepts become properties or explanatory descriptors of the "experimenting" category.

The important thing to remember is that once concepts begin to accumulate, the analyst should begin the process of grouping them or categorizing them under more abstract explanatory terms, that is, categories. Once a category is identified, it becomes easier to remember it, to think about it, and (most important) to develop it in terms of its properties and dimensions and further differentiate it by breaking it down into its *subcategories,* that is, by explaining the when, where, why, how, and so on of a category that are likely to exist.

Naming Categories and Subcategories

Students often ask where names of categories come from. Some names come from the pool of concepts already discovered in data. As the analyst examines the lists of concepts, one might stand out as broader and more abstract than the others. For example, the concept of "flight" is more comprehensive than "plane," "bird," or "kite" in the earlier example. Thus, broader or more comprehensive and more abstract labels can serve as headings for classes of objects that share some similar characteristics. Or, an analyst might be working with data when suddenly he or she has an insight that seems to explain what is going on. For instance, suppose that a researcher was studying children at play and noticed acts that he or she labeled as **"grabbing,"** **"hiding,"** **"avoiding,"** and **"discounting."** Then, on observing the subsequent incident, it suddenly dawns on the researcher that what the children are doing is trying to avoid something through those actions. Thus, grabbing, hiding, avoiding, and discounting are grouped under the more abstract heading of **"strategies."** But strategies for what? The most probable answer is to avoid "toy sharing." In this manner, it emerges that one of the important phenomena to study in relation to groups of children at play is **"toy sharing,"** with "strategies" for either sharing or not sharing being a subcategory of concepts under that larger heading.

Another source of concepts is the literature. Terms such as **"caretaker fatigue,"** **"illness experience,"** and **"status passage"** all are strong concepts and come with established analytic meanings. If they have proven relevance to the present study by emerging from the data as well, then by using these established concepts rather than coining a new name, the analyst can extend development of concepts that already might be important to the discipline or profession. On the other hand, the use of established concepts might pose a serious problem. "Borrowed" concepts or names for phenomena often bring with them commonly held meanings and associations; that is, when we think about them, certain images come into our minds. These meanings might bias our interpretations of data and prevent analysts and their readers from seeing what is new in the data. Therefore, although it might be advantageous at times for the analyst to use concepts from the literature, he or she should do so with care, always making certain that they are embodied in these data and then being precise about their meanings (similarities, differences, and extensions) in the present research.

Another important source of category names is in vivo codes. When applied to categories, these are catchy terms that immediately draw our attention to them (Glaser and Strauss, 1967; Strauss, 1987). Again, we illustrate this with an example from one of our research projects. The scene was a hospital ward, where we were doing a study of articulation of work by head nurses. While a head nurse and the investigator were discussing the policies and procedures of the unit, the head nurse pointed to one of the licensed vocational nurses (LVNs) and said, "She is the tradition bearer of the unit." The head nurse explained that the LVN had taken on the responsibility of initiating all new employees and patients to the traditions, rules, and policies of the unit. The LVN also acted as rule enforcer, reprimanding others whenever she noticed that the rules were broken. The term "tradition bearer" is a good name for a category. It is catchy and explains what is going on. We also know that it is likely that other units also must have tradition bearers, for every ward has its own policies, procedures, rules, and traditions that must be carried out and enforced for social order to prevail. If there is no tradition bearer, then what happens?

Developing Categories in Terms of Their Properties and Dimensions

Once a category is identified, the analyst can begin to develop it in terms of its specific properties and dimensions. For example, we labeled "bird," "kite," and "plane" as objects that share the characteristic of flight because each could soar in the air. We came up with the word "flight" because as we compared each event against itself and other events in the data, we noted that these objects held the following trait in common: They remained in, and moved through, the air, whereas automobiles and bicycles remained on the ground. What we want to do now is define what we mean by "flight"—why, when, how long, how far, how fast, and how high. We want to give a category specificity through definition of its particular characteristics. We also are interested in how these properties vary along their dimensional ranges. For example, birds fly lower, slower, and for shorter lengths of time than do many planes. These different objects, although similar in the sense of having the ability to fly, are dissimilar when compared against each other for specific properties and dimensions of these, giving our concept of "flight" *variation*. We have identified that it can range from high to low along the property of height, it can range from slow to fast along the property of speed, it can range from long to short along the property of duration, and so on. Notice that with each additional property and dimensional variation, we increase our knowledge about the concept of "flight."

Through delineation of properties and dimensions, we differentiate a category from other categories and give it precision. For example, if we take the concepts of "limited experimenting" with drugs versus "hard-core use" of drugs, we want to know what attributes distinguish each. Is it amount, duration, when used, and/or type of drug used?

To further clarify, whereas **properties are the general or specific characteristics or attributes of a category, dimensions represent the location of a property along a continuum or range.** For example, we might say that one of the properties that differentiates "limited experimenting" with drugs from "hard-core use" of drugs is "frequency" or the number of times a week the person is "stoned." We dimensionalize the property **frequency** by saying that with limited use, the user is stoned only *occasionally.* If we wanted to qualify or explain the term "limited experimenting" even further, then we could say that the teen uses drugs and gets stoned only when **at a party with other teens** at which **drugs are readily available** and **passed around,** whereas we might say that the hard-core user is stoned **very often,** using drugs three to four times a week, either when alone or when with selected others, and seeking out drugs on his or her own rather than having them passed around at a party. This qualifying of a category by specifying its particular properties and dimensions is important because we can begin to formulate *patterns* along with *their variations.* For example, we might say, based on frequency of use and the "type of drug used," that this situation can be classified into the pattern of "limited experimenting" with drugs. Perhaps if we do another interview and the pattern of drug use and getting stoned fits neither identified pattern, then the analyst can develop a third pattern such as the "recreational use" of drugs. **Patterns are formed when groups of properties align themselves along various dimensions.** In the earlier example, we noted that **patterns of drug use among teens can vary dimensionally from limited experimenting to hard-core use.**

To explain more precisely what we mean by properties and dimensions, we provide another example using the concept of "color."

Its properties include shade, intensity, hue, and so on. Each of these properties can be dimensionalized. Thus, color can vary in shade from dark to light, in intensity from high to low, and in hue from bright to dull. Shade, intensity, and hue are what might be called "general properties." They apply to color regardless of the object under investigation.

Whenever we come across a property of a category in the data, we attempt to locate it along a dimensional continuum. Because each category usually has more than one property or attribute, we would want to locate each property along its dimensions. For example, a flower not only has color, it also has size, shape, duration, and so on. Each of these attributes can be broken down into various dimensions. We might want to group flowers according to one specific attribute such as color qualified into subdimensions of shade, intensity, and hue. Or, we might want to do a more complex grouping, differentiating flowers not only according to color (shade, intensity, and hue) but also according to size (large, medium, and small), duration (long lasting vs. short lasting), height (tall vs. short), and shape (circular petals vs. oval petals). Once we have specified a pattern of combined attributes, we can group data according to those patterns. For instance, all flowers showing certain patterns of characteristics might be labeled as "roses" along with their variations (the different types of roses such as climbing and early blooming). **Note that when an analyst groups data into patterns according to certain defined characteristics, it should be understood that not every object, event, happening, or person fits a pattern completely.** There always are a few cases in which one or more dimensions are off slightly. This is okay within limits. People still are people, whether they have black, red, or yellow hair. It depends on how precise the analyst wants to be or to what degree he or she wants to break down the classifications into subtypes.

To summarize what we have been saying, when we compare incident to incident, we always compare according to the properties and dimensions inherent within the incident or event, grouping like with like. For example, if we take an incident of drug use, we examine it for frequency of use, type of drug used, perhaps duration of use, and then we label it as either an example of "limited experimenting" with drugs or "hard-core use" of drugs, depending on the properties brought out in each situation. It is the properties of the drug use that enable us to place the incident into a larger, more abstract classification.

Subcategories

Little has been said, up to this time, about subcategories. These will become clearer as we continue with the explanations about category development under axial coding. Basically, subcategories specify a category further by denoting information such as when, where, why, and how a phenomenon is likely to occur. Subcategories, like categories, also have properties and dimensions. For example, one subcategory of "drug using" might be "types of drugs." It explains the "what" of "drug using." Types of drugs might be classified according to the specific properties that they demonstrate such as the forms in which they come, the body's response to use, how they are used (e.g., inhaled, injected, ingested), and so on.

Variations on Ways of Doing Open Coding

There are several different ways of doing open coding. One way is *line-by-line analysis.* This form of coding involves close examination of data, phrase by phrase and sometimes word by word as demonstrated in the chapter on microanalysis (Chapter 5). This is perhaps the most time-consuming form of coding but often the most generative. Doing line-by-line coding is especially important in the beginning of a study because it enables the analyst to generate categories quickly and to develop those categories through further sampling along dimensions of a category's general properties, a process of sampling we call "theoretical sampling." Although theoretical sampling is explained in detail in Chapter 13, a short example is given here to illustrate our point. If a researcher is studying restaurants, then analysis of a very busy upscale restaurant with a large staff and a person to coordinate the work might lead the analyst to question what happens to the service in a very busy restaurant in which there are fewer staff members and no coordinator. (Notice that we are comparing along dimensions—how busy, how many staff members, presence or absence of a coordinator.) If we then go out and look for a restaurant with fewer staff members, no coordinator, and heavy lunch traffic and observe what happens to the quality and quantity of service, then we are doing theoretical sampling. Notice that we are not sampling restaurants per se but rather sampling along the dimensions of the different properties of "service" (our category). We want to know what happens to service when the conditions under which it occurs vary.

Moving on with different ways of coding, the analyst also might code by analyzing a whole *sentence or paragraph*. While coding a sentence or paragraph, he or she might ask, "What is the major idea brought out in this sentence or paragraph?" Then, after giving it a name, the analyst can do a more detailed analysis of that concept. This approach to coding can be used at any time but is especially useful when the researcher already has several categories and wants to code specifically in relation to them.

A third way in which to code is to *peruse the entire document* and ask "What is going on here?" and "What makes this document the same as, or different from, the previous ones that I coded?" Having answered these questions, the analyst might return to the document and code more specifically for those similarities and differences.

Writing Code Notes

One way in which to begin coding is to write concepts down in the margins or on cards as they emerge during analysis. This suffices if one is just labeling. We find that we work better by putting our analysis immediately into memos, as illustrated earlier in the chapter. Some of the newer, more complex computer programs allow the analyst to move from text, to concepts, to integrating concepts, doing memos, doing diagrams, and so on in the process of theory development (Richards & Richards, 1994; Tesch, 1990; Weitzman & Miles, 1995). The writing of memos is discussed further in Chapter 14. There are many different ways of recording concepts and theoretical ideas (see, e.g., Dey, 1993; Miles & Huberman, 1994; Schatzman & Strauss, 1973). Each person must find the system that works best for him or her.

SUMMARY

The purposes of procedures and techniques discussed in previous chapters now become clear. They are designed to help analysts carry out the steps of theory building—conceptualizing, defining categories, and developing categories in terms of their properties and dimensions—and then later relating categories through hypotheses or statements of relationships. Conceptualizing is the process of grouping similar items according to some defined properties and giving the items a name that stands for that common link. In conceptualizing, we reduce large amounts of data to smaller, more manageable pieces of data. Once we have some categories, we want to specify their properties. We also want to show how our concepts (categories) vary dimensionally along those properties. Through specification and dimensionalization, we begin to see patterns such as patterns of flight and patterns of drug taking. Thus, we have the foundation and beginning structure for theory building.

9 Axial Coding

Axial coding: The process of relating categories to their subcategories, termed "axial" because coding occurs around the axis of a category, linking categories at the level of properties and dimensions

The paradigm: An analytic tool devised to help analysts integrate structure with process

Structure: The conditional context in which a category (phenomenon) is situated

Process: Sequences of action/interaction pertaining to a phenomenon as they evolve over time

---

Humans the world over cannot avoid giving explanations for events and happenings. The desire for understanding is universal, although the explanations may differ by person, time, and place. Whereas some lay explanations draw on religious or magical beliefs, others are derived from practical experience or science. Explanatory schemes not only guide behavior but also provide some control and predictability over events. Scientists operate with such schemes, often highly detailed and sophisticated ones. A quotation from the writing of sociologist Leonard Schatzman is very useful here in telling us what such explanations should contain:

> An explanation . . . tells a story about the relations among things or people and events. To tell a complex story, one must designate objects and events, state or imply some of their dimensions and properties . . . , provide some context for these, indicate a condition or two for whatever action/interaction is selected to be central to the story, and point to, or imply, one or more consequences. (quoted in Maines, 1991, p. 308)

The *purpose* of *axial coding* is to begin the process of reassembling data that were fractured during open coding. In axial coding, categories are related to their subcategories to form more precise and complete explanations about phenomena. Although axial coding differs in purpose from open coding, these are not necessarily sequential analytic steps, no more than labeling is distinct from open coding. Axial coding does require that the analyst have some *categories*, but often a sense of how categories relate begins to emerge during open coding. As stated by Strauss (1987),

> Among the most important choices to be made during even these early sessions is to code intensively and concertedly around single categories. By doing this, the analyst begins to build up a dense texture of relationships around the "axis" of the category being focused upon. (p. 64)

In this chapter, we describe the logic behind axial coding and demonstrate how to link data at the property and dimensional levels, forming dense, well-developed, and related categories.

THE CODING PROCESS

Procedurally, axial coding is the act of relating categories to subcategories along the lines of their properties and dimensions. It looks at how categories crosscut and link. As stated previously, a category stands for a *phenomenon*, that is, a problem, an issue, an event, or a happening that is defined as being significant to respondents. The phenomenon under investigation might be as broad as negotiating a peace agreement between two nations or as narrow as self-perceived body image changes after an amputation. A phenomenon has the ability to explain what is going on. A *subcategory* also is a category, as its name implies. However, rather than standing for the phenomenon itself, subcategories answer questions about the phenomenon such as when, where, why, who, how, and with what consequences, thus giving the concept greater explanatory power. Early in the analysis, the researcher might not know which concepts are categories and which are subcategories. This usually becomes evident as coding proceeds.

For example, suppose that an analyst asks himself or herself, after each interview conducted with teens about drug use, "What seems to be going on here?" If the answer repeatedly is that most teens are "experimenting" with drugs and doing so mainly on a "limited basis," meaning they are trying drugs out only occasionally and restricting their use to less potent types, then "limited experimenting" with drugs might be designated as a *category*. Other categories such as "drug talk," "novel experience," "easy access," and "challenging the adult stance" help to explain why teens use drugs, how they go about sharing their experiences, and what they get out of using.

A major point must be made here. Although the text provides clues about how categories relate, the actual linking takes place not descriptively but rather at a conceptual level. To illustrate, let us return to the first paragraph of our interview with a teen about drug use. Notice that our respondent is giving us an explanation for why she experimented with drugs.

> **Respondent:** I think teens use drugs as a **release** from their parents. Well, I don't know. I can only talk for myself. For me, it was an **experience.** You **hear** a lot about drugs. You hear they are **bad** for you. There is a **lot of them around.** You just get into them because they're **accessible** and because it's kind of a **new thing.** It's **cool!** You know, it's something that is bad for you, **taboo,** a "no." Everyone is **against it.** If you are a teenager, the **first** thing you are going to do is **try** them.

Whereas this teen is telling us **why** teens use drugs in **text** form, when we analyze data, we convert that text into **concepts** that stand for those words such as **liberated self** (release from), **easy access, novel experience, negative drug talk, and challenging the adult stance.** It is by means of these concepts, which may be subcategories, that the analyst develops explanations about why some teens use drugs.

Procedurally, then, axial coding involves several basic tasks (Strauss, 1987). These include the following:

1. Laying out the properties of a category and their dimensions, a task that begins during open coding
2. Identifying the variety of conditions, actions/interactions, and consequences associated with a phenomenon
3. Relating a category to its subcatgories through statements denoting how they are related to each other
4. Looking for cues in the data that denote how major categories might relate to each other

Crosscutting at the Dimensional Level

In axial coding, the analyst is relating categories at a dimensional level. Notice that all of the codes just listed are qualified dimensionally. For example, the self is **"liberated,"** access is **"easy,"** drug talk is **"negative,"** the experience is **"novel,"** and teens are **"challenging"** the adult stance. When we relate these codes to the category "experimenting with drugs," we actually are relating "limited experimenting" with the "liberating" in self, the "easy" in access, the "novel" of experience, the "negative" of drug talk, the "challenging" of the adult stance, and so on. In this way, we can differentiate "limited experimenting" with drugs from, say, "hard-core use" of drugs, which might look quite different when compared dimensionally along these same subcategories.

Analysis at Two Levels

As readers might have noticed, when we analyze data, there really are two levels of explanations. These are (a) the actual words used by our respondents and (b) our conceptualization of these. "Limited experimenting" is what the analyst is calling the type of drug use engaged in by most teens. The teens might refer to drug use as "trying just a few," being careful about "which drugs you use," using only at "parties" and with "friends" as part of a "social act," using the "less potent" drugs, and so on. In other words they tell us when, how, with whom, and where they are using. Our translation and definition of this phenomenon or what is going on in this situation is that teens are engaged in "limited experimenting" with drugs. It is our interpretation of events.

THE PARADIGM

When analysts code axially, they look for answers to questions such as why or how come, where, when, how, and with what results, and in so doing they uncover relationships among categories. Answering these questions helps us to contextualize a phenomenon, that is, to locate it within a conditional structure and identify the "how" or the means through which a category is manifested. Put another way, by answering the questions of who, when, where, why, how, and with what consequences, analysts are able to relate structure with process. Why would one want to relate structure with process? Because structure or conditions set the stage, that is, create the circumstances in which problems, issues, happenings, or events pertaining to a phenomenon are situated or arise. Process, on the other hand, denotes the action/interaction over time of persons, organizations, and communities in response to certain problems and issues. Combining structure with process helps analysts to get at some of the complexity that is so much a part of life. Process and structure are inextricably linked, and unless one understands the nature of their relationship (both to each other and to the phenomenon in question), it is difficult to truly grasp what is going on. If one studies **structure** only, then one learns **why** but not **how** certain events occur. If one studies **process** only, then one understands **how** persons act/interact but not why. One must study both structure and process to capture the dynamic and evolving nature of events.

The answers to questions such as why, when, and where may be implicit or explicit in the field notes; that is, persons sometimes use words that cue us, such as "since," "due to," "when," and "because," followed by some event or action, for example, "Because I did not like the look of the cafe [structural conditions], I left quickly" and "Then I decided to go to my usual hangout down the street" [action/interactional strategies for handling a problematic situation]. In their talk or actions, persons also provide us with consequences, for example, "There, I was able to get a good cup of coffee and sit down and think without all of the crowding and noise of the first cafe."

In the preceding example, the logic is quite easy to follow. However, when working with actual data, the relationships between events and happenings are not always so evident. Because linkages among categories can be very subtle and implicit, it helps to have a scheme that can be used to sort out and organize the emerging connections. One such organizational scheme is what we call the **paradigm.** In actuality, the paradigm is nothing more than a perspective taken toward data, another analytic stance that helps to systematically gather and order data in such a way that structure and process are integrated. The terminology used in the paradigm is borrowed from standard scientific terms and provides a familiar language facilitating discussion among scientists. In addition, the basic terms used in the paradigm often follow the logic expressed in the language that persons use in their everyday descriptions (e.g., "for that reason," "what happened was," "my reaction was to," "this is what resulted"). The basic components of the paradigm are as follows. There are *conditions*, a conceptual way of grouping answers to the questions why, where, how come, and when. These together form the structure, or set of circumstances or situations, in which phenomena are embedded. There are *actions/interactions*, which are strategic or routine responses made by individuals or groups to issues, problems, happenings, or events that arise under those conditions. Actions/interactions are represented by the questions by whom and how. There are *consequences*, which are outcomes of actions/interactions. Consequences are represented by questions as to what happens as a result of those actions/interactions or the failure of persons or groups to respond to situations by actions/interactions, which constitutes an important finding in and of itself.

Take Note

Before proceeding with our discussion of the paradigm, there are some important points to be made.

1. During open coding, many different categories are identified. Some of these will pertain to a phenomenon. Other categories (later to become subcategories) will refer to conditions, actions/inter-actions, or consequences. The actual conceptual names placed on categories will not necessarily point to whether a category denotes a condition, an action/interaction, or a consequence. The analyst has to make this distinction. Also, every category and subcategory will have its own set of properties and dimensional qualifiers.

2. **An analyst is coding for explanations and to gain an understanding of phenomena and not for** terms such as conditions, actions/interactions, and consequences. This is a common misunderstanding among beginning analysts, who tend to be very dogmatic about their approach to analysis. They rigidly code for the paradigm components without having an understanding of the nature and types of relationships these denote. Then, they become confused when events or happenings are coded as a condition in one instance but as a consequence in another, such as how becoming ill from taking drugs at one party (a consequence) affects the willingness to try drugs at the subsequent party (another situational context), or when consequences of one set of actions become conditions in the subsequent action/interactional sequence. We realize that beginners need structure and that placing data into discrete boxes makes them feel more in control of their analyses. However, we want them to realize that such practices tend to prevent them from capturing the dynamic flow of events and the complex nature of relationships that, in the end, make explanations of phenomena interesting, plausible, and complete. Analysts who rigidify the analytic process are like artists who try too hard. Although their creations might be technically correct, they fail to capture the essence of the objects represented, leaving viewers feeling slightly cheated. Our advice is to let it happen. The rigor and vigor will follow.

3. We are not talking a language of **cause and effect.** This is too simplistic. Easy access alone does not lead to drug use, although it might make drugs more readily available. Teens can make choices; thus, there are multiple factors operating in various combinations to create a **context** (sets of conditions that come together to produce a specific situation) that makes it more likely that certain teens will try drugs, but **only** certain teens, certain drugs, at certain times, and so on. Identifying, sifting through, and sorting through all of the possible factors showing the nature of the relationships does not result in a simple "if . . . then" statement. The result is much more likely to be a discussion that takes readers along a complex path of inter-relationships, each in its own patterned way, that explains what is going on. With this in mind, we now are ready to turn to a fuller discussion of the components of the paradigm.

Explanations of Components of the Paradigm

Phenomenon, as we have stated, is a term that answers to the question "What is going on here?" In looking for phenomena, we are looking for **repeated patterns of happenings, events, or actions/interactions that represent what people do or say, alone or together, in response to the problems and situations in which they find themselves.** In coding, *categories* stand for phenomena. For instance, "limited experimenting" with drugs is a category. It also is a phenomenon—in this case, a pattern of drug use among teens. Other patterns of drug taking might include "abstaining" and "hard-core use," which, in essence, represent different dimensional patterns of drug use among teens. Each pattern will have its own set of conditions that pertain to it.

Conditions are sets of events or happenings that create the situations, issues, and problems pertaining to a phenomenon and, to a certain extent, explain why and how persons or groups respond in certain ways. Conditions might arise out of time, place, culture, rules, regulations, beliefs, economics, power, or gender factors as well as the social worlds, organizations, and institutions in which we find ourselves along with our personal motivations and biographies. Any one (or all) of these things is a potential source of conditions. (For further discussion on conditions, see Chapter 12.) Unless research participants are extremely insightful, they might not know all of the reasons why they do things, although they might give researchers some rationales for their behavior. Conditions must be discovered in data and traced for their full impact by analysts. Although researchers should seek to discover all relevant conditions, **they never should presume that they will discover all conditions or that any condition or set of conditions is relevant until proven so by linking up to the phenomenon in some explanatory way.**

Conditions have many different properties. Their path of influence on actions/interactions may be direct or indirect, more or less linear. Conditions may be micro (i.e., closer to the source of action/interaction such as peer pressure and wanting to defy parental authority) or macro (such as the degree of availability of drugs in the community and cultural attitudes toward drug use). To be complete, explanations must include both micro and macro conditions as well as indications of how these intersect with each other and with the actions/interactions (again, see Chapter 12).

Labeling Conditions

Conditions, as we have stated, may be micro or macro, shift and change over time, affect one another, and combine in various ways along different dimensions. In addition, there may be new ones added along the way. Labels placed on conditions such as *causal, intervening,* and *contextual* are ways of trying to sort out some of the complex relationships among conditions and their subsequent relation to actions/interactions.

Causal conditions usually represent sets of events or happenings that influence phenomena, for example, being at a party and being offered drugs. *Intervening conditions* are those that mitigate or otherwise alter the impact of causal conditions on phenomena such as a teen suddenly feeling that taking drugs is not right for him or her. The latter often arises out of contingencies (unexpected events), which in turn must be responded to through a form of action/interaction. For example, teens might purposefully attend a party knowing that drugs will be passed around, so that they might try them. However, if the parents of the teen throwing the party return home unexpectedly, then the teens might have to change their plans. To circumvent this situation, they might go to an outdoor teen hangout and pass the drugs around there. Or, they might decide to forgo drug taking that night, putting off their experimenting to another time and place. Intervening conditions also can help explain why some teens continue to experiment, whereas others do not. Some teens might get invited to a party not knowing that there will be drugs, try them, decide that drug taking is fun, and continue to use them. Other teens might try drugs, get sick, and never try them again. Both causal and intervening conditions may arise from micro- or macro-level conditions. *Contextual conditions* are the specific sets of conditions (patterns of conditions) that intersect dimensionally at this time and place to create the set of circumstances or problems to which persons respond through actions/interactions. They explain why a phenomenon such as why the pattern of "experimenting with drugs" is "limited" for some teens, whereas it might lead to "hard-core use" of drugs for others. Contextual conditions have their source in causal (and intervening) conditions and are the product of how they crosscut to combine into various patterns dimensionally. For example, if we were to specify that "degree of accessibility of drugs" is one of the causal conditions related to teen drug use in general, and we know that this concept can vary dimensionally from "easy" to "difficult," then we might note that it is the "easy" dimension of accessibility that makes it one of the conditions for teens trying drugs. Usually, there are many different conditions that enter into a context, each having its own specific dimensions. By grouping conditions along their dimensions, the analyst is able to identify patterns or sets of conditions that create a context. (For an excellent example of contexts along with a discussion, see Strauss, 1978.) **The important issue is not so much one of identifying and listing which conditions are causal, intervening, or contextual. Rather, what the analyst should focus on is the complex interweaving of events (conditions) leading up to a problem, an issue, or a happening to which persons are responding through some form of action/interaction, with some sort of consequences. In addition, the analyst might identify changes in the original situation (if any) as a result of that action/interaction.**

Another point that can be made about conditions is that explanations require **assumptions about the relevance of causality.** However, what these assumptions are and just what the "nature" of causality is have been much debated by philosophers of science and some scientists. Different scientific disciplines and specialties differ considerably in what they consider causality, causal elements, and causal sequences. In evolutionary biology, causality is not the same as it is in genetic biology and certainly not much like sub-atomic physicists' ideas of probability. In social science and in many of the practice disciplines, there undoubtedly also are arguments and discussions regarding the nature of causality. Our concern, as analysts, is not so much with causality as with conditions of various types and the way in which they crisscross to create events leading to actions/interactions. When people act, we want to know why, how come, and to what situations, problems, or issues they are responding. This brings us to our next paradigmatic feature, which is action/interaction.

Strategic or routine tactics or the **how** by which persons handle situations, problems, and issues that they encounter are termed *actions/interactions*. These represent what people, organizations, social worlds, or nations do or say. **Strategic actions/interactions** are purposeful or deliberate acts that are taken to resolve a problem and in so doing shape the phenomenon in some way. For example, if the phenomenon or category we are studying is "keeping the flow of work going" on a hospital unit, and one of the problems that arises is that three of the five staff members assigned to that unit call in sick one day, then we would be interested in noting how the problem of understaffing was handled so that the work could go on. Did the head nurse call in extra staff members? Was patient care cut back to basic necessities? Were patients transferred to another unit?

Routines are actions/interactions that tend to more habituated ways of responding to occurrences in everyday life such as having an established protocol to follow when the number of staff members is low. In organizations, these would take the form of rules, regulations, policies, and procedures. Although researchers tend to focus their studies on the problematic, it is just as important to examine routine matters, for they demonstrate the actions/interactions (which have been previously worked out strategically) that tend to maintain the social order.

The term "action/interaction" is an important concept. It not only denotes what goes on among individuals, groups, organizations, and the like (e.g., the passing around and sharing of marijuana cigarettes by teens at some parties) but also includes matters such as discussions about drug experiences as well as the negotiations and other types of talk that occur in group situations such as peer pressure. In addition to the "goings on"—verbal and nonverbal—that take place among individuals, action/interaction refers to the discussions and reviews that go on within individuals themselves, for example, the weighing of the pros and cons of using drugs (warnings by teachers and parents to avoid the use of drugs measured against rejection by peers if they do not use) and the actual taking of a puff, which may be a deep drag or a symbolic gesture only.

Actions/interactions among individuals acting in groups **may** or **may not** be in **alignment,** that is, coordinated. Actions/interactions evolve over time as persons define or give meanings to situations. Under some conditions, alignment does not occur, and the situation turns into one of conflict and eventually breaks down completely.

The final paradigmatic term is *consequences.* Whenever there is action/interaction or a lack of it taken in response to an issue or a problem or to manage or maintain a certain situation, there are ranges of consequences, some of which might be intended and others not. Delineating these consequences, as well as explaining how they alter the situation and affect the phenomenon in question, provides for more complete explanations. For example, although in some cases using drugs on a "limited" basis might have a detrimental affect on some persons, our interviewee actually described experimenting with drugs as a **growth** experience. It might have been a **devastating** experience, a **terrifying** experience, and so on, but for her it was not. She was able to try drugs, define their meaning for her, learn what they were really all about, and when the time came, give up using them and move on with her life. Consequences, like conditions, have inherent properties. They may be singular (not usually) or many. They may be of varied duration. They may be visible to self but not to others or to others but not to self. They may be immediate or cumulative, reversible or not, foreseen or unforeseen. Their impact may be narrow (affecting only a small part of the situation) or widespread (with consequences bouncing off each other to create a trail of events that completely alters a context). As analysts, we want to capture as much of this as possible in our analyses.

Relational Statements

Beginning with analysis of the first interviews, the researcher cannot help but notice how concepts relate to each other. In explicating these relationships, the researcher begins to link categories with their subcategories, that is, to notice that these seem to be conditions—these actions/interactions, these consequences. We call these initial hunches about how concepts relate "hypotheses" because they link two or more concepts, explaining the what, why, where, and how of a phenomenon. Examples of such statements include the following:

1. When drugs are *readily* available, there is *peer* pressure, drugs are considered a *novel* experience, and teens want to challenge the *adult negative* stance, teens are more likely to "experiment" with drugs.
2. "Drug talk" is the action/interactional means through which teens "acquire and dispense information" about drugs and their "experiences."
3. As a consequence of "limited experimenting" with drugs, teens are likely to acquire "firsthand knowledge" about drugs and gain "peer acceptance."

Although hypotheses are derived from data, because they are abstractions (i.e., statements made at the conceptual level rather than at the raw data level), it is important that these be validated and further elaborated through continued comparisons of data incident to incident. Incoming data sometimes seem to contradict a hypothesis. This does not necessarily mean that the hypothesis is wrong. When a contradiction is found, it is important to note whether the data represent a true inconsistency or whether they denote an extreme dimension or variation of the phenomenon in question. Discovering contradictions leads us to question our data further to determine what is really going on, whereas discovering variations extends the dimensional range of a category and gives it greater explanatory power (it accounts for differences). For example, a student in one of our seminars, who was studying the phenomenon of psychological pain in caretakers of persons with Alzheimer's disease, was stunned when she came across one case in which very little psychological pain was expressed by one of the respondents. After hearing so much pain expressed by the other respondents, she was confused by this finding. Finally, she realized that this case represented an extreme dimension of "experiencing psychological pain" (in this case, low). What became important, then, was to determine the conditions that were operating in this particular situation to create that variation (Khurana, 1995).

Further Development of Categories and Subcategories

As mentioned in the beginning of this chapter, axial and open coding are not sequential acts. One does not stop coding for properties and dimensions while one is developing relationships between concepts. They proceed quite naturally together, as our chapter on microanalysis demonstrated (Chapter 5). Both dimensions and relationships add density and explanatory power to a theory and will continue to emerge during analysis.

A category is considered *saturated* when no new information seems to emerge during coding, that is, when no new properties, dimensions, conditions, actions/interactions, or consequences are seen in the data. However, this statement is a matter of degree. In reality, if one looked long and hard enough, one always would find additional properties or dimensions. There always is that potential for the "new" to emerge. Saturation is more a matter of reaching the point in the research where collecting additional data seems counterproductive; the "new" that is uncovered does not add that much more to the explanation at this time. Or, as is sometimes the situation, the researcher runs out of time, money, or both.

Moving Between Induction and Deduction

The concept of induction often is applied to qualitative research. Our position on the matter is as follows. Although statements of relationship or hypotheses do evolve from data (we go from the specific case to the general), whenever we conceptualize data or develop hypotheses, we are interpreting to some degree. To us, an interpretation is a form of deduction. We are deducing what is going on based on data but also based on our reading of that data along with our assumptions about the nature of life, the literature that we carry in our heads, and the discussions that we have with colleagues. (This is how science is born.) In fact, there is an interplay between induction and deduction (as in all science). **We are not saying that we place our interpretations on the data or that we do not let the interpretations emerge. Rather, we are saying that we recognize the human element in analysis and the potential for possible distortion of meaning. That is why we feel that it is important that analyst validate his or her interpretations through constantly comparing one piece of data to another.**

Demonstration of Axial Coding

Next, we briefly demonstrate how we might code axially. The category we code around is "getting stoned." We use the same format as before, presenting a section of an interview note and then writing a memo about it. The notes were taken from the same interview about teens and drugs that we presented in Chapter 8. Notice that in axial coding, as in open coding, the analyst continues to ask all types of generative questions, makes constant and theoretical comparisons, and makes use of the analytic tools described previously. Also note that it is impossible to code around the category of "getting stoned" without bringing in concepts and ideas that evolved from the coding we did in the chapter on open coding (Chapter 8).

> **Respondent:** I started with pot. Pot, you don't get stoned the first time you try it. Most people have to take it two to three times before they feel remotely high. I did it five or six times before I felt high. I tried it at a party. Kids break it out; no one even questions it. It is just understood that it will be passed around and everyone will try it. I was pretty young, 13 I guess. It turned out I was pretty allergic to pot. It was never anything I took to.

> **Memo.** "Getting stoned" can be described as a strategic act, an *action/interaction*. It consists of the **"ingestion of drugs"** (a relationship between an individual and a substance) and also the **"bodily experience"** (both physical and mental) that results from ingesting. Getting stoned also is a *process*. It is a **learned experience** that evolves

over time. It took this teen five to six times of trying marijuana before she achieved a state of "being stoned"; you have to work with the drug or let the drug do its work. *Conditions* that are brought out in this paragraph pertain not so much to "getting stoned" as to another phenomenon, "experimenting with drugs." Her experimenting took place in the context of a "group situation." The conditions expressed were "peer expectation" and "easy availability." What is not expressed is that she went to this party willingly, apparently knowing that drugs would be there. Although age is mentioned, it is unclear what role this concept plays in drug experimentation. The relationship of age to "experimenting with drugs" will have to be explored in subsequent interviews. *Consequences* of "getting stoned" are expressed here. In her case, these include "having an adverse reaction," which probably *in turn* contributed to her experimenting only on a "limited" basis, at least with this drug. Also brought out in this paragraph is the relationship between the two phenomena of "getting stoned" and "experimenting with drugs." One has to ingest a substance or experiment with drugs to get stoned.

Interviewer: Explain.

Respondent: It made me nauseous and I threw up. At first, it was a challenge. I tried it five to six times and nothing happened. You begin to wonder what is wrong with you. You want to feel it like everyone else. I figured, I had already come this far; I want to finish it and get high. The first time I felt high, it was really fun. I felt giddy. I was with a friend. I felt I was in another world. It was fun. I have a pretty strong reaction to pot. Most people handle themselves well. For me, it is like being intoxicated with alcohol. The second time, I also was with my friend. We both laughed a lot and really let go and had fun. After that time, it stopped being fun because it started making me sick. Occasionally after that, I would try it just to see what would happen, and it always has the same reaction for me.

* * *

Memo. Some of the properties of "getting stoned" are brought out in these next sentences. She is telling us that "getting stoned" can be a **pleasant** experience (it was fun) or an **unpleasant** experience. Also, she explains that the process of experiencing a high might be **slow** or **fast**. For her, it was slow, and with that came certain consequences—"feeling different or apart from peers"—which, in turn, became part of the next set of *contextual conditions* for her wanting to continue to try pot so that she might experience a high like her peers. What is not directly said but is implied is that other teens share their experience or discuss "getting stoned" through "drug talk." Another property brought out is that one's reaction to drug taking might be **strong** or **weak**. Hers was a strong one. She also is telling us that *consequences* can evolve over time, can change from being fun (wanting to do this again) to making her sick (not wanting to take this drug again). Becoming sick is an unanticipated *consequence* that then becomes part of the next set of contextual conditions affecting willingness to experiment with marijuana again, although she would, on occasion, try it to determine whether the unpleasant effects would continue. Another aspect of the property "reaction" is that it might be **repeated** (every time) or **not repeated** (sometimes or never again). Also, we might add to our list of conditions that make up the context for experimenting with drugs that of "peer mimicry," that is, the desire to experience a high like the others.

Interviewer: Tell me more about when it was fun.

Respondent: Well, you are in a different state of mind, a different state of consciousness. You've got something in you that is kind of controlling the way you think, how you see the world. You have this foreign substance in you that is tampering with your mind. It's different from the usual good time when you are not on drugs. Instead, you are letting yourself be influenced by this substance, letting it guide you. Most people can get out of that state and be in control really fast if they want or need to. It's just that they let themselves relax, be happy. We would just sit around and talk. Sometimes, we would say off-the-wall things. It just kind of opens up your perspective on life, lets you look at things in new ways—ways that you never looked at them before. It enhances your thinking, lets you perceive things differently. You let your hair [and] your biases down. I don't know exactly how to explain it.

* * *

Memo. Here our respondent is describing the actual experience of "getting stoned" to us, enabling us to define the concept in terms of its properties. She is telling us that "getting stoned" is like being in "an altered state" of mind. It is a process of "letting go," of letting the drug have its influence over you. This probably is why "getting stoned" is a **learned experience;** one has to learn how to work with the drug and to let go. She also states that individuals have **some degree of control over this altered state** in that they can move out of the state if it is necessary to do so. One also can describe the situation as **"being relaxing,"** as **"mind opening,"** as **"encouraging exploration,"** and as **"transforming perceptions."**

Interviewer: Go on. You're doing very well.

Respondent: Whereas alcohol breaks down your inhibitions, pot doesn't break them down. You do not tell people your darkest, deepest secrets when you're high like you might with alcohol. With alcohol you lose your inhibitions, but with pot you retain them. Most people, when they are high, are in control. They know exactly what they are saying and doing. Like I said, my reaction to pot is rather rare. I have a strong reaction. [Fully] 90% of the people are in control and have no problem. It makes me nauseous. It doesn't take much for me to get super stoned. Then, I'm out of it. I'm not much in control of what I am doing. I'm in a daze. I throw up. It is not a very pleasant experience for me.

* * *

Memo. Remaining "in control," both over the self and over the drug experience, seems to be an important *property* of "getting stoned." She tells us that being "in control" for her has to do with not "losing your inhibitions" or "revealing secrets" and "knowing" what one says and does. She also gives us another concept, "super stoned," with "super" being a dimension of degree of "getting stoned," which seems to vary from being "super stoned" to "being in control," adding greater definition to our category. Some of the *consequences* of being "super stoned" (relating dimension of "super" with the consequences) are having "an unpleasant experience versus a pleasant experience." The specifics of this for her were "being dazed, not in control, and ill."

The Use of Mini-Frameworks and Other Recording Techniques

Keeping a record of one's analysis during axial coding is important. Two recording devices that we introduce here include the use of

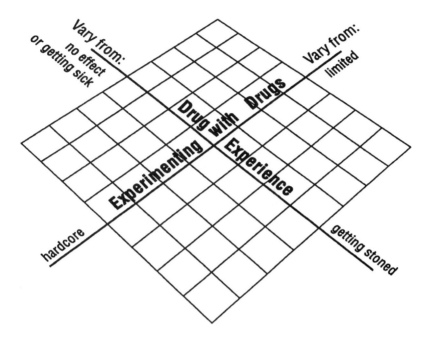

Figure 9.1. Mini-Framework Showing Cross-Cuts Between Two Major Concepts

NOTE: Heavy lines represent the intersection of major categories. Light lines represent the intersection of lesser categories with major categories and with each other.

mini-frameworks and conceptual diagrams, both of which are designed to show relationships between concepts. *Mini-frameworks* are the small, diagrammatic theoretical structures that arise as a result of our coding around a concept. Diagrams are very important devices. Their use should begin early in the analysis because they help the analyst think through possible relationships. Dey (1993) made this point very clearly when he stated, "Diagrammatic displays are not just a way of decorating our conclusions, they also provide a way of reaching them" (p. 192). More is said about memos and diagrams in Chapter 14.

Having reached this point in our analysis, we could summarize our findings using a mini-framework (Figure 9.1). This would help us to keep our relationships among concepts in mind as we proceed with our analysis. It also would point to gaps in our evolving theory and indicate what further data we should gather to more fully develop the categories. Notice how in this mini-framework, we are putting together two major concepts—"experimenting with drugs" and "getting stoned"—and are indicating how these cross-cut at a dimensional level.

SUMMARY

This chapter discussed how we code around the axis of a category to add depth and structure to it. It introduced the paradigm as a conceptual analytic device for organizing data and integrating structure with process. In axial coding, our goal is to systematically develop and relate categories. This step of analysis is important because we are building theory. Sorting out the relationships between concepts and subconcepts can be difficult. Beginning analysts should keep in mind that it is not the notion of conditions, actions/interactions, and consequences that is significant; rather, what is important is discovering the ways that categories relate to each other. The paradigm is just one device that analysts can use to think about such relationships. Although helpful, the paradigm never should be used in rigid ways; otherwise, it becomes the end rather than the means.

Also important for analysts to remember is that insights about how concepts relate can come at any time and place—in the middle of the night, while reading the newspaper, or while talking with colleagues. Keep a pencil and paper handy, jot down these "aha experiences," and bring them into the analysis. (Strauss always referred to this process as our subliminal minds at work.) Some researchers find it helpful to keep journals in which they record their thinking processes and how their concepts evolved and were transformed over the course of their research projects. These journals are referred to during the writing phase and help explain to an audience how the researchers reached their conclusions.

10   **Selective Coding**

DEFINITIONS OF TERMS

Selective coding: The process of integrating and refining the theory

Theoretical saturation: The point in category development at which no new properties, dimensions, or relationships emerge during analysis

Range of variability: The degree to which a concept varies dimensionally along its properties, with *variation* being built into the theory by sampling for diversity and ranges of properties

In open coding, the analyst is concerned with generating categories and their properties and then seeks to determine how categories vary dimensionally. In axial coding, categories are systematically developed and linked with subcategories. However, it is not until the major categories are finally integrated to form a larger theoretical scheme that the research findings take the form of *theory*. Selective coding is the process of integrating and refining categories. This chapter describes these processes.

Data Become Theory

Watching theory evolve is a fascinating process. It does not happen overnight (although one might have a sudden "insight"). It does not arise like magic out of the page. Rather, integration is an ongoing process that occurs over time. One might say that it begins with the first bit of analysis and does not end until the final writing. As with all phases of analysis, integration is an interaction between the analyst and the data. Brought into that interaction is the analytic gestalt, which includes not only who the analyst is but also the evolution of thinking that occurs over time through immersion in the data and the cumulative body of findings that have been recorded in memos and diagrams. Although the cues to how concepts are linked can be found in the data, it is not until relationships are **recognized** as such by the analyst that they emerge. Also, whenever there is recognition, there is some degree of interpretation and selectivity. But above all, integration is hard work. As Paul Atkinson, coauthor of an excellent textbook on field research (Hammersley & Atkinson, 1983), wrote in a personal communication,

> This aspect—making it all come together—is one of the most difficult things of all, isn't it? Quite apart from actually achieving it, it is hard to inject the right mix of (a) faith that it can and will be achieved and recognition (b) that it has to be worked at and isn't based on romantic inspiration, (c) that it isn't like a solution to a puzzle or math problem but has to be created, (d) that you can't always pack everything into one version, and (e) that any one project could yield several different ways of bringing it together.

This chapter presents several analytic techniques designed to facilitate integration. The techniques are especially useful when an analyst is perplexed, sensing that the data are beginning to "gel" but not quite sure how to explicate those intuitive feelings. It also discusses procedures for refining the theory once an analyst has committed to a theoretical scheme.

Important Points

There are several important ideas to keep in mind while reading this chapter. As stated earlier in the book, concepts that reach the status of a category are abstractions; they represent not one individual's or group's story but rather the stories of many persons or groups reduced into, and represented by, several highly conceptual terms. Although no longer the specific data of an individual, group, or organization, categories are derived by comparing data from each case; therefore, they should, in a general sense, have relevance for, and be applicable to, all cases in the study. It is the details included under each category and subcategory, through the specification of properties and dimensions, that bring out the case differences and variations within a category.

Second, if theory building is indeed the goal of a research project, then findings *should* be presented as a set of interrelated concepts, not just a listing of themes. Relational statements, like concepts, are abstracted from the data. However, because they are interpreted abstractions and not the descriptive details of each case (raw data), they (like concepts) are "constructed" out of data by the analyst. **By "constructed," we mean that an analyst reduces data from many cases into concepts and sets of relational statements that can be used to explain, in a general sense, what is going on.** Rarely are these concepts or statements the exact words of one respondent or case, although they could be (e.g., in vivo codes). Usually, they represent the voices of many.

Third, there is more than one way of expressing relational statements. In our own publications, they are not presented as explicit hypotheses or propositions. Rather, they tend to be woven innocuously into the narrative, as is demonstrated in the integrative memo on drug taking in teens that follows. However, there is no reason why one could not be more specific and make use of **explanatory** statements such as "under these conditions," "then," and "when this set of events occurs." It is a stylistic matter, largely the result of the theoretical perspective and the discipline for which the researcher is writing. There is *not* just *one* correct way of stating relationships. The essential element is that categories are interrelated into a larger theoretical scheme.

The first step in integration is deciding on a central category. The central category (sometime called the core category) represents the main theme of the research. Although the central category evolves from the research, it too is an abstraction. In an **exaggerated** sense, it consists of all the products of analysis condensed into a few words that seem to explain what "this research is all about." For example, returning to our hypothetical study of drug use by teens, we might conceptualize the essence of that piece of research as being "Teen Drug Taking: A Phase of Experimentation." This explanation is *our* interpretation of what the research is all about, what the salient issues or problems of the participants seem to be. Another researcher, coming from a different theoretical orientation and having another research question, might arrive at quite another interpretation. However, once an analyst explains in detail how he or she arrived at a conceptualization, other researchers, regardless of their perspective, should be able to follow the analyst's path of logic and agree that it is one plausible explanation for what is going on.

Criteria for Choosing a Central Category

A central category has analytic power. What gives it that power is its ability to pull the other categories together to form an explanatory whole. Also, a central category should be able to account for considerable variation within categories.

A central category may evolve out of the list of existing categories. Or, a researcher may study the categories and determine that, although each category tells part of the story, none captures it completely. Therefore, another more abstract term or phrase is needed, a conceptual idea under which all the other categories can be subsumed. Strauss (1987) provided a list of criteria that can be applied to a category to determine whether it qualifies:

CRITERIA FOR CHOOSING A CENTRAL CATEGORY

1. It must be central; that is, all other major categories can be related to it.
2. It must appear frequently in the data. This means that within all or almost all cases, there are indicators pointing to that concept.
3. The explanation that evolves by relating the categories is logical and consistent. There is no forcing of data.
4. The name or phrase used to describe the central category should be sufficiently abstract that it can be used to do research in other substantive areas, leading to the development of a more general theory.
5. As the concept is refined analytically through integration with other concepts, the theory grows in depth and explanatory power.
6. The concept is able to explain variation as well as the main point made by the data; that is, when conditions vary, the explanation still holds, although the way in which a phenomenon is expressed might look somewhat different. One also should be able to explain contradictory or alternative cases in terms of that central idea. (p. 36)

Choosing Between Two or More Possibilities

Analysts sometimes identify what could be two central themes or ideas in the data. Our suggestion, especially for beginning analysts, is to select one idea as the central category and then to relate the other category (or categories) to that central idea. For example, although "body" emerged as an important concept in our study of patients with chronic illness and their spouses, we focused on the work of illness management by couples. It was not until later that we took up the concept of "body" and, through analysis of other data, developed our ideas into a theoretical scheme about body.

Difficulty Deciding on a Central Category

Sometimes students, especially those in practitioner fields, become caught up in the descriptive details of a study. Or, they are so flooded with data that they are unable to obtain the distance necessary to commit to a central idea. To them, every idea in the data has equal importance. Reading memos does not help; the analyst only becomes more confused by all the information contained in them. When this happens, it is time to seek consultation from either a teacher, a colleague, or some other knowledgeable person who is willing to sit down with the analyst and help him or her brainstorm. Sometimes, students are insecure and just need reassurance that they are on the right path. Other times, they need help with distancing themselves from the details of data. The "outside person" can ask a series of directed questions, forcing the analyst to reply with abstract yet direct comments. Just having someone else listen often helps the analyst gain that distance.

TECHNIQUES TO AID INTEGRATION

There are several techniques that can be used to facilitate identification of the central category and the integration of concepts. Among these are writing the storyline, making use of diagrams, and reviewing and sorting of memos either by hand or by computer program (if one is being used).

Writing the Storyline

By the time the researcher starts to think about integration, he or she has been immersed in the data for some time and usually has a "gut" sense of what the research is all about, although the researcher might have difficulty articulating what that is. One way in which to move beyond this impasse is to sit down and write a few descriptive sentences about "what seems to be going on here." It make take two, three, or even more starts to be able to articulate one's thoughts concisely. Eventually, a story emerges. Often, returning to the raw data and rereading several interviews or observations helps to stimulate thinking. This tends to work **if one reads them not for detail but rather for the general sense,** standing back and asking the following questions. What is the main issue or problem with which these people seem to be grappling? What keeps striking me over and over? What comes through, although it might not be said directly?

To understand what a descriptive story might look like, consider the following example. The story arises from a hypothetical study on teen drug use.

> **Memo: Identifying the story.** This study consisted of 100 interviews with young adults in their 20s who used drugs during their teenage years. We were interested in finding out why teens used drugs and how they perceived or described that experience now that they are past being teenagers. They are looking back retrospectively; thus, they have more distance or perspective of what it was all about, and because of that distance, they are able to present their story with more insight than they probably would have if interviewed during their actual teenage years. Their looking back and talking about it from a "present" perspective is perhaps why we have come up with the following story:

> **Descriptive story.** What keeps striking us about these interviews is that, although many teens use drugs, few go on to become hard-core users. It seems to be a kind of teenage experimentation, a developmental phase in their lives that marks the passage from child to teen and from teen to adult. They learn about drugs and also themselves, gain acceptance from their peers, and challenge adult authority through using drugs. It is a very specific behavior that sets them apart from family but, at the same time, makes them one of the teen group. They experiment with drugs in order to discover for themselves what they are all about and learn that they can control their own behavior in relationship to drug taking. Then, when they move into more adult roles, they discover that they no longer have any desire to use drugs, or if they do, they use them recreationally. It was a teen thing that no longer interests them. Teen drug use for most teens is part of a transitional phase—a time of passage between child and adult life marked by potential experimentation with many types of behaviors, using drugs being one of these. Most limit their use of drugs to parties or when with friends.

Moving From Description to Conceptualization

Once the analyst has a grasp on the essence of the research, he or she is ready to give that central idea a name and relate other concepts to it. If no existing category seems to capture the substance entirely, then another broader concept should be used. Because we had threads about the experimental nature of drug use in teens in our memos but no real name for it, we had to come up with a concept that captured the essence of this process. We decided to conceptualize our central idea as "Teen Drug Use: A Rite of Passage." To us, this indicates that drug use was mainly limited and experimental and served as a process that marked the transition from teen to adult. Of course, this central idea must fit the data, so the next step is to write the story again but this time using the existing categories. By using concepts, we also build the *linkages* among them. The following is an example of a *storyline memo* or a memo that tells the story using concepts and their linkages. Note the statements by which the concepts are connected and their similarity to the features of the paradigm introduced in the chapter on axial coding (Chapter 9). Although not necessarily written as "these conditions are associated with this phenomenon or process" or "this action leads to this outcome," relationships such as these are implied. Also, notice that the relationships are not written in a cause-and-effect fashion. The paths of associations are more convoluted than direct, with all sorts of intervening variables entering into the analytic picture to influence the path of action (type of user that one becomes).

A storyline memo might look something like this:

Storyline memo. Although many teens try drugs, few of them go on to become hard-core users. Most of those we interviewed used drugs for a limited time and in limited quantities and then, when the novelty wore off, they stopped using. For them, it seemed more like a transitional period during their teenage years in which they experimented with different and sometimes "risky" behaviors, which they discarded when the behavior no longer held their interest or it finished serving their purpose. This was an important step in their development, for it enabled them to *challenge authority* and *take control* of events in their lives during a time when they were trying to define "who they were" as separate beings from their parents, yet very much needing the support and acceptance of their peer group because they were not ready to stand on their own as adults. They used drugs as a sort of experiment or rite marking this time in their life. That is, they usually started experimenting with drugs at a party or with friends, indicating its social interactional nature (except for those who went on to hard-core use). By taking drugs, teens showed **solidarity** with peers and a **willingness** to defy authority. It provided a way of **gaining** acceptance and, for the most part, was a **pleasurable** experience. Looking back now as young adults, they can say that it also demonstrated their **ability** to make choices and **take measures** to contain risks. They perceive that they **grew** emotionally from the experience. Conditions leading to drug use were that *access was easy,* there was *peer pressure* to use, and they *gained peer acceptance* by doing so. Most **did not** use drugs to **escape** from the realities of life, to **get away** from physical or psychological pain, to make them **feel better** or **give** them **courage;** these reasons were most often given by those who went on to become hard-core users. The amounts and types of drugs used by these teens varied. By grouping them according to their dimensions, four types or patterns of users emerged: the *nonusers,* the *limited experimenters,* the *recreational users,* and the *hard-core users.* For each type of user, the passage was different. A critical condition that determined the type of user and nature of the passage was the drug-taking experience, which we conceptualized as *"getting stoned."* "Getting stoned" created the context out of which the different types of users emerged. It was the "rite" that marked their passage, kind of initiated them into the group and determined outcome. A teen either did or did not take drugs, did and did not *get stoned.* Those who got stoned did so to various degrees with various results and varying frequencies. How a person experienced getting stoned, in turn, influenced whether and to what degree he or she continued to use drugs. Getting stoned is a learned process. One of its properties is the degree of control one retains over behavior. *Control over behavior* is a property and, at the same time, a subcategory of *getting stoned.* Getting stoned and retaining control over behavior vary, depending on the **type** of drug ingested, how **often** a drug is used, **previous** experiences, **personal** motivations, **perceptions** of what the drug seems to do for that person, **amount ingested,** and so on. Getting stoned was viewed as a *positive or negative experience.* Even when getting stoned was experienced as negative, some persons continued to use because they could not say "no," wanted to be like the others, felt that this was just a bad trip, or became physically and pyschologically dependent on the drug. Long-term consequences have to do with the looking back and perception that this was simply a phase in their lives, a behavior that was important then but that they had now outgrown. They never became physically or pyschologically addicted. Those that expressed that this was a growth phase stated they felt this way because they learned that they could *retain control over* *their behavior, minimize the risks through cautious behavior,* and *learn for themselves what drugs and getting stoned were all about.* It was risky behavior, but most did not become addicted. The action/interactional means through which teens learned about drugs, the types of drugs, where to buy them, how to use them, and their dangers, and through which teens shared their drug experiences with their peers, was termed *"drug talk."* This talk was a very important part of the "rite of passage." However, drug talk did not occur only among teens. There also was drug talk by authority figures. Drug talk could take many forms. It could be *informative, negative, pressuring,* or *boasting.*

For the nonusers, not succumbing to peer pressure, being able to say "no" to drugs, and not being willing to experiment on even a limited basis marked their rite of passage. The ceremonial "no" was proof that they could stand up to peer pressure and gain acceptance without taking drugs. So for them, nonexperimentation and not getting stoned were as much a rite of passage as was getting stoned for those who experimented with drugs. For those who became "hard-core users," early experimentation with drugs was a rite of passage, but a passage into addiction (although not always irreversible). For the "limited experimenters," drug taking and getting stoned were part of a rite or ceremonial marker that served a specific purpose during a transitional period in life. For those who went on to become "recreational users," the drug taking was an initiation into a pleasurable social process that continued into later life, but only occasionally and never interfering with daily life.

Although perhaps there might be a better explanation, our conceptualization of what is going on (i.e., drug use by teens as a rite of passage) seems to fit the data and offers one interpretation of what the research was all about. Other categories logically fit with our major category. The conceptualization also provides an explanation for our dimensional extremes: the nonusers and the hard-core users. One also could use the concept to study other types of behaviors (e.g., unsafe sex) among teens. Viewing teen drug taking as a rite of passage is an interesting idea. It takes away some of the negativity and accusatory tone associated with teen drug taking. Perhaps by understanding the meaning of drug taking to teens, adults can help teens find acceptable substitutes or other more acceptable behaviors that can serve as a rite of passage.

Using Diagrams

There are times when, either through preference or because the analyst is more of a visual person, diagrams are more useful than storytelling for sorting out the relationships among concepts. Although the subject of diagrams is taken up in depth in Chapter 14, a few words here are relevant. Diagrams can be valuable tools to integration. Diagramming is helpful because it enables the analyst to gain distance from the data, forcing him or her to work with concepts rather than with details of data. It also demands that the analyst think very carefully about the logic of relationships because if the relationships are not clear, then the diagrams come across as muddled and confused. If the analyst has made use of diagrams throughout the research process, then the succession of operational diagrams should lead up to the integrative story. However, if the analyst has few diagrams or if, after reviewing previous diagrams, he or she still is unclear about the nature of relationships among concepts, then sitting down with a teacher, consultant, or colleague to explain what is going on diagrammatically can facilitate the integrative process. Again, asking directed questions or "running" through a few representative cases can stimulate thinking about relationships. Sometimes, there are several attempts before a diagram "feels right."

Integrative diagrams are very abstract representations of data. They need *not* contain every concept that emerged during the research process, but they should focus on those that reach the status of major categories. Diagrams should flow, with the logic apparent without a lot of explanation. Also, integrative diagrams should not be too complicated. Diagrams with too many words, lines, and arrows make it difficult for viewers to "read" them. The details should be left to the writing (see Figure 10.1).

Reviewing and Sorting Through Memos

Memos are a running log of analytic sessions. They are a storehouse of ideas. Although there are many different types of memos (these are discussed in greater depth in Chapter 14), generally as the research proceeds, memos become more abstract. They also contain the clues to integration, especially if the analyst has systematically identified the properties of concepts along with their dimensions. For

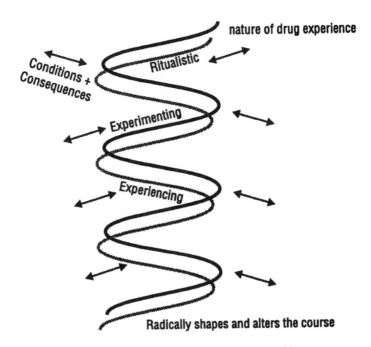

Figure 10.1. Experimenting With Drugs: A Rite of Passage

example, researcher awareness of the different patterns of drug use emerged first by noting dimensional differences in types of drug use such as why, how often, where, with whom, what drugs, with what results, and so on. Looking at the differences across dimensions enabled us to identify different patterns of "types of users." By looking at the "getting stoned" experience dimensionally (how often, what drugs were used, when, where, with whom, what the drug talk was about, degree of control maintained, etc.), we were able to connect that category with type of user. We noted that the "hard-core users" used drugs more frequently, used harder drugs such as amphetamines and heroin, and used mostly alone, compared to the "limited experimenters," who tended to get stoned only occasionally, used marijuana and psychedelic drugs rather than harder drugs, and tended to use only at parties or when with friends as part of a social act.

Memos usually are sorted by categories. However, sorting by categories becomes more and more difficult as cross-relationships among categories evolve. The analyst can become confused about appropriate placement of a memo and become concerned about "which pile do I put it in?" If one has multiple copies of each memo, then a copy can be place into the pile of each category to which it seems to apply. (It always can be pulled out later.) Once memos are sorted, they can be reviewed. It can be fun to go back and reread memos and, thereby, watch a concept evolve (and to note our false starts and leads). By reviewing and sorting memos according to categories and then for their cross-dimensional linkages, researchers should be able to arrive at a considerable amount of integration.

It is our experience that students do quite well with their memo writing up to the point of integration. They might have identified one or more patterns (e.g., "types of users") and a process (e.g., "getting stoned") and even perhaps some relationships among these. The difficulty students seem to have is coming up with the more abstract theoretical scheme that explains all of their data. It is with final integration that most beginning analysts seem to need help. Yet, final integration is necessary. Without it, there might be interesting description and some themes but no theory because there are no statements telling us how these themes relate to each other. Of course, if one's ultimate research goal is to arrive at a set of findings rather than theory development, then integration is not as relevant.

Some researchers turn to the literature to look for a unifying concept that might fit their data. They do this when they have sorted through and reread all their memos and have an intuitive sense of what the central idea is but have no name for it. Sometimes, they attempt to locate a concept that is similar in nature to the central idea identified in their research (see, e.g., Miles & Huberman, 1994). This system helps analysts to locate their findings in the larger body of professional knowledge and to contribute to further development and refinement of existing concepts in their field.

However, this is not our usual approach because, more often than not, existing concepts only partially fit the data. It might also prevent researchers from arriving at new perspectives and approaches, and these are important to the advancement of knowledge in every field. We prefer that students be more creative, that they provide their own names for what is going on and then describe their conceptualizations in terms of the particular properties and dimensions that were evident in their data. Later, in writing up their findings, they can make comparisons describing how their conceptualizations of data extend or fit with the existing literature. Sometimes, however, an existing concept so aptly describes what is going on that it is fortuitous to use it. For example, the concept of "trajectory," which evolved out of earlier studies of chronic illness management (Fagerhaugh & Strauss, 1977; Glaser & Strauss, 1975; Strauss, Fagerhaugh, Suczek, & Wiener, 1985), was so pertinent to our study of chronic illness in couples (it was found in every interview) that we decided to use it as our central organizing concept, although modifying and extending it (Corbin & Strauss, 1988). Or, a researcher may embark on a study with the intent of examining a concept under different sets of conditions; for example, he or she might use the concept of "awareness" (developed during a study of dying [Glaser & Strauss, 1965]) to do research on spies, thereby increasing the concept's generalizability. All of these are variations on approaches to naming the central integrative concept. Whatever method the analyst chooses, the unifying concept should meet the criteria of a core category described earlier in this chapter.

REFINING THE THEORY

Once the researcher has outlined the overarching theoretical scheme, it is time to refine the theory. Refining the theory consists of reviewing the scheme for internal consistency and for gaps in logic, filling in poorly developed categories and trimming excess ones, and validating the scheme.

Reviewing the Scheme for
Internal Consistency and Logic

A theoretical scheme should flow in a logical manner and should not have inconsistencies. If the story line memo and diagrams are clear, then consistency and logic should follow. However, sometimes during the final writing, the researcher senses that something is not quite right and still needs to be worked out. Under these conditions, the researcher should go back and once more make use of diagrams and review the memos. But unless the analyst knows what he or she is looking for or what is missing, diagramming will not help.

A place to begin is with the central category itself. A central category, like any category, must be defined in terms of its properties and dimensions. If we call teen drug taking a "rite of passage," then we must define what we mean by the terms "rite" and "passage." Like all categories, the definition comes out of the properties and their dimensions. Even if the central category was not named in earlier memos, when the analyst reviews the memos, he or she should find references to the idea in the data along with properties and dimensions. For example, although the term "rite of passage" was not used earlier in the research, the memos were replete with references to the social aspects of drug taking and its meaning to teens, the discovery about self, and the maturational process that occurred. In the memos, we were able to identify that the passage varied in **nature, type, duration, form, and outcomes** (i.e., the properties of this passage). Therefore, we might define "rite of passage" as an interactive social process that will vary according to type of user and that is marked by "getting stoned" or not and having certain outcomes in terms of growth. We go on to further explicate the definition when we write up the rest of the theory showing how the passage varied dimensionally according to type of user and by relating "types of users" to "getting stoned" and then tracing out the consequences, a major one being becoming more adult-like in making choices and handling peer pressure.

To check for consistency and logical development, the analyst can stand back and ask himself or herself (because by now the analyst is so immersed in the data) what he or she thinks the properties are and then go back and see how much of this has been built into the scheme. If it still is not clear, or if there are areas that seem to be missing, then the analyst should go back to data and sort this out. Sometimes, it is simply that the analyst is almost there but, without realizing it, has taken the wrong stance toward the data; that is, it is easy to look at the data from the perspective of the analyst and not the respondents while thinking that he or she is doing just the opposite. For example, while one of us (Corbin) was writing her dissertation, which looked at management by women of high-risk pregnancies, something seemed awry with the logic; it just did not seem to fit; that is, the behaviors of the women did not always match with perceptions of risks, which varied from high to low, changing sometimes over the course of their pregnancies. Finally, it dawned on her that although she thought she was being impartial, in reality when she was classifying incidents, she was defining degree of risk from the perspective of a health professional rather than from the perspectives of respondents, who sometimes viewed the risk quite differently from health professionals and then acted on the basis of those perceptions.

Filling in Poorly Developed Categories

In theory building, the analyst aims for density. By "density," we mean that all (within reason) the salient properties and dimensions of a category have been identified, thereby building in variation, giving a category precision, and increasing the explanatory power of the theory. Poorly developed categories usually become evident when making diagrams and sorting memos. For example, if we went back and found that we had written many memos about "limited experimenters" but few on "hard-core users" of drugs, then we would have to return to the field to gather more data about this category to fill in that gap.

Filling in can be done through review of memos or raw data, looking for data that might have been overlooked. Or, the analyst can go back into the field and selectively gather data about that category through theoretical sampling (see Chapter 13). Filling in often continues into the final writing phase. The analyst always will find gaps when he or she begins to write. The problem is deciding when to let go. Not every detail can be well developed or spelled out. Of course, large gaps should be filled in. A category should be sufficiently developed in terms of properties and dimensions to demonstrate its *range of variability* as a concept. In the previous example, achieving variation would mean being able to show that even within a category, there are differences in how one experiences a rite of passage and that such differences can be accounted for by examining the dimensions of what types of drugs were used, how often, and so on.

The ultimate criterion for determining whether or not to finalize the data-gathering processes still is *theoretical saturation*. This term denotes that during analysis, no new properties and dimensions emerge from the data, and the analysis has accounted for much of the possible variability.

Trimming the Theory

Sometimes, the problem is not insufficient data but rather an excess of data; that is, some ideas do not seem to fit the theory. These usually are extraneous concepts, that is, nice ideas but ones that never were developed, probably because they did not appear much in data or seemed to trail off into nowhere. Our advice is to drop them. If they are interesting, then the analyst can pursue them at a latter date, but there is no reason to clutter a theory with concepts that lead nowhere or contribute little to its understanding.

Validating the Theoretical Scheme

When we speak of validating, we are not talking about testing in the quantitative sense of the word. This can be left to future studies, if desired. What we mean by "validating" is the following. The theory emerged from data, but by the time of integration, it represents an abstract rendition of that raw data. Therefore, it is important to determine how well that abstraction fits with the raw data and also to determine whether anything salient was omitted from the theoretical scheme. There are several ways of validating the scheme. One way is to go back and compare the scheme against the raw data, doing a type of high-level comparative analysis. The theoretical scheme should be able to explain most of the cases. Another way to validate is to actually tell the story to respondents or ask them to read it and then request that they comment on how well it seems to fit their cases. Naturally, it will not fit every aspect of each case because the theory is a reduction of data, but in the larger sense, participants should be able to recognize themselves in the story that is being told. They should be able to perceive it as a reasonable explanation of what is going on even if not every detail quite fits their cases. In this short section, we have taken up only one aspect of validating theory. This topic is discussed further in Chapter 16.

What if a Case Does Not Fit

It is not unusual to find outlying cases, those that fall at either extreme dimensional range of a concept or that seem quite contrary to what is going on. For the most part, these outliers represent variations of the theory or present alternative explanations. For example, in the study example about teens and drug use, suppose that we found cases in which participants became addicted to drugs and dropped out of school. How does our explanation of drug taking as a rite of passage fit with them? It was a passage for them too, but a passage into addiction rather than a step toward adulthood. They started out like other teens, being ceremoniously introduced to drugs at a party. However, getting stoned became an end unto itself rather than remaining a social act through which they shared an experience with other teens. The difference lies in where the passage led rather than in whether or not it was a passage per se. Sometimes, a case represents a state that is in transition between types or phases. For example, a teen might not fit the profile of either a recreational or a hard-core user; that is, he or she might have some properties of both. When an odd event arises in the data, there usually are intervening variables or conditions that explain that variability. These too must be identified. Discovering these outlying cases (sometimes referred to as "negative cases") and building explanations into the theory for them increases its generalizability and explanatory power.

Building in Variation

One of the problems with some theoretical schemes is that they fail to account for variation. This is problematic because it makes the theory appear artificial, as though every person or organization falls into these neat and distinct types or steps in a process. We know that life does not fit into neat little boxes. There always are variations of every process. Some persons move slower, some move faster, some drop out, and some take a different passage. This means that even within patterns and categories, there is variability with different people, organizations, and groups falling at different dimensional points along some properties. For example, if we were to take the category of "limited experimenters," there could be many variations within this category, with some teens limiting their use to only one type of drug, other teens trying drugs but getting stoned once or twice, others trying five different drugs but each drug only once, others engaging in a lot of drug talk with their peers about their experiences, and still others keeping their experiences personal. In writing about our theory, we want to bring out the variations both within and between categories.

SUMMARY

Selective coding is the process of integrating and refining the theory. In integration, categories are organized around a central explanatory concept. Integration occurs over time, beginning with the first steps in analysis and often not ending until the final writing. Once a commitment is made to a central idea, major categories are related to it through explanatory statements of relationships. Several techniques can be used to facilitate the integration process. These include telling or writing the storyline, using diagrams, sorting and reviewing memos, and using computer programs.

Once the theoretical scheme is outlined, the analyst is ready to refine the theory, trimming off excess and filling in poorly developed categories. Poorly developed categories are saturated through further theoretical sampling. Finally, the theory is validated by comparing it to raw data or by presenting it to respondents for their reactions. A theory that is grounded in data should be recognizable to participants, and although it might not fit every aspect of their cases, the larger concepts should apply.

11 Coding for Process

DEFINITION OF TERM

Process: Sequences of evolving action/interaction, changes in which can be traced to changes in structural conditions

Bringing process into the analysis is an essential part of our approach to theory building. In the chapter on axial coding (Chapter 9), we introduced the notion of "process." In this chapter, we take our discussion further by explaining what we mean by this term and how one might go about discovering process in data. To reassure our readers, we are not introducing a new form of analysis. The standard procedures of *asking questions* and *making comparisons* remain *the essential* analytic processes. What is somewhat different is the analytic focus. Rather than analyzing data for properties and dimensions, we are looking at action/interaction and tracing it over time to note how and if it changes or what enables it to remain the same with changes in structural conditions. Changes in conditions may be anticipated, planned for, and predicted. Or, they may occur quite unexpectedly (contingency) and require some on-the-spot problem solving. So, to move on with our purpose, we ask the following questions. What is process? Why is it such an important part of our analysis? The purpose of this chapter is to answer these questions. It begins with a general description of our view process and ends with an example of how one might analyze data for process. Because process is such an elusive term, one that is just as difficult to explain as it is to capture in data, perhaps the best way in which to begin our discussion is to present two scenarios.

When listening to a piece of music (well, most music anyway), one cannot help but be struck by all the variations in tone and sound. We know that music, whether it be jazz, popular, or classical, is composed of a series of notes, some played fast, some slow, some loud, others soft, sometimes played in one key, sometimes in another, often with movement back and forth between keys. Even the pauses have purpose and are part of the sound. It is the playing of these notes, with all of their variations and in coordinated sequences, that gives music its sense of movement, rhythm, fluidity, and continuity.

To us, process is like a piece of music. It represents the rhythm, changing and repetitive forms, pauses, interruptions, and varying movements that make up sequences of action/interaction. The next scenario is perhaps an even more graphic illustration of our notion of process. Recently, one of us (Corbin) was seated in the waiting room of a small airport. Having nothing to do but wait, she began to take an interest in what was going on in the coffee shop nearby. It was a modest shop of a type that can be found in any small town in the United States. There were between 20 and 25 persons seated around the room at tables and at the counter. There was one waitress and one cook. The waitress moved from table to table, taking orders and bringing the orders to the cook, who, after preparing the food, gave it back to the waitress to be delivered to the waiting customers. The same waitress also received the money from customers and rang it up in the cash register. From time to time, the waitress stopped to talk to customers, poured more coffee, cleared the tables, and generally kept moving, her ever watchful eyes alert for signs of customer needs. Although her actions/interactions differed in form and content over the time she was observed, all were part of a series of acts pertaining to a phenomenon that might be called "food servicing work." While the waitress was doing her work, the patrons were eating, talking, and watching the small private planes come and go.

The scene was not a very dramatic one. In fact, it was quite routine, surely repeated day after day in much the same way in coffee shops all over the country. Although routine, the action/interaction was a flow of continuous activity, with one sequence of actions flowing into another. This is not to say that there were no interruptions or problems, but these tended to be resolved as part of the ongoing flow of action. Watching the scene made the observer realize, "Ah, now *that* is process."

Process, then, can be described as a series of evolving sequences of action/interaction that occur over time and space, changing or sometimes remaining the same in response to the situation or context. The action/interaction may be strategic, taken in response to problematic situations, or may be quite routine, carried out without much thought. It may be orderly, interrupted, sequential, or coordinated—or, in some cases, a complete mess. What makes the action/interaction process is its evolving nature and its varying forms, rhythms, and pacing all related to some purpose.

THE INTERPLAY BETWEEN STRUCTURE AND PROCESS

As stated in the chapter on axial coding (Chapter 9), action/interaction occurs within a set of conditions or situational context. As such, structure and process are related in very complex ways. Just as the sound of a piece of music changes with a change in key, action/interaction evolves or can change in response to shifts in the context. In turn, action/interaction can bring about changes in the context, thus becoming part of the conditions framing the next action/interactional sequence. For instance, take the same restaurant described previously and imagine what the action/interaction or the "flow of work" would look like if we varied the conditions. We could have several large groups of persons come in at the same time with still only one waitress and one cook to service them. Imagine how this would change the pacing of the work and the ability to talk with customers, to pour that extra cup of coffee, to prepare the food and serve it before it cooled down, and so on. What if the cook suddenly became ill and the waitress had to both cook and serve the food, or what if there were 5 waitresses but only 20 customers? Suppose that the waitress was inexperienced and slow and the customers got tired of waiting for their food. Would the pleasant and friendly action/interaction taking place between customers and the waitress turn to one of impatience and frustration? Each of these different scenarios has the potential to alter or shift the nature of the action/interaction. Structure, then, creates the context for action/interaction, with the latter flowing or being interrupted as individuals or groups attempt to align their acts to the situation. Because structure over time tends to change (think of customers coming and going from the restaurant), action/interaction has to change to stay aligned with it. In this way, process and structure are inextricably linked.

The Variable Nature of Process

One could say that, at best, process is like a coordinated ballet or symphony, with each movement graceful, aligned, purposeful, sometimes thoughtful and other times habitual, and with one action leading into another. At its worst, it might resemble a soccer riot, with the acts misaligned, disrupted, uncontrolled, nondirected, and sometimes hurtful. Most human action/interaction, however, probably lies somewhere in between. It is not always as graceful as a ballet or as chaotic as a riot. In fact, it can be dull and routine but also novel and creative. Process demonstrates the ability of individuals, organizations, and groups to respond to and/or shape the situations in which they find themselves. In addition, process illustrates how groups align or misalign their actions/interactions and, thereby, are able to maintain social order, put on a play, have a party, do work, create chaos, or fight a war. As researchers, we want to capture these dynamic qualities and varied scenarios of action/interaction (see Figure 11.1).

Conceptualizing Process

Process in data is represented by happenings and events that may or may not occur in continuous forms or sequences. It always can be located in a context. How one conceptualizes or describes process is variable. Although process often is described by analysts as stages or phases, it also can be examined in terms of sequences or shifts in the nature of action/interaction. The choice of form depends on the data

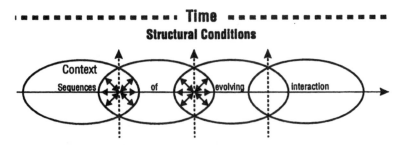

straight lines = evolving inter/action
circles = context for inter/action
overlaps in circles = intersection of conditions and consequences leading to change of
variation in context and adjustments made in interaction to keep it flowing

Figure 11.1. Process

and the research question. For example, "experimenting with drugs" is a process. One could examine it from the perspective of the stages or phases that lead to experimenting with drugs. However, stages or phases might not be the best way of explaining what is going on in this situation. Perhaps it is the action/interaction that surrounds the "acquisition" and "use" of drugs that is more descriptive of what is going on. Not everything that is process can be reduced to stages or phases, nor should it be.

ANALYZING DATA FOR PROCESS

Analyzing data for process is not a separate aspect of analysis. Coding for process occurs simultaneously with coding for properties and dimensions and relationships among concepts. It is part of axial coding and the building of categories. Instead of looking for properties, one is **purposefully looking at action/interaction and noting movement, sequence, and change as well as how it evolves (changes or remains the same) in response to changes in context or conditions.** An example would be the changes in the movements of a ballerina princess when the context changes by the entrance of an evil prince, as in *Swan Lake*. Her dance, which is peaceful and dreamy, takes on a more frightful and intense quality.

Analyzing the data for process has certain advantages. In addition to giving theory a sense of "life" or movement, it aids with integration and discovery of variation. Examining data for how action/interaction changes over time and space and in response to contingencies forces an analyst to look for patterns. Also, by relating process to structure, one is, in fact, connecting categories. As an example, recall that in the chapter on selective coding (Chapter 10), we stated that "experimenting with drugs" could take several forms. There were the nonusers, the limited experimenters, the recreational users, and the hard-core users. The type of user was connected with the category "getting stoned" (a process). Whether or not one got stoned, when, how often, to what degree, with what drugs, and so on determined an individual's experience with drugs and his or her willingness to continue to use or not use drugs, how often, and when; therefore, it was related to the type of drug user that a teen became. Note again that the linkages among concepts occur at the dimensional level.

Just because an action/interaction is repeated and routine does not mean that it is not processual. Studying the routinization of action/interaction, especially in organizations, and discovering what conditions make it possible to stay routine in the face of contingencies (unanticipated happenings) can be just as important a contribution to knowledge development as is studying the novel and problematic action/interaction.

Some questions that might be asked of data when analyzing for process include the following. Generally, what is going on here? What problems, issues, happenings are being handled through action/interaction, and what forms does it take? What conditions combine to create the context in which the action/interaction is located? Why is the action/interaction staying the same? Why and how is it changing? Are actions/interactions aligned or misaligned? What conditions or activities connect one sequence of events to another? What happens to the form, flow, continuity, and rhythm of action/interaction when conditions change, that is, it becomes misaligned or is interrupted or disrupted because of contingency (unplanned or unexpected changes in conditions)? How is action/interaction taken in response to problems or contingencies similar to, or different from, action/interaction that is routine? How do the consequences of one set of actions/interactions play into the next sequence of actions/interactions to either alter the actions/interactions or allow them to stay the same? The latter question is extremely important because it enables researchers to see how actions/interactions have consequences, and these often become part of the conditional context in which the next action/interactional sequence is located. For instance, a bad experience with getting stoned might be the deciding factor that moves the recreational drug user into becoming a non-drug user, just as a pleasurable experience with getting stoned might be the deciding factor that explains why the recreational user continues to use drugs into adulthood.

Subprocesses

Process usually can be broken down into subprocesses. These usually are the individual tactics, strategies, and routine actions that make up the larger act. These might change or remain the same with changing conditions. If we were to take the process of experimenting with drugs, we might break it down into subprocesses such as "engaging in drug talk," "obtaining the drugs," "ingesting the substance," "having the experience," and "sharing the experience." Each one of these subprocesses can further be broken down into action/interactional tactics.

An Approach to Analysis

We are not opposed to coding for stages or phases when this fits the data. What is important to us is that process be related to structure, that is, the alignment of actions/interactions to conditions, how these change from one stage to another, variations within a phase, and how the outcomes of one set of actions/interactions feed back into the context to become part of the conditions influencing the next set of actions/interactions. The following materials are *biographical* ones. Let us say that the question we are asking is how larger historical events take on personal meaning for individuals. This historical event in this case was World War II. We have termed the process for which we are coding "personalizing," meaning that an event takes on personal significance. We present parts of the raw data from an interview, followed by a brief analysis to illustrate how we code for process.

Respondent: Well, you know in the beginning, okay, Pearl Harbor got bombed, but it was far away, it doesn't mean anything. It was far away.

Analysis. Here our interviewee is telling us that to her, the bombing of Pearl Harbor is an "invisible event." The word "invisible" here means "far way," with the war not directly touching her.

Respondent: But then it becomes close to home when you hear people talking abut it and this one's son has to go. Then my brother had to go. My brother was overseas, and he didn't even know how to shoot a gun and still they sent him over. Other families' boys . . . it was terrible.

Analysis. Now, the event becomes a "visible event"; that is, it comes closer to home. The conditions for it becoming a visible event were "hearing people talking" and "hitting at a personal level" (her brother and sons of friends having to go to war).

Respondent: So, I will never forget, we were walking along the streets shopping, and my mother met this woman she knew, and this woman, my mother was crying because her son had to go overseas, and this woman said, "You should be so proud. He is fighting for his country." Well, sometime later, this woman's son-in-law had to go. She wasn't feeling so happy then, you know.

Analysis. With her brother being drafted, the war is beginning to take on "significant meaning." Because this woman is recalling events that probably happened 50 years ago, it seems that the brother's going to war, the mother's crying, and the neighbor's comment affected her sufficiently to be retained in her memory all these years. In terms of the larger process of what seems to be going on, this event appears to be a "turning point," a beginning step in the process of incorporating the war, with all its potential ramifications, into her identity.

Respondent: Then, you start reading the paper about the wounded. This friend of my husband was a doctor over in Italy. His wife had two kids. She went into a vegetable store to buy some oranges. I can't exactly remember, but they were only selling four at a time. She asked for a couple more. The man yelled at her, "Lady, don't you know there is a war on!" Things like that.

Analysis. The "significant meaning" of the event is being reaffirmed each day through the daily reading of the newspaper and the way in which she and friends are being affected in terms of their daily lives such as ability to purchase food. Sacrificing becomes an event shared with others. This particular event, unlike her brother being drafted, is not so much a turning point as a "reinforcer." The war hits her over and over again at a personal identity level, in all types of "indirect ways." One can see here how, although there is a series of events, these events are processed within the individual, so that each becomes part of the ability to move on to the next step in the process of a historical event taking on personal meaning.

Respondent: You roll bandages and knit socks and scarves. You go to the Red Cross and help.

Analysis. Now, our interviewee is moving from "passive involvement" to "active or direct involvement." This is a shift in action/interaction as she begins to do her part in the larger community war effort. Everyone pulls together and works toward a common goal. It is expected. We are not sure what the conditions were that brought about this shift. One can only hypothesize. It could be the fact that a friend asked her to come along, or there was societal pressure. Or, perhaps it was because her husband was drafted and she needed something to do to fill her time. To find out which (if any) of these conditions was (or were) operating, we would have to go back and ask the interviewee.

Respondent: Then I went. Well, first my husband was drafted. I traveled with him after he got his commission. But before he got his commission, he was down at Camp Crop and I went to see him. All these young women on the train and everybody talking to them.

Analysis. Another turning point comes when her husband is drafted. Not only is he pulled into the war, but the war becomes a direct experience for her. She is not only doing things like rolling bandages, she is part of the event itself. She is going to the places where her husband is staying, living as the wife of a soldier. Each of these turning points (conditions) shifts and moves our process along. The words "I went" are very interesting because we do not know whether she meant she went to see him or, in her way, she felt she too was going to war symbolically.

Respondent: He went overseas with his very good friend. They were in the service together. By that time, they were both 1st lieutenants. They got their orders at the same time. We were at Fort Smith then. So, they had to get back in a hurry, and they wanted us home. The other couple had a little girl. The only thing they could get was the drawing room for the five of us, so we got on the train and they decided that the friend's wife and the baby would sleep in a little berth. There was a bed on the other side that the friend would have. Then, my husband and I would sleep in the upper berth. So, they [the other couple] let us go in first when evening came and we got ready for bed. They are knocking on the door, "Are you ready yet?" The whole train started laughing, it was so funny. It was the most miserable night of my life because I got swished, pushed, you know, in an upper berth with a big man. But we got home, and they went down to Camp Mead and then overseas. It was sheer hell.

Analysis. The war experience had its lighter moments, especially early when the interviewee was able to travel with her husband. The incident on the train was one of those lighter moments. However, another turning point in the process occurs when her husband is sent overseas. The war has now taken on very direct and "significant meaning" because her husband is now "in" the war. She describes this period as one of "sheer hell."

Respondent: My husband's friend was taken prisoner within 4 weeks. My husband lasted 6 weeks before he was wounded. My friend kept calling saying, "I don't hear from [her husband]. Does your husband say anything in his letters?" It was really horrific. I read in the paper that Patten says the life expectancy of a platoon is 4 to 6 weeks, so I figured that my husband wasn't coming home.

Analysis. Things that this woman now reads in the newspaper take on "personal meaning," especially in light of her husband being wounded and the friend becoming a prisoner of war. She is directly affected. The war no longer is a thing "out there" or a time of traveling as a soldier's wife but rather is something that is very significant, and because of it, she feels the "threat of loss."

Respondent: I kept reading the paper every day, looking for names in the paper because they would list the names, you know. It was not a good time.

Analysis. Reading the newspaper and looking at the list of wounded or dead has taken on new meaning for her. It no longer is an abstract act of looking at names. She is purposefully looking to see whether the name of her husband or that of her friend is listed. This is now **her** war as well, indirectly through her husband's active participation, and she lives in "biographical limbo" while she anxiously awaits his return. The question is "Will he return?" and, if he does, "Will he be the same mentally and physically?"

Respondent: When he first got wounded, I got letters written by a Red Cross person. Then, he wrote himself. He had beautiful handwriting, but his writing was like chicken scratches. He couldn't control the pen. They really didn't think he would come back to himself. But he did. He came back all the way.

Analysis. This woman's husband "came back" not only alive but also without physical limitations from his wounds. Thus, she was able to put "closure" on the event. The war's significance in her life stands out because 50 years later, she brings it up in a biographical interview that did not focus on the war.

Summary

Although there are many different ways of conceptualizing the preceding process, for the purposes of this book, we refer to it as "personalizing." In keeping with our research question (the phenomenon we are studying), we can say that the interviewee is "personalizing a historical event." In this case, it is a war, but it could be an earthquake, a revolution, and so on. We can break the process down into several steps. Again for the purposes of this chapter, the first step is called "bringing the event home"; that is, the event no longer is invisible or way out there but rather is something that moves closer to her sense of self, hitting at her personal identity. The turning point in the process occurred when she began internalizing the fact that her brother had to go to war and when she started hearing people whom she knew talk about the war in personal ways, as when shopping with her friend. The second step is "doing your part." This means making a personal commitment and getting the self directly involved by doing something active rather than remaining a passive bystander. However, the war still was rather impersonal in the sense that although she was doing things, the war still had yet to hit her at the core of her identity. The bandages were for "unknown" soldiers, not for her brother or husband. The external events that seemed to lead to this second turning point were reading about wounded soldiers, a friend having the war thrust in her face by the grocer, and her facing restrictions on what she was allowed to buy—small events that, taken together, made the war seem more real. Thus, our interviewee got caught up in "doing one's part" for the war effort. In the third step, "becoming an active participant," we see a major step in the personalizing process occurring. The turning point was her internal response to her husband being drafted. Her self, her core identity, now was directly involved in this historical event. Her husband was a soldier, and she was traveling as a war wife. However, although she was physically involved in the traveling and certainly emotionally involved because she never was sure when her husband would be sent abroad, the "real significance" of war still had not yet hit her. We see that in the fourth step. Finally, when her husband was sent overseas, she read about the deaths of others, then her husband was wounded, and now we see our interviewee reaching the fourth step of the personalizing process—"emotionally signifying" the event. Now, the event was completely fused with her identity as she waited in "biographical limbo" for her husband's return.

Although we do not have much detail in this interview, we can hypothesize that it was the internal process of making past, present, and future mental reviews of actual and anticipated events that led to the personalizing process; that is, external events were played against biographical implications of those events in a series of self- and other dialogues. For example, when her husband was sent overseas (she refers to this period as "sheer hell"), one can hypothesize that because she now was closely reading the obituaries, she imagined that something awful might happen to her husband, brother, or friend. Actions/

interactions with her neighborhood friend and with family, and the reading of the newspaper, were conditions that prompted mental dialogues or reviews and subsequent overt action/interaction. Then, when her husband was wounded, she perceived that he might be left handicapped, and she held this image until he came home and his functioning returned to normal.

Each step represents categories. Each has its own properties, action/interactional strategies, and outcomes. Because this is only our first interview, the products of analysis are only tentative and are compared against future data from further interviews. One would expect that with further analysis of other documents, there might be added steps, considerable variation in the steps, and much more detail about the reviews (self- and other dialogues) that move the process along. To extend our analysis, the researcher would want to sample other biographically impacting events to determine how individuals incorporate these into their selves. Such events might include natural disasters, major political upheavals, and scientific breakthroughs that change the ways in which individuals think, act, or work (e.g., the computer). One also might want to compare an individual process such as "personalizing" against the national process of "personalizing" and try to determine how these are related. Do the steps of a nation as a whole compare with those of the individual, and what is the relationship between them? Again, there is much more that could be said or done with this analysis. However, the purpose here is to point the way and not to do an exhaustive examination of data. We now turn to looking at some macro processes to show that process can be found at different micro/macro levels of analysis.

Process Analysis at Both Micro and Macro Levels

One can analyze data for process at any level of analysis, that is, at either the micro or macro level. (See Chapter 12 for a description of the micro and macro conditions.) Examining the impact of historical events, say on American citizens as a collective, refocuses the analyst's attention away from the individual to the larger, more macro impact such as women filling in for men in the workforce and then many of these women staying in the workforce once the war ended. Although the interviews were done with individuals, the phenomenon of responding to war is a collective and national one because the nation (not individuals) is at war, and most everyone in the country is undergoing the event (even though persons responded in individual ways). There is an interplay between what is going on at the national level (e.g., changes in social order, discussions in the press, sacrifices that citizens are called on to make) and what is going on at the biographical level as reflected in the experiences and responses of these persons. Before closing this chapter, we provide some additional examples of processual analysis. We use published studies to illustrate our points. In these studies, process forms the central or core category around which all the other data are organized.

First, a researcher may write a paper or book organized around processes that are specifically named, conceptually developed, and systematically connected within a theoretical framework with other concepts. Carolyn Wiener did this in her monograph, *The Politics of Alcoholism: Building an Arena Around a Social Problem* (Wiener, 1983), a study of the many ideological positions in contest over definitions, etiologies, treatments, ethics, and policies with regard to "widespread" and "severe" alcoholism. Wiener's analysis was broken down into arena processes and related subprocesses, which were evident in the section headings and chapter titles. They were as follows:

Animating the Problem

1. Establishing Turf Rights

2. Developing Constituencies

3. Funneling Advice and Imparting Skills and Information

Legitimating the Problem

4. Borrowing Prestige and Expertise

5. Redefining the Problem

6. Building Respectability

7. Maintaining a Separate Identity

Demonstrating the Problem

8. Competing for Attention and Combining for Strength

9. Selecting Supportive Data

10. Convincing Opposing Ideologies

11. Enlarging the Bound of Responsibility

By our reading of the monograph, its subtitle, "Building an Arena Around a Social Problem," constitutes Wiener's (1983) core category (a process in this case). Her major subprocesses are "animating," "legitimating," and "demonstrating." These subprocesses constitute the action/interactional mechanisms for carrying out that larger process of "building." Under each of the subprocesses are strategies and tactics (e.g., "establishing turf rights," "developing constituencies") that explain how the subprocesses are actually carried out. This focus on process enables the researcher to order a great mass of substantive data and also to achieve considerable conceptual density.

Finding process in researchers' writings sometimes is like finding mushrooms buried slightly beneath the forest leaves. The researchers do not always spell it out for us, yet if one looks carefully, process is there at the organizing core. An example of such can be found in Fujimura's (1988) article that reported findings from her study of cancer laboratories. Data were collected by extensive field observations and interviewing as well as scrutiny of documents. Although Fujimura never mentioned process in the article, it is clear from her section headings that process played a major role in the "evolution of a scientific bandwagon," her core category. This evolution was characterized by the rapid and immensely influential spread of recombinant DNA theory, the oncogene theory, and its accompanying techniques to a number of biological specializations and to other disciplines. The section headings in her article were as follows:

Standardizing Recombinant DNA Technologies

Building "One Size Fits All" Oncogene Theory

Marketing the Package

Buying the Package: Many Prizes in the Box

In the final section of her article, Fujimura (1988) detailed extensively the consequences derived from the bandwagon on the oncogene theory. She called this the "bandwagon snowball effect." Filling out her analysis, Fujimura provided dense data regarding funding and policies of the foundations, universities, laboratories, and government agencies—all involved in the development and spread of the oncogene theory. In summary, her core category was the "evolution of a scientific bandwagon," and her section headings indicated the action/interactional processes through which that evolution occurred. Filling in the theory were detailed linkages among a large number of substantive objects and events.

A third publication that we briefly comment on here reported findings from a study conducted by Melville Dalton. In the study, Dalton (1954) examined the workings and concerns of several industrial and commercial firms. He gathered data through both participant observation and informal interviews. His very interesting book describing the study contained both a largely implicit theoretical framework and some useful concepts as well as an enormous amount of ethnographic detail. We mention it here because his theoretical analysis revolved around the concept of negotiation and was largely processual. According to Strauss (1978), in another publication, Dalton found that the essential interactional mechanism for keeping these organizations functioning was making commitments to carry out the many agreements derived via continual negotiation at every level of the organization. In Strauss's words,

> A web of commitments grows up, continuously renewed, albeit continuously changing, evolving as a consequence of typically repeated, serial, and linked negotiations. . . . One can easily discern, both in his [Dalton's] data and in his own analysis, at least the following strategies: trading off, the paying off of accumulated obligations, the overt making of deals and other kinds of secret bargains, the use of additional covert negotiations for keeping hidden the results of previous covert arrangements, the bypassing of negotiations, and the mediating of negotiations; also [one can discern] a very complex balancing of accumulated favors and obligations, along with the juggling of commitments within the negotiation itself. (p. 139)

Although process was central in Dalton's analysis, it was very much connected to structure.

Analyzing for Process at a General Theory Level

Thus far, our discussion has focused on analyzing for process when building substantive theory. But what happens when one is building general theory? Is the analysis much different? The answer is both yes and no. The questions that the analyst asks of data remain essentially the same, although perhaps broader. However, comparisons are made on a much broader scale, that is, between different substantive areas rather than being limited to one area.

For example, in Strauss's (1978) book on *Negotiations*, he used processual analysis to formulate a formal or general theory about negotiations. This theory was developed by examining negotiations in a variety of contexts (different substantive areas) including representatives of nations, judges in law courts, political machines, clans and ethnic groups, and insurance companies and their clients. By comparing and contrasting these various groups, he was able to identify the components of the negotiative process that transcended all groups (thereby formulating his general theory) and also was able to describe the individual variations in the negotiation process specific to each group.

SUMMARY

Process represents the dynamic and evolving nature of action/interaction. Process and structure are inextricably linked. Structure creates the context for action/interaction and, as such, is what gives it rhythm, pacing, form, and character. Regardless of whether the researcher is aiming to develop general or substantive theory, bringing process into the analysis is essential. Process can be the organizing thread or central category of a theory, or it can take a less prominent role. Regardless of what role it plays, process can be thought of as the difference between a snapshot and a moving picture. Each one pictorial form presents a different perspective and gives insight, but if one wants to see what happens or how things evolve, then one must turn to the moving picture. Theory without process is missing a vital part of its story—how the action/interaction evolves.

12 The Conditional/ Consequential Matrix

DEFINITIONS OF TERMS

Conditional/consequential matrix: An analytic device to stimulate analysts' thinking about the relationships between macro and micro conditions/consequences both to each other and to process

Macro conditions/consequences: Those that are broad in scope and possible impact

Micro conditions/consequences: Those that are narrow in scope and possible impact

Paths of connectivity: The complex ways in which macro and micro conditions/consequences intersect to create a context for action/interaction

Contingencies: Unanticipated or unplanned events that change conditions that can call for some sort of action/interactional (problem-solving) response to manage or handle them

If a researcher wants to build theory, then it is important for him or her to understand as much as possible about the phenomenon under investigation. This means locating a phenomenon contextually or within the full range of macro and micro conditions in which it is embedded and tracing out the relationships of subsequent actions/interactions through to their consequences. Because beginning researchers often become lost while attempting to sort out all of these complex relationships, we looked for a practical means for helping analysts to keep track of these various components of analysis. We call our analytic device the "conditional/consequential matrix," henceforth referred to as "the matrix." This chapter presents an overview of the matrix. It describes the matrix's purposes, offers an explanation of its diagrammatic features, and suggests how an analyst might use it to trace the paths of connectivity among conditions, actions/interactions, and consequences.

THE MATRIX

The *conditional/consequential matrix* is a coding device to help analysts keep in mind several analytic points. Among these are (a) that macro conditions/consequences, as well as micro ones, should be part of the analysis (when these emerge from the data as being significant); (b) that the macro conditions often intersect and interact with the micro ones and (c) thereby, in direct or indirect ways, become part of the situational context; and (d) that the paths taken by conditions, as well as the subsequent actions/interactions and consequences that follow, can be traced in the data (the paths of connectivity). The paradigm (Chapter 9) introduced the notions of conditions, actions/interactions, and consequences and suggested that structure and process were interrelated. This chapter takes that notion further by detailing the full range of conditions from micro to macro that might influence actions/interactions and the widespread nature of consequences that flow out of these.

The relevance of the matrix is as follows. Locating a phenomenon in context means more to us than simply depicting a situation descriptively, as would a good journalist or novelist. It means building a systematic, logical, and integrated account, which includes specifying the nature of relationships between significant events and phenomena. Although the paradigm is helpful in thinking about relationships, in and of itself it is incomplete. What the paradigm does not do is (a) address the many theoretical sampling choices that an analyst must make during the research process; (b) explain the varied, dynamic, and complex ways in which conditions, actions/interactions, and consequences can coexist and affect each other; (c) account for the different perceptions, constructions, and standpoints of the various actors; (d) put all the various pieces together to present an overall picture of what is going on; or (e) **emphasize that both micro and macro conditions are important to the analysis. Events that occur "out there" are not just interesting background material. When they emerge from the data as relevant, they too should be brought into the analysis. Sorting all this out is where the matrix is helpful.**

THE NOTION OF THE MATRIX

The matrix (Figure 12.1) is a diagrammatic representation of a set of ideas. The ideas contained therein are as follows.

1. *Conditions/consequences do not stand alone.* They always are integrated into the text and are related to action/interaction as it evolves and changes over time (process). The focus of a research project might be on different aspects of a phenomenon, its properties and dimensions, its structure, or process. Or, one might focus on structure and process. (It depends on the analyst and the data; however, the focus on one aspect, say process, does not mean that the other areas should be neglected. Structure [conditions], properties, dimensions, and consequences are important to the understanding of process.) The relationship between conditions and consequences and subsequent actions/interactions rarely follows a linear path. In other words, "A" (condition) rarely leads to "B" (action/interaction) and then to "C" (consequence) in a direct manner. This is too simplistic an explanation of events and is not consistent with real life. Rather, action/interaction may be taken in response to multiple conditions, some of which occurred in the past, some of which are happening in the present, and/or some of which are anticipated in the future

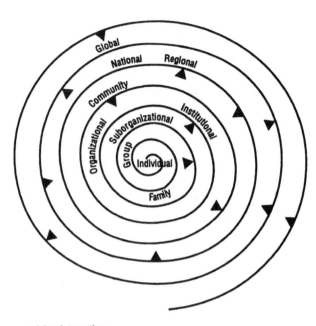

dark lines = evolving interaction
spaces between = sources of conditions/consequences which make up structure or context
arrows = intersection structure with process

Figure 12.1. The Conditional/Consequential Matrix (Represents constant interplay inter/action [process] with conditions/consequences [structure] and the dynamic evolving nature of events.)

(Dewey, 1934). Furthermore, one event often leads to another, and then to another, like the links in a chain, making the relationships among events very difficult to sort out. Consider the following example in which the author clearly describes events (conditions) and the relationships among them to subsequent actions/inter-actions. (However, each participant was not necessarily aware of what happened before or after or was aware what others were thinking or doing.) The event is the "announcement" of an impending storm. Notice how this announcement initiated a chain of conditions/consequences and actions/interactions. The outcome of the previous acts became conditions for further acts, and when an unanticipated event (contingency) entered the picture, it too had its consequences. Although each event was a distinct occurrence, it was in some direct or indirect way related to the event that preceded it and that which followed. The quote is about the announcement of an oncoming major storm and what happened as a result.

> The effects of the forecast tended to spread out link by link until they formed long chains. The shrewd proprietors of several restaurants called up the factory and reduced their orders for ice cream. The manager of the factory found his needs for milk and cream lessened and passed on his word to the dairy. Since the cows could not be forced to cooperate, the dairy company diverted the surplus to its subsidiary corporation, which manufactured butter and cheese. The manager then hired two extra men, whose wives, on the strength of the prospective jobs, spent more freely than usual at one of the smaller retail stores. The retailer optimistically imagined an up-swing of business and said he would take the new car over which he had been hesitating. At this point, however, the chain of effects turned back upon itself and ended. For the storekeeper, later in the day, read the forecast, and believing that his retail business always suffered in rainy weather, he called up the automobile salesman and canceled the order. (Stewart, 1941, p. 118)

2. *The distinction between micro and macro is an artificial one.* Micro conditions often have their origins in macro conditions, and when appropriate, the analyst should trace the relationships between these. For example, if an interviewee mentions that access to drugs is easy because there are several gangs operating near campus, then the researcher would want to know more about the connection between gangs and access to drugs, with the notion of gangs being the more macro condition. (One could go on to trace the whole notion of international drug rings, but this could take the researcher off course and change the focus of the study from a micro focus to a more macro one. However, if the notion of drug rings comes up during the interviews, then the researcher should follow up to determine what this means for the problem under investigation.) This information could be gained through further questioning of informants but also perhaps by talking with school and police officials and even gang members (if possible). As analysts, we are interested in the interplay between micro and macro conditions, the nature of their influence on

each other and subsequent actions/interactions, and the full scope of consequences that result as well as how those consequences feed back into the next conditional context to influence further actions/interactions. Part of our sampling in the preceding example, then, would be to try and determine what happens to "access" when the gangs are broken up or no longer are operating near the high school. Does the change in access affect drug use by teens? The full extent of relationships between micro and macro is not always visible to individual research participants. Each comes to the situation from his or her own standpoint or perspective and rarely has a grasp of the whole. Rather, each participant might make some reference to an event during an interview or observation such as "A new team of undercover narcotic agents has been assigned to our school," and it is up to the researcher to trace out the impact of the on-site presence of that team on drug access and drug use. **This is not to say that a researcher wants or has to trace every event that happens over the course of the research.** One could become hopelessly caught in a never-ending process of data collecting. It is only when such incidents emerge from the data as significant, such as noticing a "change in drug use" when gangs move into the neighborhood, that one would follow up on the incident.

3. *Conditions and consequences usually exist in clusters and can associate or covary in many different ways, both to each other and to the related actions/interactions.* Furthermore, with time and the advent of contingencies, the clusters of conditions and consequences can either change or rearrange themselves, so that the nature of relationships or associations that exists between them and the actions/interactions also changes. To find an example of this statement, one only has to look at the cumulative mess of health care delivery as it presently stands in the United States. Somehow and at some point in time, control of health care delivery slipped out of the hands of physicians and patients and into those of insurance companies and other organizations such as health maintenance organizations. This event occurred before most Americans knew what was happening. Among the chain of events (conditions/consequences) that have interacted and fed back on each other leading to this situation were a downward

turn in national economics; the need for retrenchment in industrial and other work organizations (they no longer wanted to pay for costly insurance premiums for their employees); the increased sophistication and costs of diagnostic procedures, medications, and treatments; the lack of accountability for spending on the part of physicians, hospitals, and patients; an increase in longevity; an increase in the incidence of chronic conditions; and individual demands and expectations for costly medical interventions. At the individual level, it is not until a person tries to go to the doctor for health care that he or she begins to understand the full impact of all that has transpired. A simple visit to a podiatrist first involves a visit to a primary physician, who may or may not be willing to refer the patient to the specialist. Even if the physician is willing to refer, permission for the visit first must be obtained from the insurance company, which also must okay any subsequent visits. The patient can wait around in pain, can complain to the doctor and/or insurance company, or simply give up and live with the medical problem until it becomes more advanced and more costly to treat. The way in which individuals are affected depends on the amount of money they have (to pay for additional insurance or supplements) and the type of doctors and health care plans with which they might, through chance or choice, become connected. Meanwhile, health care has become a for-profit rather than a nonprofit industry. Government continues to be ineffective in controlling access or costs, being more concerned with bipartisan politics than with equitable access, and doctors and patients keep trying to figure out how to get around the system so that they might obtain the medical care that they need. No one yet knows for certain where it eventually will lead. In the meantime, feedback from consumers to their employers, legislators, and insurance companies or health maintenance organizations are bringing about small changes aimed at easing the transition into a very different set of expectations about health care and the form it will take.

4. *Action/interaction is not confined to individuals per se; rather, it can be carried out by nations, organizations, and social worlds, albeit by the individuals within these who are representing the nations, organizations, and social worlds.* Furthermore, actions/interactions carried out by

nations, organizations, and so on can be directed at, or have an impact on, individuals, other nations, and other organizations and vice versa. For instance, legislation passed at a national level very often has its impact at the individual level. Taxes are a good example. On the other hand, a mobilization of individuals at a grassroots level can affect the passage of legislation at a national level. Some grass-roots efforts, such as environmental ones, often go beyond the community or national level to reach international stature.

DIVERSE PATTERNS OF CONNECTIVITY

The analytic picture presented in the preceding discussion is one of **multiple and diverse patterns of connectivity** with discernible shifting patterns of action/interaction over time. Although experienced researchers often have their own devices for keeping track of these complex sets of relationships, a researcher new to qualitative analysis might feel overwhelmed. It is important to remember that not every path a researcher attempts to follow will lead to discovery of an analytic gold mine, nor is it ever possible to discern all the possible connections among conditions, actions/interactions, and consequences. Every analyst has to accept that there are limitations to what can be discovered based on access to data, degree of analytic experience, and amount of personal reserves. We acknowledge that doing this complex type of analytic work is not easy, but to some degree it is necessary.

> Making explicit linkages between interaction and conditions that affect it is a complex analytic enterprise because conditions can be of varying substantive character (economic, political, religious, occupations) and of varying scope (international, national, occupational, organizational, suborganizational, interpersonal). The same is true of the consequences of interaction. Potentially, our analyses are even more complex because the interaction itself can vary in substantive aspects and in scope. (Corbin & Strauss, 1996, pp. 139-140)

MAKING ANALYTIC CHOICES

Of course, not every event or incident in the data must be traced out extensively. To do so would be exhaustive and would complicate the analytic explanation with unnecessary detail. The analyst has to trace out only those linkages that emerge as pertinent and that will further explain what is going on. This means making sampling choices about what questions to ask, what observations to make, and what other forms of data to collect. These choices, although directed by the data, often confuse the analyst. If there are too many choices, then he or she might not be sure about where to go next to collect data that will maximize discovery. The matrix can help the analyst to systematically think about what data to collect next, where to go for them, and then how to trace and connect those data to emerging concepts. In the end, there should be fewer loose analytic threads. (For an excellent example of how the matrix actually has been used to examine and organize data gathered on how employees working together across geographic distances negotiate common work practices, see Guesing, 1995.)

To give an example, if a researcher is studying nursing students and their program of study, and he or she *repeatedly* hears words of anger expressed about recent curriculum changes, then the researcher might want to pursue further the concept of "expressed dissatisfaction." This would entail theoretically sampling informants and events from the different areas represented in the matrix to discern the details of the changes (i.e., their nature and extent), how the curriculum changes were presented to students and by whom, what the changes mean for students in terms of their passage through the program, and who instituted the changes and why. In addition, the researcher would want to determine whether students are dissatisfied about other aspects of the program and if there is an interplay between their dissatisfaction with these other aspects and their dissatisfaction with the curriculum changes. Furthermore, the researcher would want to examine broader issues such as the role the university played in bringing about or supporting those changes; how the department and the university are responding to the students' concerns; how the curriculum changes will affect students' ability to get jobs in the community; what the national nursing curriculum trends are; and what larger professional, economic, and political issues might be at stake in the curriculum changes. Finally, the researcher would want to add a temporal dimension to all of this by determining whether or not these complaints appear under particular sets of conditions. Is there a history to them? Are complaints by nursing students cyclic, that is, repeated but changed as they move through the curriculum? These analytic issues and questions are not data. They are ideas for theoretical sampling and become important, for instance, if the researcher, when interviewing faculty members, learns that the curriculum changes were made in response to national trends and input from local hospitals; that the university administrators, although not against the changes, were not overly supportive either; and that when students complain, faculty members redirect them to the nursing department for an explanation.

In the preceding example, we are saying something more than "It is important to sample other nursing students, faculty members, or administrators in terms of their satisfaction or dissatisfaction with the changes." The questions we are raising are relational ones and allow us to penetrate more deeply into the issues. This penetration requires a far more extensive and theoretically directed data-gathering and analysis technique than just asking whether students are satisfied or not, to what degree, and why. By thinking in terms of the matrix and using it as a guide or reminder, even a beginning analyst can obtain a grasp on the complex nature of events and the interplay between these. In other words, the matrix can be used to direct theoretical sampling. It can help the analyst to make decisions about what analytic threads are important to pursue, where those data might be found, and how events might link to each other.

PURPOSES OF THE MATRIX

The purposes of the matrix can be summarized as in the following box (Corbin & Strauss, 1996):

PURPOSES OF THE MATRIX

1. To assist the analyst in locating the area or scope (micro/macro) of the research project being undertaken and in not losing sight of where that area stands in relationship to the areas above and below it

2. To extend the range of conditions and consequences considered by the analyst, that is, to consider more than just the micro conditions

3. To help the analyst in identifying and in making choices about which combination of conditional or consequential factors in the data might be relevant to this particular situation

4. To trace the often intricate web of connections that exists between contextual factors (conditions/consequences or structure) and actions/interactions (process)

5. To develop explanatory hypotheses about these relationships that can be verified or modified through further data collection and analysis

6. To make it more probable that explanatory hypotheses incorporate variation

7. To enable the researcher to organize materials and present a more complete and persuasive explanatory account of the phenomenon under investigation

8. To provide direction for theoretical sampling

DESCRIPTION OF THE MATRIX

All this time, we have been talking about the matrix as a set of ideas. The problem lies in translating these ideas into an easily understood diagram. The one that we have devised does not capture the complexity of what we just explained. In fact, it is quite simple, but purposefully so to make it easier for beginning students to grasp its significance and to use it more easily (see Figure 12.1).

The matrix consists of a series of concentric and interconnected circles with arrows going both toward and away from the center. The arrows represent the intersection of conditions/consequences and the resulting chain of events. Conditions move toward and surround the action/interaction to create a conditional context. Other arrows move away from actions/interactions, representing how the consequences of any action/interaction move from action/interaction to change or add to conditions in often diverse and unanticipated ways. One of the limitations of the diagram is that the flow appears linear. In reality, the paths taken by conditions/consequences as they move within and through the various areas from macro to micro are anything but linear. A more likely metaphor would be billiard balls, each striking the others at different angles, setting off a chain reaction that ends with knocking the appropriate balls into the pockets. Another would be a kaleidoscope that, with every turn of the frame, realigns the little pieces of colored glass (or plastic) to form a new picture.

Explanation of the Diagram

Conditions/consequences represent the structural context in which action/interaction occurs. Structural context has been broken down into different areas ranging from more macro to more micro. This arrangement is arbitrary. It is important to keep in mind that placement of an area within the circles does not denote degree of importance or potential impact of any set of conditions/consequences. It is just that some are considered more macro and some more micro. For example, legislation passed at the national (more macro) level has the potential to affect all citizens and the action/interaction that they take or are able to carry out, whereas policies and procedures of an organization potentially affect only the employees of that organization. In the center of the matrix stands the phenomenon under investigation. Around it is action/interaction as it evolves over time and place (process). The action/interaction may take many forms and may be purposeful or routine, aimed at shaping phenomena (i.e., handling problems, issues, contingencies, or everyday occurrences) within a given structural context. The structural context consists of conditions originating from any one or a combination of sources, each circle representing a different possible area from the more micro to the more macro. Action/interaction may be aimed at any of the sources within one or more areas, bypassing some, going through others, and so on. Keep in mind that when we speak of structure or context, we do not think of it in a deterministic sense. Rather, conditions/consequences create sets of events such as the storm (a context) to which actors respond through action/interaction. For us, even a nonresponse is a way of acting because it also has the potential consequences. (If you do not repair your leaking roof before the storm, then you are likely to get wet.) The interplay between conditions, the responses of actors, and the consequences that result is what we are trying to capture in our analysis with the help of the matrix.

Moving progressively outward from the center of the matrix are several concentric circles. As already stated, each represents a different source of potential conditions/consequences from the more macro to the more micro. Not every possible source has been delineated. **The matrix is meant only to be a conceptual guide.** Persons may fill in, add to, or modify the matrix to fit their studies and data. Another important point is that conditions and consequences from any of the defined areas can have relevance to a study. Even when a researcher is studying a phenomenon that can be clearly located in one of the inner areas of the matrix (e.g., community, a family), consideration of broader conditions and consequences still is important. For example, acting/interacting individuals in the community bring with them their personal motivations, values, and beliefs. However, they also bring with them those of the larger culture at the community, regional, and national levels. A person might take part in an effort to bring more industry into the community because he or she is motivated by a personal desire to become mayor someday. However, like other community representatives, this person might also be influenced by the sales pitch made by representatives of the prospective industries that their companies "will create more jobs for the community." Further influences might include a trend toward population growth in this region, creating a need for more jobs, and a national economic boom of which both the community and the industries want to take advantage. If relevant, this will emerge from the data, but the researcher needs to be aware that these broader conditions are just as important to the analysis as the personal motivations of each representative.

Moving on, to maximize the generalizability of the matrix as an analytic tool, each area is presented in its most abstract form. Items (sources of conditions/consequences) to be included in each area will emerge from the study; thus, they depend on the type and scope of the phenomenon being studied. Researchers using the matrix usually alter the classification scheme to suit their own purposes (Guesing, 1995).

Areas

Beginning at the outer edges of the circle, we have placed the most macro area, represented by the term "international" or "global" area. This area includes, but is not limited to, items such as international politics, governmental regulations, agreements or differences among governments, cultures, values, philosophies, economics, histories, and international problems and issues such as "global environmental warming." The next area we have designated as the "national" or "regional" area. Included in this area are potential conditions such as national/regional politics, governmental regulations, institutions, histories, values, and national attitudes toward gender relationships and behaviors. For example, the rules governing the role of women in society in Islamic countries are considerably different from, say, those in the United States. However, even in the United States, one can find gender role differences such as in earning power, managerial status in organizations, "harassment," and access to certain jobs.

The next source of conditions comes from what has been designated as the "community" area. Included in this area are all of the preceding items but as they pertain to a particular community, giving it singularity among all other communities. The next circles represent the "organizational" and "institutional" areas. Each organization or institution has its own purposes, structure, rules, problems, histories, sets of relationships, spatial features, and so on that provide sources of conditions. (Some institutions, such as religious ones, might be international in scope, but how they are interpreted and practiced often is individualized to communities or even to individuals.) Still another circle represents the "suborganizational" and "subinstitutional" areas. For example, in our study of articulation work by head nurses, we studied the work being done by nurses on each of the various hospital wards. However, those wards were part of a hospital and stood in relationship to that hospital as well as the Veterans Administration hospital organization. Moving inward in our group of circles, we finally reach the group, family, or individual areas. These areas include conditional sources such as the biographies, experiences, motivations, educations, status, gender, beliefs, attitudes, and values held or expressed by those individuals or groups.

Substantive Areas

A researcher could study any substantive topic within any area of the matrix. For example, one might study health care at a national level, focusing on recent legislation, policies, and emerging organizations and trends, or one might study the management of chronic illness by families. Regardless of the topic or area of focus, it is important for the researcher to remember that issues of health policy will affect individual and family management of illness and, conversely, that problems that arise in individual or family management eventually can have an impact on legislation and the evolution of health care policy. Other substantive areas that might be studied include, but are not limited to, identity, decision making, social movements, arenas, conflict and consensus, awareness, social change, work, information flow, and moral dilemmas. Each of these can be studied within any area. Time, history, biography, space, economics, gender, power, politics, and so on all are potential conditions that *can be* relevant to any substantive area studied at any area outlined in the matrix. The important thing is that no item (be it gender, age, power, or whatever) should be considered relevant to the evolving theory unless it emerges from the data as being so; that is, one would want to show how power, age, or gender acts as a condition in one or more areas to influence action/interaction. When we talk about verifying a hypothesis, what we mean is that we want to know when, where, and how this relational statement is demonstrated in the data. Does this particular phenomenon come up repeatedly? If so, then what forms does it take under varying conditions?

How One Traces a Path

To trace a conditional path, the researcher begins with an event or incident that leads to a happening (some form of action/interaction) and then attempts to discern the chain of related events, that is, what the conditions were at the time, what sequence of action/interaction followed, what consequences resulted, and what else happened down the line. In other words, he or she attempts to systematically follow the chain of events (the interplay between events), tracing them as they occur either within or between matrix areas, as described earlier in the quotation about the storm and in the example that follows on the disruption of work flow in a hospital. Throughout the tracing process, the researcher also might attempt to examine the nature of association among conditions to each other, to action, and to consequences. Are there inverse associations? Do some conditions seem more important than others? Does action/interaction always follow from a set of conditions, or are there contingencies and intervening conditions that come into play to provide variation or bring about unanticipated problems? Why do certain consequences result from an action/interaction under one set of conditions, whereas other consequences result from the same action/interaction when conditions differ. To clarify what we mean by "tracing," we present an analysis of a simple episode from one of our research projects.

While observing on a hospital medical unit, the researcher (Corbin) noted the following incident. A physician came to the unit to make patient rounds and, in so doing, made known her desire to check the colostomy of one of the patients. She asked the nurse who was accompanying her for a pair of Size 6 sterile gloves—a relatively small size. The team leader checked the unit's storage area, but the smallest size gloves available were a Size 7. These were offered to the physician. She refused to accept them because she felt that the extra length in the fingers would interfere with her ability to conduct a proper patient examination. At a loss for what to do, the accompanying nurse presented the problem to the head nurse. Given that the needed size was not available on the unit, the head nurse also attempted to persuade the physician to use the larger gloves so that she might get the work done and continue with her medical rounds. Again, the physician refused the offer. Now, the head nurse was faced with the problem of locating the smaller sized gloves elsewhere in the hospital or telling the physician to forget it. Not wishing to do the latter, she needed to find the smaller sized gloves. First, she called the central supply office. She was told that gloves in the requested size were temporarily in short supply because of the large demand for gloves created by the AIDS epidemic, which put a strain on the hospital's supply. Also, the head nurse was told that because latex gloves were in short supply at this time, their distribution was being closely monitored by a designated person in central supply, who presently was attending a meeting. The head nurse and the physician would have to wait until the meeting was over if they insisted on having a Size 6 pair of gloves. Meanwhile, the physician was getting impatient. She had other patients to attend to and wanted to get on with her work. Consequently, the head nurse began to telephone other hospital wards. She eventually located a pair of Size 6 gloves in the recovery room. She quickly went to fetch these, and the physician was able to proceed with her examination. The entire action/interaction took about 30 minutes of the head nurse's and the physician's valuable time.

The concept of focus in our analysis was "disrupted work flow," and although the event described was just one example of this concept, it represented an opportunity to trace out the impact that events outside the hospital might have on the flow of work within it. Following through on the chain of events, one notes that the work is **interrupted because a needed resource (Size 6 gloves) is unavailable.** To keep the flow of work going, the head nurse must locate the Size 6 gloves. But the researcher is forced to ask the question: Why is finding these smaller sized gloves, at this time, so problematic? After all, gloves are not controlled substances, like narcotics, to be kept under lock and key. Following through with this event, the researcher, beginning with the interrupted action, traces the following conditional path.

We begin with **action/interaction,** which was interrupted because a needed resource was lacking. Next, we move to the *individual area* of the **matrix.** The head nurse attempted to persuade the physician to accept the larger sized gloves. However, the physician refused. Moving to the *suborganizational area,* the head nurse contacted the central supply department. Here too, the head nurse attempted to persuade central supply to give her the gloves but was unsuccessful because the person who controlled access was at a meeting. Finally, the head nurse located a pair of Size 6 gloves in the recovery room (suborganizational area) and went to fetch them. But still, the larger question remains unanswered: Why were gloves in such short supply that they were affecting the flow of work? To answer this question, we move to the *organizational area.* Gloves are in short supply in this organization. Why? Because there is an increased demand on the units. Why the increased demand? Because (jumping up to the *national area*) newly published national guidelines on infection control advise the wearing of gloves to protect patients and health workers against AIDS, hepatitis, and other contagious diseases. This brings us back to the *community area*. Are other hospitals and nursing homes also experiencing this same shortage, or is this problem particular to the Veterans Administration hospitals (*regional area*)? It appears that an increased demand for supplies and competition among organizations for supplies are two conditions affecting the availability of gloves. This raises questions about production, distribution, and supply of latex gloves (sterile and nonsterile) at the retail industrial sphere and within this *community*. Obviously, suppliers were caught unaware. We return to the *national area*, where the new guidelines originated, and ask why there are guidelines. What do they actually state? These can be traced back to the AIDS epidemic occurring throughout the nation (in fact, *internationally*) and a concern for the transmission of all contagious diseases. Now, we can show a relationship between a "national public health problem" (the larger event that set off a chain of conditions) and "disruption of the work flow" in one hospital ward. We can see that a series of events ranging from macro to micro created a context of shortage at this particular time. Obviously, the supply of gloves increased to meet the demand because several months later, obtaining sterile gloves of any size was not a problem in this hospital.

Avoiding a Common Error

What we are attempting to help researchers avoid through the use of the matrix is an error common to many beginning researchers, that is, writing a chapter or page outlining the relevant conditions operating in a situation but making no connection between those conditions and the explanation of the series of events (actions/interactions) that follow. Demonstrating how work flow is disrupted because of the AIDS epidemic by a revision in national guidelines, which in turn leads to a shortage of gloves, is quite different from making the blanket statement that "AIDS is having an impact on hospital work," which leaves it to readers' imaginations to discern exactly what that impact might be. Of course, the preceding example is only one incident that leads to "disrupted work flow." To understand this concept better, the researcher has to examine other instances of disrupted work flow on the units and follow through with them in the same manner. In the next instance of disrupted work flow, macro issues might not be involved at all. It might be that two aides cannot agree between themselves on a division of labor or that several people called in sick on a particular day because of personal problems. The conditions/consequences surrounding work flow will emerge from the data.

SUMMARY

This concludes our rather complicated chapter on the conditional/consequential matrix. The chapter emphasized the interplay between macro and micro conditions (structure) and their relationship to actions/interactions (process). The main point is that macro conditions are not merely backdrops against which to present the theory. When relevant, they are very much part of the analytic story and should be woven into the analysis. The matrix was presented as an analytic device to help the analyst keep track of the interplay of conditions/consequences and subsequent actions/interactions and to trace their paths of connectivity. Although the concepts contained within the matrix are quite sophisticated, by keeping a picture of the matrix in mind while analyzing data, even a beginning qualitative analyst can capture some of the complexity and richness of life expressed in data.

13 Theoretical Sampling

DEFINITION OF TERM

Theoretical sampling: Data gathering driven by concepts derived from the evolving theory and based on the concept of "making comparisons," whose purpose is to go to places, people, or events that will maximize opportunities to discover variations among concepts and to densify categories in terms of their properties and dimensions

One of the major issues that often confronts researchers is where to sample, that is, where to go to obtain the data necessary to further the development of the evolving theory. This chapter explores the meaning of *theoretical sampling*. Questions that we address include the following. What is theoretical sampling? Why does one use theoretical sampling rather than some other form of sampling? How does one proceed? How does one keep the sampling systematic and consistent without rigidifying the process? How much sampling must be done? At what times? How does one know when he or she has done enough? How does theoretical sampling differ from the more traditional forms of sampling?

Recollect that concepts are the basis of analysis; they form the building blocks of theory. All procedures are aimed at identifying, developing, and relating concepts. To say that one samples theoretically means that sampling, rather than being predetermined before beginning the research, evolves during the process. It is based on concepts that emerged from analysis and that appear to have relevance to the evolving theory. They are concepts that are found to (a) repeatedly be present (or, in some situations, noticeably absent) in the data when comparing incident to incident and to (b) act as conditions that give variation to a major category. The aim of theoretical sampling is to maximize opportunities to compare events, incidents, or happenings to determine how a category varies in terms of its properties and dimensions. The researcher is sampling along the lines of properties and dimensions, varying the conditions. For example, if a researcher were studying the care of patients in hospitals and it emerged that "work flow," a major category, varied in degree, type, amount, and so on by type of ward and time of day, then the researcher might spend some time observing on all three shifts as well as on different types of hospital wards (i.e., some devoted to care of children, premature and sick infants, cancer patients, and cardiac patients) to determine how and why work flow varied. Maximizing opportunities for comparing concepts along their properties for similarities and differences enables researchers to densify categories, to differentiate among them, and to specify their range of variability.

Theoretical sampling is important when exploring new or uncharted areas because it enables the researcher to choose those avenues of sampling that can bring about the greatest theoretical return. Notice that earlier we said sample incidents, events, or happenings and not persons per se. Incidents or events represent situations (leading to problems, issues, or phenomena) in which persons, organizations, communities, or nations find themselves that are somehow problematic or routine and to which there is a response through some form of action/interaction. For example, to return to our study of work in hospitals, an earthquake (it really did happen) represents an event or a happening. The fact that it happened was significant, but what was more relevant to our study was what happened to the "work flow" (an important category) on the wards during and immediately after the earthquake. How did the workers organize themselves, the environment, and the patients to keep the work flow going? This natural event provided a fortuitous opportunity to sample "work flow" under conditions that maximized response to problematic and disrupted work situations.

Theoretical sampling is cumulative. Each event sampled builds from and adds to previous data collection and analysis. Moreover, sampling becomes more specific with time because the analyst is directed by the evolving theory. In the initial sampling, the researcher is interested in generating as many categories as possible; hence, he or she gathers data in a wide range of pertinent areas. Once the analyst has some categories, sampling is aimed at developing, densifying, and saturating those categories.

A certain degree of consistency is important to theoretical sampling in the sense that comparisons are made systematically on each category, ensuring that each is fully developed. A certain degree of flexibility also is needed because the investigator must be able to take advantage of fortuitous incidents that occur while out in the field such as an earthquake (although perhaps not quite so drastic).

For the most part, theoretical sampling should be worked out carefully rather than letting it occur haphazardly, the latter of which can lead the analyst to unproductive paths and away from the focus of study. However, rigid adherence to any procedure can hinder the analytic process and stifle creativity. Sampling and analysis must occur sequentially with analysis guiding data collection. Otherwise, categories could be unevenly developed, leaving the analyst with more work at the end of the study to fill in poorly developed categories.

GENERAL CONSIDERATIONS

Guiding data collection during theoretical sampling are analytic questions and comparisons. The types of questions that an analyst might ask are as follows. What would happen if . . .? When? How? Where? The answers to these questions serve as the basis for sampling and then making comparisons across those various conditions. Asking questions and making comparisons serve different purposes in each of the three modes of sampling that will be discussed in the following.

At the beginning of a study, there are many sampling matters that the researcher must consider. The initial decisions made about a project give the researcher a sense of direction and a place from which to launch data gathering. What happens once data collection is underway becomes a matter of how well the initial decisions fit the reality of the data. Initial considerations include the following.

1. *A site or group to study must be chosen.* This, of course, is directed by the main research question. For example, if a researcher is interested in studying decision making by executives, he or she must go to those places where executives are making decisions to observe what they do and say verbally, in memos, and so on. Also important is obtaining permission from appropriate sources to use those sites.

2. *A decision must be made about the types of data to be used.* Does the investigator want to use observations, interviews, documents, biographies, audiotapes, videotapes, or combinations of these? The choice should be made on the basis of which data have the greatest potential to capture the types of information desired. For example, a researcher might want to use memos and other written documents as well as interviews and observations when studying executive decision making.

3. *Another consideration is how long an area should be studied.* If an investigator is studying a developmental or an evolving process, he or she might want to make some initial decisions about whether to follow the same persons or places over time or follow different persons or places at different points in time.

4. *Initially, decisions regarding the number of sites and observations and/or interviews depend on access, available resources, research goals, and the researcher's time schedule and energy.* Later, these decisions may be modified according to the evolving theory.

INTERVIEW AND OBSERVATIONAL GUIDES

Once the researcher has decided on the respondents, the place, the time, and the types of data to be gathered (not precluding the use of others), he or she is ready to develop a list of interview questions or areas for observation. (Usually, this must be done to satisfy the requirements of human subjects committees.) Initial interview questions or areas of observation might be based on concepts derived from literature or experience or, better still, from preliminary fieldwork. Because these early concepts have not evolved from "real" data, if the researcher carries them with him or her into the field, then they must be considered provisional and discarded as data begin to come in. Nevertheless, early concepts often provide a departure point from which to begin data collection, and many researchers (and their committee members) find it difficult to enter the field without some conception of what it is that they are going to study.

Once data collection begins, the initial interview or observational guides (used to satisfy committees) give way to concepts that emerge from the data. To adhere rigidly to initial guidelines throughout a study, as is done in some forms of both qualitative and quantitative research, hinders discovery because it limits the amount and type of data that can be gathered. It has been our experience that if one enters the field with a structured questionnaire, then persons will answer only that which is asked and often without elaboration. Respondents might have other information to offer, but if the researcher does not ask, then they are reluctant to volunteer, fearing that they might disturb the research process. More unstructured interviews with general guidelines only, such as "Tell me what you think about . . . ," "What happened when . . . ?," and "What was your experience with . . . ?" give respondents more room to answer in terms of what was important to them. Answers to these questions will be compared among respondents, and concepts that evolve will then be the basis for further data gathering, always leaving room for other answers and concepts to emerge.

SAMPLING PROCEDURES

Sampling is directed by the logic and aim of the three basic types of coding procedures described earlier in this book: open coding, axial coding, and selective coding. It also is closely related to the sensitivity that a researcher has developed to the emerging concepts. The more sensitive a researcher is to the theoretical relevance of certain concepts, the more likely he or she is to recognize indicators of those concepts in the data. Sensitivity usually grows throughout the research project and enables the researcher to decide what concepts to look for and where he or she might find indicators of them.

Because sensitivity to the theoretical relevance of certain concepts grows with time, an interesting feature of combined data collection and analysis is that one can sample from previously collected data as well as from data yet to be gathered. It is not unusual in the early stages of a project for the investigator to overlook the significance of certain events. Later, when more sensitivity has developed, the investigator can legitimately return to data and recode them in light of these new insights.

Sampling in Open Coding

Because the aim of open coding is to discover, name, and categorize phenomena according to their properties and dimensions, it follows that the aim of data gathering at this time is to keep the collection process open to all possibilities. Sampling is open to those persons, places, and situations that will provide the greatest opportunity for discovery.

During **open sampling**, selection of interviewees or observational sites is relatively open in the sense that one could choose every third person who came through the door or could systematically proceed down a list of names, times, or places. No concepts yet have proven theoretical relevance, so one does not know where to go to look for variations of them along the lines of their properties and dimensions. At first, the investigator is open to all possibilities during interviews, during observations, when reading documents, and so on and will want to take full advantage of every opportunity that comes up, exploring each as much as is feasible. To ensure openness, it is advantageous not to structure data gathering too tightly in terms of either timing or type of persons or places, even though one might have some theoretical conceptions in mind, because these might mislead the analyst or foreclose on discovery. Open sampling requires considerable interviewing and observational skills as well as a researcher who feels comfortable while waiting for something to happen or someone to say something interesting. Interviewing skill evolves over time. The first interviews or observations tend to be very sketchy and awkward, whereas later ones tend to be much richer in data. Open sampling requires a researcher who knows how to probe (e.g., "Tell me more about that") without putting respondents on the defensive or, worse, unconsciously signaling them to reply or to act in expected ways. In open sampling, it is crucial to maintain a balance between systematically gathering data that will enable development of categories and flexibility that allows events, happenings, and the direction of interviews to flow openly.

Knowing how to approach respondents, ask questions, make observations, obtain documents, and record videotapes is crucial to the research process. Analysis is only as good as the data that are collected. Further information regarding interviewing or field observational techniques can be found in Hammersley and Atkinson (1983), Johnson (1975), and Schatzman and Strauss (1973).

Data collection should be followed immediately by analysis. Beginning researchers often are so enthusiastic about collecting data that they rush out and do five or six interviews or observations before sitting down to analyze what they have. They quickly become overwhelmed by the sheer amount of analytic information that emerges during analysis. More important, they miss opportunities to sample on the basis of emerging concepts. As analysis proceeds, the questions that arise by making comparisons among incidents become the guides for further data gathering. Also, during actual interviews or observations, because of increasing sensitivity on the part of the researcher, he or she often adjusts the interviews or observations on the basis of emerging relevant concepts. If something pertinent comes up, then the researcher might ask for further explanation or opportunities to observe. The ability to sample "on site" can save time later because a researcher does not have to return to the site or person to follow up on what appears to be a relevant lead.

Variations in Open Sampling Techniques

Open sampling can be carried out using different approaches. Because each approach has its positive and negative aspects, a combination of all techniques probably is the most advantageous way in which to proceed. As with all research, there is the **ideal** way of conducting a study and the **practical** way (or that for which one has to settle).

1. The researcher may look for persons, sites, or events where he or she purposefully can gather data related to categories, their properties, and dimensions. For example, when a research team was doing a study on medical work in hospitals, one team member noted that machinery in hospitals had several properties (Strauss et al., 1985). These included cost, size, and status. The team then proceeded quite deliberately to sample events and sites where the similarities and differences among these properties of machinery would be maximized. Team members went to observe the CAT (computerized axial tomography) scanner, a big and expensive machine that has been given considerable status among diagnosticians. However, CAT scanners represent just one extreme type of hospital machinery, a fact to keep in mind when collecting data. It also is important to sample other machinery that varies dimensionally along the properties of costs and so on, that is, machinery that is less costly, less prestigious, and less reliable. In the preceding case, the researchers were driven to sample by the conceptual notion that the work of patient care might be influenced by the particular properties that the medical machinery brought into service as part of their care, thus integrating two categories: "patient care" and "medical technology."

2. Another way in which to openly sample is to proceed very systematically, going from one person or place to another on a list (or going by whoever walks through a door or whoever agrees to participate), sampling on the basis of convenience. This is a more practical way in which to gather data and probably is the method used most often by beginning researchers. In other words, the researcher takes who or what he or she can get in terms of data. This does not mean that comparisons are not being made on the basis of concepts during analysis, for they are. It is just that the researcher must accept the data that he or she gets rather than being able to make choices of to whom or where to go next. Differences in data often emerge naturally because of the natural variations in situations. For example, when we began our study of "work flow" in hospitals, we knew little about the particular hospital, wards, or head nurses; we simply proceeded from unit to unit, spending time with any head nurse who was willing to

participate in the study. In the end, we found that each unit was different in terms of organizational conditions, the number of patients and types of work done, and how the work flow was organized and maintained over time. Because of those differences, there was ample opportunity for making comparisons based on emerging concepts.

3. Then, too, differences often emerge quite fortuitously. The researcher happens on theoretically significant events quite unexpectedly during field observation, interviewing, or document reading. It is important to recognize the analytic importance of such an event or incident and to pick up on it. This comes with having an open and questioning mind and with being alert. When an analyst happens on something new or different, he or she must stop and ask the questions: What is this, and what can it mean? Thus, evolving theoretical sensitivity emerges and is linked with theoretical sampling during open coding.

4. Another form of sampling is to return to the data themselves, reorganizing them according to theoretically relevant concepts. For example, during a study of high-risk pregnant women, when it became evident to the researcher (Corbin) that she was categorizing women according to her own perception of risks (which was medical) yet women were acting on the basis of their perceptions (which was not always the same as the medical definition), the researcher went back and reshuffled incidents, placing them in categories according to how the women perceived those incidents. Note that in any one interview or observation, there often are several incidents pertaining to the same concept and that each is coded separately. For example, in the study of high-risk pregnant women, sometimes even during the course of 1 week, perceptions of risks varied depending on what was going on with the chronic condition, the baby, and the pregnancy. This meant coding each incident separately because risk management strategies on the part of the women tended to vary accordingly, bringing out the variations within the concept of "risk management."

Relational and Variational Sampling

Open coding soon leads to axial coding. Sampling still proceeds on the basis of theoretically relevant concepts (categories), but the focus changes. Recall that in axial coding, the aim is to look for how categories relate to their subcategories as well as to further develop categories in terms of their properties and dimensions. In data gathering and analysis, the researcher will want to sample incidents and events (from either new or previously collected data) that enable him or her to identify significant variations. By asking what difference the type of machinery makes to the type of care the patients receive, the researcher is putting together two concepts to discover the relationship between these: "type of care" and "type of machinery." Questions to be asked include the following. How is the patient prepared. How are risks managed? How is the work parceled out? Who schedules and coordinates it? Relationships among concepts, like the concepts themselves, are compared across sites or persons to uncover and verify similarities and differences.

During **relational and variational sampling,** the researcher is looking for incidents that demonstrate dimensional range or variation of a concept and the relationships among concepts. As in open sampling, there are different ways in which a researcher can proceed, and most of the ways described heretofore also apply here. Again, the ideal form of theoretical sampling might be difficult to carry out if a researcher does not have unlimited access to persons or sites or does not know where to go to maximize similarities and differences. Realistically, the researcher might have to sample on the basis of what is available. Contrary to what one might think, the act of purposefully choosing sites or persons based on potential of maximizing differences among emerging concepts is a deductive process. Unless the analyst has "deja vu," he or she can only presume that by going to such and such a person or to such and such a place, the analyst will find the dimensional variation that he or she is looking for. Until the persons get there, the researcher does not know for certain that the place actually will maximize those similarities and differences. In reality, the analyst's hunch that a place, person, or group will provide that added dimensional variation might not be borne out. A researcher never should become upset by not being able to choose a site or obtain access to a theoretically relevant site or person(s). Rather, the researcher should make the most out of what is available to him or her. When it comes to events and incidents, rarely will a researcher find two or more that are identical. Rather, there nearly always will be something different—be it conditions, actions/interactions, or consequences—that will provide the basis for making comparisons and discovering variations. If the analyst is comparing incidents and events in terms of how these give density and variation to the concepts to which they relate, then he or she is doing theoretical sampling. It might take longer to uncover process and variation, as well as to achieve density, when a researcher cannot purposefully choose persons or sites to maximize variation, but through continued and persistent sampling, differences eventually will emerge, even if the researcher must settle for what is available.

Sampling in Selective Coding: Discriminate Sampling

Highly selective sampling (choosing sites purposefully to maximize or minimize differences) does become important, however, when one is engaged in selective coding. Why this is important is explained in the next section. The aim of selective coding is to integrate the categories along the dimensional level to form a theory, validate the statements of relationship among concepts, and fill in any categories in need of further refinement. Sampling becomes very deliberate at this point.

The Process of Discriminate Sampling

When engaged in *discriminate sampling*, a researcher chooses the sites, persons, and documents that will maximize opportunities for comparative analysis. This might mean returning to old sites, documents, and persons or going to new ones to gather the data necessary to saturate categories and complete a study. Throughout a study, validation of the products of analysis is a crucial part of theory building. Validation is built into each step of analysis and sampling. We are not talking about testing in a statistical sense of counting. Analysts constantly are comparing the products of their analyses against actual data, making modifications or additions as necessary based on these comparisons and then further validating the modifications and additions against incoming data; therefore, researchers constantly are validating or negating their interpretations. Only the concepts and statements that stand up to this rigorous constant comparison process become part of the theory. Recall that negative cases also are very important. For us, they denote a possible extreme example of variation in a concept.

Theoretical Saturation

A question that always arises is how long a researcher must continue to sample. The general rule when building theory is to gather data until each *category is saturated* (Glaser, 1978, pp. 124-126; Glaser & Strauss, 1967, pp. 61-62, 111-112). This means until (a) no new or relevant data seem to emerge regarding a category, (b) the category is well developed in terms of its properties and dimensions demonstrating variation, and (c) the relationships among categories are well established and validated. Theoretical saturation is of great importance. Unless a researcher gathers data until all categories are saturated, the theory will be unevenly developed and lacking density and precision.

SOME ANSWERS TO IMPORTANT QUESTIONS

1. Can I sample data from a library, and how? Some investigations require the study of documents, newspapers, or books as sources of data. Just how does one go about this?

The answer is that one samples exactly as he or she does with interview or observational data, with the usual interplay of coding and sampling.

If one is using a cache of archival material, then this is the equivalent of a collection of interviews or field notes (Glaser & Strauss, 1967, pp. 61-62, 111-112). However, the documentary data might not be located in one place; rather, they might be scattered throughout a single library or several libraries, agencies, or other organizations. Then, one must reason, just as with other types of data, where the relevant events or incidents are to be found and sampled. Will they be in books about particular organizations, populations, or regions? One answers that question by locating the materials using the usual bibliographic research techniques including browsing purposefully in the library stacks.

A special type of document consists of the collected interviews or field notes of another researcher. It is customary to call the analysis of such data by the term "secondary analysis." A researcher building theory can code these materials as well, employing theoretical sampling in conjunction with the usual coding procedures.

2. How does one theoretically sample when a team is gathering the data and still maintain consistency?

When working with a team of researchers, each member must attend group analytic sessions. Each also must receive copies of any memos that are written by individual data gatherers as well as those that are written during group sessions. Data must be brought back to the group and shared. The important point is that each team member knows the categories being investigated, so that each can systematically gather data on them during his or her own fieldwork. Equally important is that the team meets regularly and frequently for analyzing portions of its data. Working as an analytic unit enables team members to remain firmly within the same conceptual framework. Of course, each must participate in major decision making regarding theoretical sampling. As the data pile up, it might become impossible for team members to read all of each other's interviews or field notes, so each has the responsibility to code his or her own materials. Everyone must read all the memos; otherwise, team members will miss out on the evolving nature of the theory development.

3. Can my theory be tested further by others?

Of course, a theory can be tested. Although validated during the actual research process, a theory is not tested in the quantitative sense. This is for another study. Usually, parts of a theory are tested quantitatively. Although a researcher might not formally explicate the propositions or statements of relationship that connect the major concepts of a theory, these usually are woven into the text and can be explicated and tested in a subsequent study by the same or other researchers. Remember that a theory is just that—a theory. A proposition that does not seem to hold up under further testing does not necessarily indicate that the theory is wrong; rather, it indicates that its propositions have to be altered or expanded to encompass additional and specifically different conditions.

4. How does sampling in theory-building studies differ from more traditional forms of sampling?

In quantitative forms of research, sampling is based on selecting a portion of a population to represent the entire population to which one wants to generalize. Thus, the overriding consideration is representativeness of that sample or how much it resembles that population in terms of specified characteristics. In reality, one never can be certain that a sample is completely representative. In quantitative research, however, certain procedures, such as randomization and statistical measures, help to minimize or control for that problem. When building theory inductively, the concern is **with representativeness of concepts and how concepts vary dimensionally.** We look for instances in which a concept might be present or absent and ask why. Why is it there? Why is it not there? What form does it take? Because we are looking for events and incidents that are indicative of phenomena and are not counting individuals or sites per se, each observation, interview, or document may refer to multiple examples of these events. For instance, while following a head nurse around over the course of a day, the researcher might note 10 different examples of the use of power. Naturally, the more interviews, observations, and documents obtained, the more incidents that will accumulate (evidence of their validity as representative concepts) and the greater the likelihood of discovering significant variation.

5. When is the theoretical sampling complete? How long does one have to continue?

Sampling is completed when categories are saturated. However, sampling often continues right into the writing because it often is at these times when persons discover that certain categories are not fully developed. Then, data gathering functions in the service of filling in and refining exactly as described previously.

6. Is theoretical sampling difficult to learn?

It is relatively easy to understand the logic of theoretical sampling. However, just like other theory development procedures, sampling must be practiced by doing actual research investigations to make the process more routine.

> 7. What about research design? What is its relationship to theoretical sampling?

Unlike statistical sampling, theoretical sampling cannot be planned before embarking on a study. The specific sampling decisions evolve during the research process. Of course, prior to beginning the investigation, a researcher can reason that events are likely to be found at certain sites and populations. Realistically, when writing proposals for funding agencies, it is important to explain how one will sample and the rationale for such. Examples of how sampling was done during preliminary research always should accompany this discussion.

SUMMARY

In this method of theory building, the investigator samples events and incidents and not persons or organizations per se. During sampling, the investigator looks for indicators (events or happenings) representative of theoretically relevant concepts, then compares these events or happenings for their properties and dimensions, always looking for dimensional range or variation. Persons, sites, and documents simply provide the means to obtain these data. The focus of sampling changes according to the type of coding one is doing (open, axial, or selective). Sampling tends to become more purposeful and focused as the research progresses. Sampling continues until all categories are saturated; that is, no new or significant data emerge, and categories are well developed in terms of properties and dimensions.

14

Memos and Diagrams

Memos: Written records of analysis that may vary in type and form

Code notes: Memos containing the actual products of the three types of coding: open, axial, and selective

Theoretical notes: Sensitizing and summarizing memos that contain an analyst's thoughts and ideas about theoretical sampling and other issues

Operational notes: Memos containing procedural directions and reminders

Diagrams: Visual devices that depict the relationships among concepts

When most people think of *memos,* what comes to mind are those written or typed forms of communication that are passed among members of organizations or families. The usual function of these memos is to serve as reminders or sources of information. When the term *memo* is used in this book, it refers to very specialized types of written records—those that contain the products of analysis or directions for the analyst. They are meant to be analytical and conceptual rather than descriptive. *Diagrams* are visual rather than written memos. They are devices that depict the relationships among concepts. Both are important ways of keeping records of analysis and can be done the old-fashioned way (i.e., by hand) or by using one of the newer computer programs designed for that purpose, such as ATLAS or NUD·IST.[1]

Memos can take several forms—*code notes, theoretical notes, operational notes,* and subvarieties of these. In fact, a single memo may contain elements of any of these different types. It is important, especially for beginning researchers, to maintain the distinctions among types when they are working on their memos. If several different types of memos are placed on one typed page, or if types of memos are mixed together, then some memos might become lost or forgotten.

Memos and diagrams evolve. Perhaps the most important point to keep in mind is that there are no wrong or poorly written memos. Rather, they grow in complexity, density, clarity, and accuracy as the research progresses. Later, memos and diagrams may negate, amend, support, extend, or clarify earlier ones. It is truly amazing to observe how a database accumulates and grows theoretically over time while still maintaining its grounding in empirical reality. Memos serve the dual purpose of keeping the research grounded and maintaining that awareness for the researcher.

Writing memos and doing diagrams are important elements of analysis and never should be considered superfluous, regardless of how pressed for time the analyst might be. Memoing and diagramming should begin with **initial analysis** and continue throughout the research process. Although memos and diagrams themselves rarely are seen by anyone but the analyst (and perhaps committee members), they remain important documents because they record the progress, thoughts, feelings, and directions of the research and researcher—in fact, the entire gestalt of the research process. From a practical standpoint, if memos and diagrams are sparsely done, then the final product theory might lack conceptual density and integration. At the end, it is impossible for the analyst to reconstruct the details of the reseach without memos.

Memos and diagrams help the analyst to gain analytical distance from materials. They force the analyst to move from working with data to conceptualizing. We believe that memos and diagrams are so important to the developing theory that we suggest that readers also consult Glaser (1978, pp. 283-292, 116-127), Glaser and Strauss (1967, pp. 108, 112), Schatzman and Strauss (1973, pp. 94-107), and Strauss (1987, pp. 109-128, 170-182, 184-214) for further information on this subject.

SOME GENERAL AND SPECIFIC FEATURES ABOUT MEMOS AND DIAGRAMS

There are some general features of memos and diagrams with which readers should be familiar. We turn to these next.

1. Memos and diagrams vary in content, degree of conceptualization, and length, depending on research phase, intent, and type of coding.

2. In the beginning stages of analysis, memos and diagrams appear awkward and simple. This is of no concern. Remember, no one but the analyst (and possibly committee members) sees the memos and diagrams.

3. Although the analyst can write on the actual interview or field notes, this is not practical, except perhaps in the earliest phases of open coding. We say this for several reasons. First, it is difficult to write memos of any length or to diagram on field notes because there usually is insufficient space to develop ideas. Second, some of the original concepts might be revised as the analysis proceeds, and these might be misleading and confusing when the analyst returns to a document to recode and sees the old codes written in the margins. Third, it is difficult to retrieve information (i.e., to combine or sort memos) if the margin is the only place in which information has been coded. Fourth, there are many computer programs available to assist with memo writing and other functions of analysis, making it unnecessary to write in the margins of a document. (For reviews of some of these and their use with grounded theory, see Fielding & Lee, 1991; Kelle, 1995; Lonkilla, 1995; Pfaffenberger, 1988; Tesch, 1990; Weitzman & Miles, 1995.)

4. Each analyst develops his or her own style for memoing and dia-gramming. Some analysts use computer programs, others use color-coded cards, and still others prefer putting written memos into bind-ers, folders, or notebooks. The method that one uses for recording and managing memos is not important. What is relevant, however, is that memos and diagrams are done and that they are orderly, progressive, systematic, and easily retrievable for sorting and cross-referencing.

5. Whereas the contents of memos and diagrams are crucial to the developing theory, they have functions in addition to storing infor-mation. Among the most important of these is that they force the analyst to work with concepts rather than with raw data. They also enable the analyst to use creativity and imagination, with one idea often stimulating another.

6. Another function of memos and diagrams is to act as reflections of analytic thought. A lack of logic and coherence quickly manifests itself when the analyst is forced to put his or her ideas down on paper.

7. Memos and diagrams provide a storehouse of analytic ideas that can be sorted, ordered and reordered, and retrieved according to the evolving theoretical scheme. This ability becomes useful when it comes time to write about a topic or when the analyst wants to cross-reference categories or evaluate his or her analytic progress. Studying diagrams and reviewing memos also can reveal which concepts are in need of further development and refinement.

8. It is *necessary* to code after every analytic session. However, it is not always necessary to write **long** memos or diagrams. When stimu-lated by an idea, the analyst should stop whatever he or she is doing and capture that thought on paper. This need not be a lengthy memo; a few generative ideas or sentences will suffice. Otherwise, important thoughts can be lost. Then, when the analyst has more time, he or she can write more.

9. Memos also can be written from other memos. The writing or reading of one set of memos often stimulates new insights, which in turn inspire other memos. Also, summary memos can be written that

synthesize the content of several memos. Integrative diagrams can be used to incorporate the ideas of several unconnected ones.

SPECIFIC TECHNICAL FEATURES OF MEMOS AND DIAGRAMS

In addition to the general features of memos, there are some technical ones including the following.

1. Memos and diagrams should be dated. They also should include references to the documents from which ideas were derived. Each reference should include the code number of the interview, observation, or document; the date on which the data were collected; the page number (and line number for those using computer programs); and any other means of identification that might prove useful when retrieving the data later.

2. Memos and diagrams should contain headings denoting the concepts or categories to which they pertain. Memos and diagrams that relate two or more categories to each other or to subcategories should cross-reference the concepts in the headings.

3. Short quotes or phrases of raw data (as well as date, page number, and all other identifying information for easy retrieval) can be included in the memos. They are handy reminders of the data that gave rise to particular concepts or ideas. Later, when writing, these can be used as illustrations.

4. It is helpful in the title or heading to describe the type of memos being written (see definitions at beginning of chapter) for quick reference.

5. Any theoretical or operational note derived from a code note should reference the code note that stimulated it.

6. Although it might be possible to code an incident or event into two different categories, it is advisable to code each incident sepa-

rately to keep memos and categories specific and distinct. If in doubt, then cross-reference the item in another memo. Later, as more data are collected and analyzed and as distinctions among categories are clarified, an incident can be categorized correctly.

7. The analyst should not be afraid to modify the content of memos and diagrams as the analysis progresses and as new data lead to increased insights.

8. The analyst should keep a list of emergent codes available for reference. In the later stages of coding, refer to the list for possible categories or relationships that might have been overlooked during final integration. Keeping a list also helps to avoid duplication of categories.

9. If several memos on different codes begin to sound alike, then it becomes important to re-compare the concepts for similarities and differences. Perhaps important differences are being overlooked. If there are more similarities than differences noted in the concepts, then it might be advantageous either to collapse the concepts under the one heading that seems most explanatory or to choose a higher order or more abstract concept that combines both.

10. The analyst should keep multiple copies of memos for later organizing and sorting. Also, if one copy is lost, then there always is a backup copy. This injunction holds especially true for computer copies; anyone who has ever lost important data due to computer or user failure knows how frustrating it can be not to have backups.

11. The analyst should indicate in the memos when a category appears saturated. This enables the analyst to direct data collection toward categories still in need of development.

12. If the analyst comes up with two or more exciting ideas at the same time, then he or she should jot down a few notes about each one immediately. This way, neither idea is lost when it comes time to write a memo on each one.

13. The analyst should be flexible and relaxed when doing memos and diagrams. Rigid fixation on form or correctness can stifle creativity and freeze thoughts.

14. Most important, the analyst should be conceptual rather than descriptive when writing memos. Memos are not about people or even about incidents or events as such. Rather, they are about the conceptual ideas derived from these. It is the denoting of concepts and their relationships that moves the analysis beyond description to theory.

MEMOS AND DIAGRAMS IN THE THREE TYPES OF CODING

When coding, memos and diagrams appear differently at various points in the analysis. It is not possible in a book of this size to provide examples of each potential type of memo and diagram. To do so not only would be boring but also would tend to rigidify the process. **The analyst has to develop his or her own style and techniques.** However, to provide some examples of what is possible, we include samples from some of our studies and give reference to texts in which readers can find other illustrations.

Open Coding

Open coding is like working on a puzzle. The analyst has to get organized, sort the pieces by color (which often includes noting minute differences in shading), and build a picture by putting the individual pieces back together. The first pages of field notes often are quite puzzling. It is difficult to know where to start, what to look for, and how to recognize it when one sees it. It might appear as an undifferentiated mass. The tentative nature of analysis is reflected in early memos. The analyst writes initial thoughts and ideas without concern for what others think or whether the analysis is correct. Early memos contain impressions, thoughts, and directions to oneself. When bouts of insecurity hit, the analyst should remind himself or herself that if all the answers were known, then there would be no reason to do this particular research.

Code Notes

At first, code notes look quite sparse. During the first readings of field notes, the analyst might scan a document and identify some concepts but have little sense of what the data are all about. Eventually, by making comparisons and asking theoretically relevant questions, the theory begins to emerge. Early notes include categories, the concepts that point to categories, and some properties and dimensions. An example of an early memo might look like the following.

4/4/97 Code Note

PROPERTIES AND DIMENSIONS OF THE PAIN EXPERIENCE

The pain in my hands from my arthritis is really bad in damp cold weather. I wake up with it in the morning, and it lasts throughout the day. The only time it seems to get better is at night when I am warm in bed and under the covers. (field notes, quote from interview with Subject 1, p. 1)

This woman is describing her "pain experience." We can see that the pain has, among others, the properties of intensity, location, and duration. Another property is degree of relief. When she says that it is "really bad," she is giving us a dimension of the property of intensity. The location of the pain is in her hands, and it is of "long" duration, lasting throughout the day. Relief is possible under conditions of warmth.

Taking off from this code note, I can hypothesize that pain can vary in intensity from severe to mild, that it can be located anywhere in the body and in more than one place, and that it can last a short or a long time. Also with this type of pain and for some persons, it is possible to obtain relief under certain conditions, so that pain relief can vary from possible to impossible. There is also a property of variation; that is, the intensity of the pain can vary, depending on location in the body, degree of activity, time of day, and weather. Finally, there is the property of continuity of the pain. It can be continuous, intermittent, or temporary. In this case, one might say it is intermittent.

The analyst also might indicate in the preceding memo where along the dimensional continua for each property this particular event is located. Also, the analyst might want to designate the conditions that give rise to the particular properties (or dimensions) of this pain incident. This will provide some of the dimensional specificity that will be needed later when looking for patterns and when the analyst begins to relate categories. Examples of relational statements include the following. "Under conditions of cold damp weather, the pain increases in intensity." "Under conditions of warmth, the pain disappears or decreases in intensity." "Under conditions of morning, the pain begins." "Under conditions of night, the pain is relieved somewhat." A potential other category is "pain relief." One can make that a distinct category rather than a property of the "pain experience." Notice that the relational statements are written as hypotheses, indicating that they are provisional statements to be validated through further data collection and analysis. Notice also that these notes lead to axial coding in the sense that they begin to define the conditions under which an event occurs. The preceding example demonstrates that when coding, it is difficult to separate open from axial.

The analyst also could write a theoretical note from the preceding quotation and code note. Theoretical notes pick up where code notes leave off. In a theoretical note, the analyst might ask what some of the other possible properties of pain are and their dimensions and then use that information to carry out theoretical sampling. A theoretical note on the preceding topic might look something like this:

4/4/97 Theoretical Note (written from Code Note, "Properties and Dimensions of the Pain Experience," also dated 4/4/97)

OTHER POSSIBLE PROPERTIES AND DIMENSIONS OF PAIN

Arthritis is certainly not the only cause of pain. One can also have pain from an injury, say a pulled muscle or a mild burn. Using my own experience with each of these, what else can I learn about pain? Well, pulled muscles or mild burns are usually the result of injuries, which makes them temporary in nature rather than permanent. How might I describe the pain of either? Pain from a pulled muscle is usually intensified when I try to move whatever body part is affected. This happens with arthritis also. This gives me another condition for intensification of pain.

Under conditions of movement, pain can increase. What about the mild burn? This is different. Pain of a burn can be described as kind of a continuous burning sensation that eventually fades. This points to still another property, that is, type of pain. Pain varies in type from burning to throbbing, acute, or whatever. Another one of its properties is that pain has a course or trajectory. In the beginning, burn pain is more intense; later, the pain will decrease in intensity. Thus, I now have some ideas for theoretical sampling such as temporary versus chronic pain, pain trajectories or courses and how intensity varies over those trajectories—early, middle, late.

An analyst also might write a theoretical note from an article about pain or do an analysis of a research report about pain, play some comparative games, do a line-by-line analysis, or ask questions about one's own or a relative's "pain experience." Doing these exercises will increase awareness about what to look for and where, giving direction for theoretical sampling. Following is an example:

4/4/97 Theoretical Note (comes off of Code Note, 4/4/97, "Properties and Dimensions of the Pain Experience," also Theoretical Note, same date)

QUESTIONS ABOUT PAIN

What are some of the causes of pain besides arthritis? There are many different causes of pain, for example, cancer, injury, surgery, tooth decay, amputation, and childbirth. How is pain experienced in each of these? Is it expected or not expected? Does being expected make a difference in how it is experienced? If it is expected, are steps taken to prevent or lessen it? If yes, how? What steps? If not, why not? What reasons would there be for not taking action to prevent or lessen it? Is some pain more intense than other pain? Does the intensity vary over time? Take childbirth or cancer, for instance; is it more intense early or later in the course? Why? What is done about it? How is pain handled? How does one convince someone that one is in pain? Do factors such as culture, age, how long the pain has been going on, intensity, and so forth affect how one experiences and how one handles pain? From here, I might want to sample the pain of childbirth, that associated with advanced or dying cancer patients, pain in children, and pain in the elderly to see if these make any difference.

Theoretical notes often lead to operational notes, that is, ideas about what operations to carry out next, be it asking questions, making comparisons, or doing more observations or interviews. The specific directions and reminders we write to ourselves are operational notes. Following is an example:

4/4/97 Operational Note

SAMPLING FOR PAIN

Based on my theoretical memo of the same date, it seems that I now have several different areas from which to gather data on pain. These will further elicit properties of pain and give information about the different dimensions of those properties and the conditions that cause those properties to vary dimensionally. A good place to start is with childbirth. Another is to talk to persons with cancer. In talking to and observing these groups, I should do so in terms of the similarities and differences in properties and dimensions that were identified from the arthritis interview (chronic intermittent pain) and look for others that I might not have yet discovered. I will want to look at pain in these new areas for such properties as present status, type, intensity, trajectory, duration, degree, etc. I would also want to note the conditions under which the properties vary along their dimensions. In other words, what conditions lead to pain being described as intense at one time, by one person, but not at another time by the same or another person? Or, what causes pain to feel like a throbbing sensation one time but burning the next? Is it only the source of pain that causes this variation, or do different people experience pain differently? Why is some pain continuous, while other pain is intermittent?

There is virtually no limit to the variety of types of memos that might be written during open coding. The analyst might write initial orienting memos, preliminary theoretical or directive memos, memos that open up thought on new phenomena, memos on new categories including their properties and dimensions, memos that distinguish between two or more categories, and memos that summarize where the researcher has come from and where he or she is going. The preceding memos are rather simple, but they illustrate types of memos that might be written during early phases of a project. They help the investigator begin the process of conceptualization and thinking. Following is a more complicated theoretical note taken from a project on head nurses. It should give readers an idea of what an open coding memo might look like somewhat later in a project. Note that it still is exploratory and that it opens up thoughts about two known categories, ideas to be explored in future theoretical sampling.

AS/JC 5/31/88 LOCAL KNOWLEDGE/ROUTINE WORK

LOCAL KNOWLEDGE IS SPECIFIC KNOWLEDGE

1. Specific knowledge that is taken for granted regarding past experiences with, for instance: instruments, procedures, practices, places or spaces, schedules, timing, pacing, personal relationships, both work and sentimental moods, and climates.

2. I think these items can be expressed in terms we have used before. We talked about orders. Thus, there are interactional order, technological order, spatial order, temporal order, and sentimental order. Maybe also institutional order regarding organizational rules? See how those correspond more or less to the above.

3. This specific knowledge is supplemented with, of course, more general knowledge that is taken for granted. That would include knowledge about days of the week, weekends, holidays, how hospitals work, medical-nursing knowledge of various topics, and more general cultural taken-for-granted knowledge.

4. When a new person is recruited to the staff, he or she either has to be specifically taught the above local knowledge items in each type of order (where things are put, where to find this instrument, how we do this procedure here or, indeed, how to do this procedure that you don't know about yet, etc.). Or, [the new person] has to pick it up himself or herself. The person can do this on the job by observing others or asking others during activity. Or, [the person] can do this quite aside from usual activity, sitting them down and asking, even at coffee breaks. Or, I guess, [the person] can pick it up informally on the ward and off the ward talk.

5. But actually, there is no possible way of teaching a new person all the local knowledge items. Much of it has to be picked up during the work activities. AND THIS TAKES LOTS OF TIME. It takes even

more time if no staff member cues the new person in or makes deliberate attempts to teach or if the person is unobservant or too shy or lazy to ask.

6. IT'S IMPORTANT TO SEE that a considerable part of what we call routine action rests on local knowledge. One has only to watch people doing routine work to see that they don't have to even think about where to put things, when things have to be done (unless the schedule's gone awry), how to behave when entering a room, etc. The head and body know what to do, so to speak, by themselves! In true John Dewey fashion, it's when there is a problem, even a small one, that routines get at least somewhat mired down, that the staff person has to create something at least a bit novel or draw on some past experience in handling that problem. The latter may also be part of local knowledge of the staff. Or, it may be just her own. But note that in handling problems in new ways, local knowledge may be drawn upon as an ingredient in new action.

7. In time, as we have said before, a new way of acting may get institutionalized (either on the ward or at higher organizational levels). In that case, it becomes part of the specific local knowledge on the ward. I guess that now as I make my observations, I would want to sample for these ideas, that is, in terms of local knowledge, who has it, how they obtain it, how they use it, what for, and what happens if they don't have it.

Other examples of memos can be found in the Strauss's (1987) book, *Qualitative Analysis for Social Scientists* (especially pp. 111-127).

Diagrams

During the early phases of open coding, the analyst might have very little to diagram, for relationships between concepts have not yet emerged. Perhaps most useful at this time is what might be called a listing rather than a diagram. In a listing for each category, the analyst can delineate the properties along with the dimensions. This list could be extended as the analysis progresses. It provides the foundation that leads to the logic diagrams done during the axial coding.

Axial Coding

During axial coding, the analyst begins to fit the pieces of the data puzzle together. Each piece (e.g., category, subcategory) has its place in the overall explanatory scheme. When building a puzzle, the analyst might pick up a piece and ask, "Does this go here or there?" The analyst's first attempts often are trial and error. Later, as he or she becomes more theoretically sensitive, making the fit between conceptual indicator and category becomes easier.

Memos

Because the purpose of axial coding is to relate categories and to continue developing them in terms of their properties and dimensions, the memos written during axial coding will reflect this purpose. They present answers to the questions of what, when, where, with whom, how, and with what consequences. Early memos may reflect uncertainty, misconceptions, and feeble attempts. The analyst must trust that, with time, the data will become clearer and that the content of memos will improve in depth and quality of conceptualization. An early code note in axial coding might look like the following example. First, we present an excerpt from a field note so that readers might see the data with which we are working. The phenomenon under investigation is pain and its management. It follows our previous theoretical and operational notes, directing us to look at pain caused by factors other than disease. The pain being examined here is due to childbirth. Our interview was with a mother regarding her experience with pain during childbirth.

Code Note Axial Coding (follow-up on "Directions for Theoretical Sampling, 4/8/97. Interview #6, p. 8, para. 4, dated 4/6/97)

You asked me to tell you about my experience with pain in childbirth. It's been quite a few years since I've had a baby. The funny thing about pain, whatever its source, is that once it's over, you kind of bury it deep in your subconscious. You can say that it was awful or not so bad, but this expression is filtered through a haze. You can't really feel it anywhere. You just have images of what you think it was like. Do you know what I mean? Childbirth is weird. You kind of dread it because you hear so much about the pain of labor. On the other hand, you look forward to it because you're tired of carrying the child and anxious to see it. The pain is seen as the only way of getting there, so you know you have to go through it. You just hope that it won't be too bad or that they will give you something if it is.

The pain is expected. You think about it, dread it, [and] prepare for it by going to classes and learning how to control and tolerate it. In the beginning, it's not too bad. Toward the end, though, it kind of overwhelms you. The force of the contractions just kind of takes over. But you do have moments of rest in between, and you know it is going to end as soon as that baby comes out. And they can give you something to make it hurt less. I was lucky. I had short labors, so I didn't need any kind of medication. I just used my breathing and relaxing exercises. But I can see that if it goes on for hours and hours, how you would get tired and need something.

PAIN, PAIN MANAGEMENT CONDITIONS, AND ACTION/INTERACTION STRATEGIES AND CONSEQUENCES FOR MANAGING THE PAIN OF CHILDBIRTH

We are talking here about a particular type of pain event, one associated with childbirth. This association gives the pain experience its specific properties or location along the dimensional continua. The pain of childbirth is expected (degree of expectancy); can be controlled (degree of controllability); grows more intense as the labor progresses (degree of intensity also denotes that there is phasing); has a known beginning, onset of labor, and an end (delivery of the child indicating course of pain trajectory); and is intermittent with periods of no pain in between (degree of continuity). Oddly enough, the pain of childbirth has another quality or characteristic that is quite strange and difficult to express. Pain is part of a labor process, [with] labor, of course, serving as the end of pregnancy, the delivery of the awaited child. Hmm. How do I describe this property? The pain itself is not purposeful but [rather is] associated with a purposeful activity—labor. I'll note this, though I'm not yet sure what to do with this bit of information. It doesn't necessarily mean acceptance (though it might to some people) or tolerance, but perhaps it gives the pain a certain degree of predictability. This still doesn't quite capture this phenomenon, which is pain that leads to something good.

These properties of childbirth pain create the context in which the management of that pain takes place from the woman's perspective. From this field note, I can come up with the following potential relationships between concepts. Under conditions where the pain (childbirth) is known beforehand, one can prepare; when it is intermittent rather than continuous, it is easier to manage; when its intensity varies over the course from mild at the beginning to more intense later, one can develop management strategies that plan for this; when labor is fairly short or at least follows a predictable course, again, it allows [for] planning; and there are known techniques for controlling its intensity, and these can be learned or negotiated for. Then, one can take action to control the intensity of the pain during labor through pain management techniques such as the use of relaxation and breathing techniques, pain medication, or anesthesia (caudal, pericervical). The consequences or outcomes of the use of these management techniques may not be absolute control but [still] control of sufficient degree to get one through the labor.

One may enter labor with some predefined sense of what management techniques one is likely to use such as breathing and relaxation techniques; however, if the pain management context changes due to a contingency such as labor becoming prolonged due to complications, then one may have to alter that predefined plan of management and use supplements or alternatives to those original techniques.

Other potential categories [and] properties to come out of this field note to be explored in further memos [include] pain consciousness or memory; this seems acute at first but dulls with time. Another is phases of pain trajectory; this concept bears examining. Still another is predictability of the pain and how this acts as a condition for management.

This field note suggests but does not address [the following questions]. What about the timing and amount of medication [and] anesthesia? What are their effects [and] potential risks or consequences of pain management?

A theoretical note coming off of the preceding code note (related to but not directly off of the field note) could go in many different directions. It might further explore the questions raised in the code note or suggest strategies for the management of the pain in childbirth or the pain due to other sources such as surgery, leading to theoretical sampling of pain in postsurgical units. The researcher might want to compare strategies for pain management in childbirth to those in surgery and those in persons dying of cancer. The theoretical note might examine consequences of the use of different strategies in terms of their ability to control the level of pain. It might pull several memos together regarding pain and its management in a summary memo. This information would then be used by the researcher to carry out further theoretical sampling.

As an aside, we are not saying that the information contained in theoretical memos is actual data. Rather, what they represent are ideas for further data collection and different ways of thinking about the concepts that emerge from data. What we are spelling out is what does or should transpire in the analyst's mind as he or she works with data. Theoretical sampling means looking for how concepts vary dimensionally. To carry out theoretical sampling, the analyst has to think about the concepts so that he or she knows where to go and look for the actual data that will demonstrate that variation. That is not forcing data because the actual data that are collected through theoretical sampling will determine what form the actual analysis takes. The analyst might be, and often is, surprised at what he or she finds out when in the field. Variations that the analyst expected to find might not be there. New ones might emerge from quite unexpected sources. The analyst also must be prepared for this. But this serendipity is what makes doing qualitative research and analysis so much fun. There always is that element of discovery.

An operational note written off of the preceding lengthy memo also might go in many different directions. It might suggest where to go to do theoretical sampling or suggest questions to follow up on in the subsequent interviews. Or, it might remind the analyst of the categories or subcategories to focus on in the next analytic session. For further examples of memos showing axial coding, see the examples to follow.

Here is another instance of a memo taken from our study of head nurses that reflects axial coding. We were thinking analytically about the phenomenon of three work shifts in hospitals, where continuity of work must be maintained 24 hours a day.

AS/JC 6/25/89 SUMMARY OF CODE NOTES ON THREE SHIFT ISSUES (off field notes 6/20/89, Code #20, pp. 201-245, Notebook 31)
1. Conditions for EACH SHIFT.
   a. Conditions as parameters, resources per work flow.
   b. Conditions generative of contingencies.

   Therefore, routines (organizational and ward and shift) plus strategies for handling these internal contingencies of shift, whether large or small contingencies.
2. Same for work flow BETWEEN shifts.

Therefore, routines plus strategies for handling between shifts (A.M. shift is central, however).

3. Classic strategies for maximizing routines and minimizing contingencies information flow via $a, b, c, d, \ldots n$ types of resources (manpower, supplies, technology, skill, time, energy, motivation) via $a, b, c, d, \ldots n$ for each resource type.

   a. Routine.

   b. Prevention of foreseen contingencies.

4. Routines and strategies, however, will also be specific to particular ward conditions.

5. Relative success or failure related to appropriate routines and strategies per ward context.

6. Note that routines (especially organizationally derived) may precipitate contingencies (temporary or repeated, i.e., inappropriate).

7. So may the strategies.

8. The central role of the head nurse and her judgments, monitoring, assessing, negotiating, etc. SHE CONSTITUTES, IN OTHER WORDS, A SPECIAL SET OF STRUCTURAL CONDITIONS affecting the work on each shift.

   Note RE: the three-shift issue: All of our concepts should work here also (i.e., local knowledge, routines, resources, power, climate, mood, ideology, division of labor, etc.); therefore, sampling should proceed according to these concepts and their relationships.

Following is another memo taken from the same source. This is a theoretical note. Notice the hypotheses and how they are built into the memo.

AS/JC 7/22/88 (telephone)

IMPORTANT MEMO: ROUTINE/NOVEL

I posed the issue, long ago observed, that nurses encountered typical problems often costly of time and effort and sentiment but do not act to change institutional rules or procedures to prevent. Rather, they go on with their institutionalized routine ways of doing work [e.g., problematic dying patients or as in pain book]. Rather, they typify this patient as like one(s) they have had before. But afterward, there is no institutional change. These, I have thought for a long time, are due to the way organizations get work done, their priorities, and perhaps structural strains that precipitate recurrent semi-crises. But here is a much better and detailed set of answers.

1. When work processes break down, then there is a change of procedure.

2. If they don't change procedures, it's because the work associated with the problem is not of high priority. The nurses are SO BUSY doing the high-priority work that they don't have time [or exert the] effort to do anything else. They will, in fact, if the problem (like a problem patient) gets bad enough to call in specialists, so- cial workers, chaplains, [or] psychiatrists because their own work has to go on. Or, they will ignore the patient, perhaps making the problem worse.

3. If the work affected by the breakdown of work process is of high priority (like affecting its efficiency or patient's safety), then they have to reflect on how to prevent this from occurring again.

   a. If the change is easily done, then it is done through interac-tional processes: negotiation, persuasion, even some coersion.

   b. If the change will be difficult organizationally, this essentially means a lot of additional work must be done, but it must be done, that is: figuring out what's to be done, planning, decision making, persuading, negotiating, finding new resources, acting to raise motivation, additional supervising when the new routines are instituted, etc. And, of course, [there is] an additional drain on the total articulation process until everything is acting smoothly again.

4. So, what we are saying is that THESE ARE THE CONDITIONS FOR [ACTION TO BE INSTITUTED], AND MECHANISMS THROUGH WHICH ACTION IS INSTITUTED, TO REPLACE ROUTINES WITH NEW INSTITUTIONALIZED PROCEDURES. Notice: We have to look more closely at the meaning of routine procedures in future data collecting. At the lowest level, it means how tasks are done. But this can be done by staff agreement as well as by administrative rules.

Diagrams

In axial coding, diagrams begin to take on form. Initial logic diagrams can be useful for sorting out the various relationships. The analyst might want to do integrative diagrams to describe early relationships between a category and its subcategories or among several categories. Early diagrams are not elaborate. They become more complex with time. (For examples of the changes that take place in integrative diagrams over time, see Strauss, 1987, pp. 174-178.)

	Homogeneous Patients	Heterogeneous Patients
Easy work		
Difficult work		

Figure 14.1. Homogeneous/Heterogeneous Patients × Easy/Difficult Work

Phases of illness	Number of machines Few - Many		Frequency Few - Intermittent - Often			Duration Short - Forever	
Early							
Middle							
Late							

Figure 14.2. Illness Course: Machine-Time Dimension

Figures 14.1, 14.2, and 14.3 are examples of various types of diagrams that can be helpful in discovering relationships in data.

Selective Coding

Selective coding denotes the final step in analysis—the integration of concepts around a core category and the filling in of categories

Pain Tasks	Consequences For						
	Illness trajectory	Life and death	Carrying on	Interaction	Ward work	Sentimental order	Personal identity
Diagnosing							
Preventing							
Minimizing							
Inflicting							
Relieving							
Enduring							
Expressing							

Figure 14.3. A Balancing Matrix

in need of further development and refinement. At this time, memos and diagrams mirror the depth and complexity of thought of the evolving theory.

Code Notes

In selective coding, there tends to be fewer code notes. Theoretical notes and operational notes are likely to pertain to the filling in of categories and refinement of the theory.

A code note at this time might take the form of an integrative memo describing what the research is all about. This memo will serve as a stepping off point for the analytic story that is to follow. (See Chapter 10 of this book. See also Strauss, 1987, pp. 170-183.) As stated in Chapter 10, in the storytelling memos, the core category is identified, as are the other categories related to it.

Theoretical and Operational Notes

These will be very specific and directed at what further needs to be thought about or done to finalize the theory. Think about this or that. Go here or there to theoretically sample. Check out this or that.

Do this or that. By now, the analyst is likely to approach his or her work with confidence. He or she no longer is exploring but rather is validating the integrated scheme against data and refining the theory by following through on loose ends.

Diagrams

Diagrams in selective coding show the density and complexity of the theory. Because of this, it often is difficult to translate the theory from words into a concise and precise graphic form. Yet, the very act of doing the final integrative diagram will help the analyst finalize relationships and discover breaks in logic. In the end, it is important to have a clear and graphic version of the theory that synthesizes the major concepts and their connections. Figure 14.4 was an example of an integrative diagram, taken from our work on trajectory. This diagram went through many revisions before we arrived at the final version. Another point is that integrative diagrams can correspond to different parts of the theory. For example, an analyst might have a diagram that deals specifically with one major category and all its subcategories, as is shown in Figure 14.5.

THE SORTING OF MEMOS AND DIAGRAMS

Although already discussed in Chapter 10, this procedure is reviewed briefly here. An image that comes to mind when we think about sorting memos is of an inexperienced researcher standing with stacks of memos in his or her hands and then dropping them one by one, letting them fall where they will. The piles that result represent a fortuitous sorting of the concepts. There are times when everyone feels this way, especially in those darkest days when we are inundated with data and ideas but cannot quite comprehend how they come together. We know that there is order, but it seems beyond our ability to pull it all together.

Yet, those of us with experience know that, indeed, there is order and that our memos and diagrams hold the key to that order. By reading and rereading them, and then by sorting them, we can begin to discover how the categories come together around a core category.

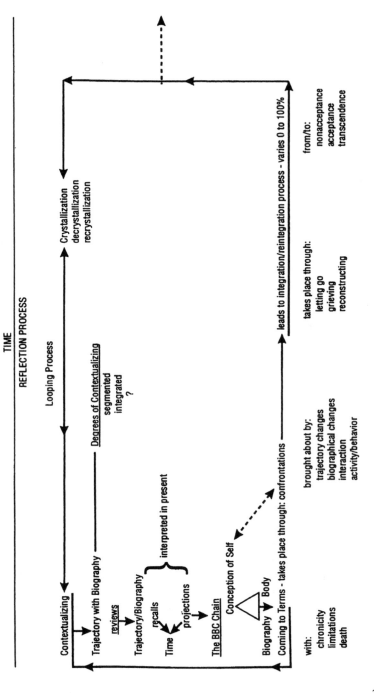

Figure 14.4. Integrating the Memo Sequence

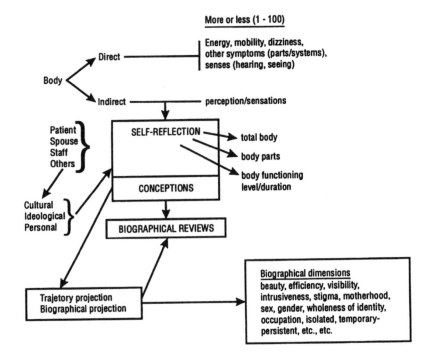

Figure 14.5. Body, Biography, and Trajectory

From our general reading of the memos, we write a descriptive story. Then, using the categories (analytic terms) in our memos, we translate our descriptive story into an analytic one. The logic and order are there (or should be if the procedures in this book were followed).

In practical terms, once we have some idea of how our categories come together, or some organizing scheme (worked out through the writing of our descriptive and analytic stories and integrative diagrams), we can group our memos according to this scheme. Sorting is important because it is a final step in the analytic process. With this finalization, the researcher can try out the scheme on research participants, colleagues, committee members, friends, spouses, and/or companions. The final sorting enables the researcher to write on each topic in detail as well as on the integrated whole.

SUMMARY

Memos and diagrams are essential procedures in research aimed at theory building because they enable researchers to keep a record of the analytic process. Memos and diagrams will vary in form and comply over time and by type of coding. Memos contain the products of coding, provide direction for theoretical sampling, and enable the analyst to sort out ideas in his or her mind. Any breaks in logic quickly become evident as thoughts are put down on paper. Diagrams are visual representations of the relationships among concepts. Both memos and diagrams are useful later when writing for publications and giving talks about the research.

NOTE

1. Readers may obtain these programs from:

   SCOLARI Sage Publications Software
   2455 Teller Road
   Thousand Oaks, CA 91320-2218
   phone: (805) 499-1325; fax: (805) 499-0871
   e-mail: order@scolari.com
   World Wide Web: http://www.sagepub.com.

Part III
Gaining Closure

Becoming a writer is about becoming conscious. When you're conscious and writing from a place of insight and simplicity and real caring about the truth, you have the ability to throw the lights on for your reader. (Lamont, 1994, p. 225)

We become conscious of, and gain insight and understanding from, our research and, in turn, pass this consciousness on to others through presentations and by writing. As difficult as this might be for some, it is only by putting forth our findings and the discussion, dialogue, and critique that ensues that ideas take root and science is born. Although professional recognition and tenure are important, most of us do research because we care and want to make a difference. These final few chapters are meant not only to give suggestions for presenting and writing research and doing critiques but also to give readers the confidence to bring forth their findings. By writing and preparing presentations, researchers will see their theories gain form and solidify. By examining and applying the criteria for evaluation to their own research, they can gain respect for their accomplishments. Finally, by reading the chapter on questions and answers, readers will discover that they are not alone in their questions and concerns regarding qualitative research. Their questions, and those of critical others, are legitimate. Hopefully, by reading our responses, they will discover that there also are legitimate ways of addressing those concerns. In our final words to students, we want them to take pride in their research findings and to recognize that each study, however small, has the potential to make a difference.

15 Writing Theses and Monographs and Giving Talks About Research

Finally, there are those inevitable questions about writing for publication that are associated with every research project. When should I begin writing the research for publication? How do I know when the research is ready to put into print? What shall I write about? What form(s) should the writing take—a paper(s), a monograph, something else? Is writing papers different from writing monographs or theses? What about oral presentations? Should I try to publish? Where should I publish? What audience(s) am I writing for (including when I am writing a thesis)? What should the styles of writing look like? How do I get started on the actual writing or the outline for it? How will I know when the writing is good enough to submit for publication?

In this chapter, we attempt to give useful answers to such questions. There are three sections. The first addresses verbal presentations, the second addresses monographs and theses, the third addresses various types of papers. (Other works that readers might consult regarding the communication of qualitative research findings include Alvermann et al. (1996); Chick, Crisp, Rodgers, and Smith

(1996); Dey (1993, pp. 235-263); Glaser (1978, pp. 128-141); Lofland (1974); Morse and Field (1995, p. 194); Strauss (1987, pp. 249-264); Street (1996); and Wolcott (1990).

FROM ANALYSIS TO WRITING

Before reading the following pages, we suggest that readers review, or at least scan, Chapter 14. There, readers are reminded that when the time comes to actually sit down to write about their research or to outline preliminary talks or papers, a great many aids are available in the form of memos and diagrams. There also is the analytic story on which to draw, as presented in Chapter 10. This should provide an overview of the research. The problem is how to translate these materials clearly and effectively into papers and presentations so that others can benefit from them. One of the interesting features about writing is that the theory often becomes more refined. The act of writing helps clarify thoughts and elucidates breaks in logic. As one of our ex-students, Paul Alexander, stated in a memo dated September 19, 1996,

> Writing forced me to see the whole theory and highlighted those parts that didn't fit so well. . . . So, I would go back to the data. . . . This kind of building and verifying of various aspects of the theory continued throughout the writing process, especially in specifying the relationships between areas of the theory.

WHY PUBLISH?

A few prefatory words should be said before beginning our discussion. Why publish at all? There are a variety of reasons for publishing. One or more may lie behind the considerable effort it takes to get something written, edited, and approved by editors of journals or publishing companies. Without reviewing the many motivations (such as self-pride, career advancement, and desire to contribute to reform or to illuminate the lives of the people studied), there is the paramount obligation to communicate with colleagues. No professional body of knowledge can be accumulated, nor can its implications for practice and theory be usefully developed, without the fulfillment of this obligation. Experienced researchers generally have this obligation built into their psyches. The less experienced researchers, and especially graduate students doing research for the first time, not only might lack motivation to publish but also might undervalue their own research. If a researcher believes this about his or her work, and if this belief is supported by the researcher's committee members or colleagues, then reluctance to go public might have a legitimate basis in fact. If not, then collegial obligation should be honored.

VERBAL PRESENTATIONS

Researchers often present materials orally as a trial run to see how a given audience will react to these presentations. Indeed, those who are being studied sometimes will directly or indirectly press a researcher, for example, "What are you finding?" or "Can't you give us at least preliminary findings or interpretations?" Either in an attempt to satisfy their curiosities and get feedback or for other reasons, many investigators find it useful to make oral presentations. They even do this fairly early in their research projects. Qualitative research studies lend themselves to relatively early reporting because the analyses begin at the outset of the projects. It is not at all necessary to wait until a finer grained analysis is completed to satisfy listeners, whether they are just curious, are avid for results, are skeptical, or merely want to test the researcher.

Naturally, before preparing a presentation, the investigator should try to determine the aspects of the research findings in which this particular audience might be most interested and the style of presentation to which the audience might be most responsive. Collegial audiences can absorb a greater amount of talk couched at more abstract levels and even talks devoted to research strategies and experiences. Other audiences will respond well to discussions of concepts and conceptual relationships only if they are spiced with sufficient descriptive narrative or case materials to make them interesting. The researcher also needs to choose carefully the appropriate level of vocabulary for each audience. A bad choice can turn off an audience; a good one can make all the difference in getting ideas across. If there is a discussion or question-and-answer period after the talk, then no matter how early or late in the life of the research project, this extra time can be turned into an informal collective interview that adds to the data. The audience unwittingly functions to corroborate the theoretical formulations or to prompt the researcher to qualify them.

It should be obvious from the preceding sentences that knowledge about the audience is very important for a successful verbal presentation. No less important is that the researcher *does* have something to say to a particular group of listeners. If the audience is a collegial one, for example, then good theoretical or professional-practitioner sensitivity improves the chances of having appreciative listeners.

All of this advice may sound rather general, although perhaps somewhat reassuring. What about the practical question of how one actually decides on the topic of a talk or speech? In qualitative research studies, given the considerable number of categories generated through coding, how does one decide which ones to talk about in a speech? Keeping in mind that a talk's content should be matched to the audience so far as possible, we suggest the following answers. First, it is generally preferable not to present the entire theoretical framework. This usually is too complex for an audience to absorb in an oral presentation. It also takes a great deal of skill to present the many categories and their relationships clearly enough so that listeners can both understand them and keep them in mind. The researcher can, of course, sketch the main descriptive story before turning to an elaboration of one of the theory's more interesting features. However, we believe that a verbal presentation will be more effective, and certainly better grasped and remembered, if it focuses on one or two catchy categories and includes many descriptive examples. For instance, say a researcher discovers that the medical work performed by hospitalized patients themselves is virtually invisible to nurses and physicians. This category of "patient work" can then be discussed in terms of why, when, and how it occurs, touching on how it relates to the staff's work and subsidiary categories such as "comfort work" or "safety work" (Strauss, Fagerhaugh, Suczek, & Wiener, 1981). The different subtypes of patient work also can be worked into the presentation. Focusing on one or two categories enables the speaker to convey meaningful ideas without overloading the presentation with details (Strauss, Fagerhaugh, Suczek, & Wiener, 1982).

Developing a presentation around one or two categories involves writing a clear outline of the main story and clearly thinking through the categories' relationship to that story. Through careful planning and the use of descriptive quotations, the researcher should be able to present an intriguing story. The larger framework remains in the background but provides the invisible springboard from which the speech is constructed. It should be made clear to the audience that the researcher is presenting only one or more aspects of the total story.

WRITING MONOGRAPHS OR THESES

When writing a monograph or thesis, the researcher should begin with reliance on several instruments. Over the course of a research project, the investigator develops a strong theoretical sense of what the research is all about. He or she also has learned a great deal substantively about the problem under investigation. Both of these will come into play during the writing. Of course, the researcher also needs other skills such as a sense of how to construct sentences and how to clearly present an idea. Unfortunately, a writer can be his or her own worst enemy. Aside from poor writing skills, a writer might have all the usual blocks described in books designed to help people write (Becker, 1986; see also Lamont, 1994). Fortunately, by this time in a project, the researcher has a cache of memos and diagrams that can provide the basis for writing. The writing requires the following:

1. A clear analytic story
2. A sense of what parts of the story the writer wishes to convey
3. A detailed outline
4. A stack of pertinent memos to fill in the details of the outline

Procedures

When beginning to think about writing up the results of a project, the investigator should review the most recent integrative diagrams and sort the memos until he or she is clear about the main analytic story. This review is followed by further sorting of memos until there is sufficient material to write a detailed outline. The sorting might even raise some doubts about the analytic story or point out some of the breaks in logic. If so, the researcher should not be discouraged; the worst that could happen is that the analytic story becomes qualified and, therefore, improved. At any rate, the story must be translated into an overall outline. Some people do not work well with detailed outlines. Yet, because of our own experiences and those of our students, we give the following advice: At least sketch an overall logic outline; otherwise, there might be gaps in the presentation of the theory. There are additional procedures that can be of help in bridging the leap between analysis and outline. The first is to think intently about the logic that informs the story. Every research monograph (indeed, every research paper) will have such logic. Each has a few key sentences or paragraphs that signal the author's underlying logic (Glaser, 1978, pp. 129-130), although sometimes the author seems not to be aware of this. This signal of what is central to any given publication (or thesis, for that matter) often is found in the first paragraph or pages and then again in the closing page or pages. As for a manuscript, even the first draft should have its essential analytic story presented clearly. When writing a thesis or monograph, unlike giving a presentation or even writing a paper, there should be an explication of the entire analytic story.

A second procedure for translating analysis into writing is to assemble a workable outline and then write statements that link each section together so that the writer remains clear about the progressive development of the theoretical story. Chapter outlines are detailed and ordered by thinking through what should be included in each section and subsection, keeping in mind the relation of the parts of the chapter to the entire book. Essential to these decisions, again, is the sorting of the memos that seem relevant. Even when finally writing a chapter, the researcher will find himself or herself relying on the memos. The preface or opening chapter explains the purpose of the manuscript and perhaps even summarizes the analytic story, that is, what this thesis or monograph is all about. This statement, as well as the outline itself, can be revised if the investigator later deems it necessary.

A third procedure involves visualizing the architecture of the written manuscript, that is, the conceptual form that the author wants the book or thesis to take. Visualizing the structure can be compared with creating a type of spatial metaphor. For example, when writing *Unending Work and Care* (Corbin & Strauss, 1988), we carried in our minds the following metaphor. Imagine walking into a house. First, a visitor would enter and pass through a porch, then pass through the foyer, then enter a large room that had two prominent subsections, and then leave the house through the back door. At that time, the visitor would walk slowly around the entire house, looking into the main room through several different windows but now observing carefully the relationships of the various objects in the room. When our manuscript was finished, its form corresponded to this spatial metaphor—an introduction, a preliminary chapter, a large theoretical section composed of three chapters, and then another long section consisting of several chapters that elaborated and drew implications from the theoretical formulations presented earlier. If faced with writing a thesis, the researcher might find this third procedure (visualization) difficult to use. After all, theses in most university departments, even qualitative research theses, have fairly standard formats. These usually begin with an introductory chapter, followed by a review of the literature, then a presentation of the findings (in two or three chapters), and then the summary/conclusions/implications section. For all that, the thesis writer might be able to think architecturally about the middle (content) chapters. At any rate, when constructing a thesis based on the findings from a qualitative research study, the researcher should rely on the first two procedures touched on here: (a) developing a clear analytic story by sorting through the diagrams and memos and then (b) working out a main outline that will fully incorporate all important components of that story.

What to Write?

Qualitative researchers often encounter a difficult problem when trying to decide what to write about their findings. The source of the problem is the fairly complex body of data generated through the entire research process. The big questions, then, are the following. What of all this analysis should be included? How can one compress all of these findings into a couple of chapters? After all, the standard format for writing theses does not allow one to expound infinitum. In other words, into how much depth does one go when reporting the research? The answer is that, first, the writer must decide on what the main analytic message will be. Then, he or she must give enough conceptual detail to convey this to readers. The actual form of the central chapters should be consonant with the analytic message and its components.

This answer, nevertheless, fails to specify, whether for writing a thesis or a monograph, how much and which conceptual details to include and which can be excluded. It all goes back to answering the questions "What was this research all about?" and "What were the main issues and problems with which these informants were grappling?" Then, there should be sufficient conceptual detail and descriptive quotations to give readers a comprehensive understanding of these. Participants and those professionals familiar with the theoretical area should feel satisfied that the story has been told and understood.

The Issue of Self-Confidence

The increasing ease in accomplishing what is, after all, quite specialized writing also is related to the issue of a researcher's confidence in his or her own analytic and compositional abilities. In this regard, we shall quote from one of our books because the quotation expresses succinctly what an inexperienced researcher is likely to experience. The quotation refers more to analysis than to writing, but in writing itself the two skills are, as we have noted, tightly joined.

> Researchers may find themselves blocked when they begin to write, let alone later during the writing itself, if they lack confidence in their analyses. Do I really have it right? Have I left out something essential? Have I really identified the core category? And if yes, still, do I have all of this in enough detail (conceptual density)?
>
> The answers may be yes, no, or maybe! But the issue here is not whether the analysis has been adequately and sufficiently done, but confidence that one really knows the answers to those questions. Even experienced researchers may not always be certain before they have chewed on their suspended pencils long enough to know

where precisely are the holes—or to be certain that, after review, they know there are no important holes—in their analyses. Whether experienced or inexperienced, a common tactic for reducing uncertainty is "the trial"—try it out on other people, individuals, groups, informally or formally.

Seminars can give presenters confidence in their analyses, whether in preliminary or almost final form, as well as confidence in the analyses embodied in their writing. Speeches given at conventions, if favorably received, can add further validation of an analysis and its effective reflection in readable prose.

Nevertheless, when approaching or even during the writing period, there is almost invariably a considerable amount of anxiety about whether this can be, or is being, accomplished effectively. After all, some people are perfectionists and cannot seem to settle for less than an ideal performance. That can mean, of course, no performance at all or a greatly delayed one. Others lack some measure of confidence in themselves generally, and this spills over into questions about ability to accomplish this particular kind of task.

This anxiety and anguish . . . can be further mitigated (also) by writing a paper or two before embarking—at least seriously—on the long and major writing task. . . . Getting a paper or two accepted for publication can give a considerable boost to flagging confidence or lingering doubts about one's ability at research (and writing it up effectively). (Strauss, 1987, pp. 259-260)

Letting Go

Having edited what probably should be the final draft, a researcher also can have difficulty letting go of a manuscript. This problem might be due not so much to a lack of self-confidence (although it can be that) as to a temporary failure of nerve. Have I really got the last details in—and got them right? These doubts are stimulated by the almost inevitable discovery of additional details, both conceptual and editorial, and the relocation and rephrasing that occurs during each rewriting of a draft. Part of an increasing maturity as a research writer is to understand that no manuscript ever is completely finished. If the writer is fortunate enough not to have a personal, departmental, or publisher deadline, then he or she may profit from putting aside the final draft for some weeks or even months to gain a bit of editorial and analytic distance from it. Also, a colleague or two might be pressed to read part or even all of the manuscript and to provide constructive feedback. Eventually, the writer does have to let go of his or her work, convinced that the manuscript is as finished as it ever will be. One can rest assured that, once off to a publisher or committee, there always will be feedback about improvements to make. The logic of letting go is that writing is only part of a cumulative stream of conveying ideas to which the writer may return later to criticize in this or a later work. Incorporating one's own criticisms is no different from responding to other people's criticisms. The psychology of letting go is, however, more complex. Basically, it comes down to avoiding the trap of dreaming of the perfect manuscript and, instead, allowing oneself to be open to new projects, new ideas, and new data. It is important to strike a balance between profitable reworking of drafts and cutting loose from them. How to do this is difficult to convey. Of course, an experienced researcher who actually is familiar with the investigator's work can help with this problem, but in the end, every writer must rely on his or her inner sense of rightness and completion.

If the researcher is writing a dissertation and is fortunate enough to study in a department that allows a certain degree of latitude in style, then he or she can write for audiences other than committee members and wider departmental faculty. Moreover, book publishers usually reject theses, as such, sent to them as possible publications, preferring a different format of presentation instead. So, if one is allowed to write a thesis in a style that approximates a monograph, then the conversion to a potential publication is rendered that much easier.

Audiences

There also is the question of a writer's conception of the audiences for his or her thesis. Perhaps this issue is less complicated than for other forms of publication (this is discussed later) and for speeches, but it is one that plagues many students. After all, the immediate readers are the thesis adviser and other members of the doctoral committee. If they do not approve of the dissertation, then the entire enterprise will be a personal disaster. When doctoral committees consist of faculty members who strongly disagree on their criteria for adequate work, students can be hurt by these methodological discrepancies. If fortunate or astute, students choose committee members whom they know will agree among themselves about the desired standards and format acceptable for their dissertations, although perhaps with some revisions. There is no tried-and-true rule to suggest how this variable situation can be managed. Our best counsel is to choose, if possible, a supportive yet critical adviser and to write as good a manuscript as possible. If the student produces solid research, then he or she is likely to earn a degree unless some of the committee members are skeptical of qualitative studies. If that is a possibility, then the student should keep to a minimum the number of such potentially adverse critics on the committee.

There are some crucial differences between monographs and theses, although heretofore we have tended to blur this distinction. Chief among their differences is that the discussion in a monograph should be conceptually fuller, that is, include greater depth and detail. Because there is more space and fewer constraints with which to work than when working on a thesis, the author is freer to develop an analytic message. Moreover, the monograph can be more complex, not only in more extensive elaboration of categories and their relationships but also in a much greater amount of substantive material. The latter may include case studies and even long quotations from interviews, field notes, and documents. The author always may choose to digress sometimes, discussing minor and side issues, so long as these are consonant with the main thrust of the monograph. Also, some issues are likely to be explored that were omitted from the more restricted dissertation or not fully worked out during the dissertation research. Inconsistencies that crept into the more hurried writing of the thesis should be corrected in the monograph. Dissertation committees tend to emphasize findings, whereas the readers of monographs are more likely to appreciate, or at least accept, an analytically based argument and a broader discussion of the research materials.

The author of a monograph also has more latitude in choosing the style of presentation. In some part, the style should reflect the author's message while taking into consideration the audience for whom the message is intended. Questions to consider include the following. Are the readers restricted to disciplinary or professional colleagues or to some types of them? Does the writer hope to have readers from several fields, perhaps including those from practitioner fields? What about lay readership? For a monograph to be maximally effective, the author should ask "What do I wish to say to each of these audiences?" or, if several audiences are intended, then "What style can I use to reach each audience?" Usually, a blend of theory with sufficient descriptive detail to make it vivid and clear is the preferable combination. In short, the style and shape of presentation should be sensitive to and reflect the targeted audience(s).

Suppose that the author wants to address both disciplinary colleagues and laypersons. To reach both audiences requires giving considerable thought to the use of vocabulary, terminology, case materials, overall mood, and other aspects of writing style. Many monographs published by sociologists have both collegial and nonprofessional readers as targeted audiences. (Among the monographs that have been published are Biernacki, 1986; Broadhead, 1983; Charmaz, 1991; Davis, 1963; Denzin, 1987; Fagerhaugh & Strauss, 1977; Rosenbaum, 1981; Shibutani, 1966; Star, 1989; and Whyte, 1955.) Sometimes, the targeted readers are nonprofessionals, for instance, patients and their families such as the book on epilepsy written by Schneider and Conrad (1983). Occasionally, monographs are directed at lay audiences, colleagues, and professionals. Then, they are published as trade books, for instance, a book on remarriage after divorce (Cauhape, 1983).

Writing for multiple audiences generally is more complicated than writing for one's colleagues. Yet, many researchers are eager or feel obligated by conscience to write for more than scientific or professional readers. Sometimes, they also use their research as a platform for writing books that are not monographs. For example, we wrote a book about policy following our study of chronic illness (Strauss & Corbin, 1988) to address some of the larger social and political issues that the chronically ill and their caregivers face in trying to manage their conditions at home. It was not a research report per se, but it arose directly out of our reseach nevertheless. Or, books can be written for practitioners, full of information based on research (Strauss et al., 1964).

Converting Theses to Monographs

How is a thesis converted into a monograph? Guidelines bearing on how to do this were suggested implicitly in the preceding section.

However, the prior question that faces the author of a dissertation is whether it should be written next in monograph form. Several questions pertaining to this decision should be thought through carefully and preferably in the following order.

1. Are the substantive materials, findings, or theoretical formulations presented in the thesis sufficiently interesting to be worth my time and effort to write up for a wider audience(s)? Some theses are natural candidates for such presentation. Other dissertations, no matter how important they might be to some colleagues, are not good candidates, but portions of their materials are likely to be published as articles and later may be widely cited.

2. If deemed sufficiently important, then how do I decide which are the most relevant topics or conceptualizations to include in a monograph?

3. Do I have sufficient time and energy to translate this thesis into a monograph? Am I really still interested in this subject matter? Am I saturated or bored with it? Have I had it? Is it really my forté, or should I move on to other, now more interesting topics or areas? Of course, sufficient interest in doing it successfully can lead to very great personal satisfaction. Part of the commitment and resulting satisfaction also may derive from a sense of obligation to audiences, who ought to know about what one has discovered through the research.

4. There still is another question that many potential authors consider: Given a certain level of interest and sufficient time and energy, is it worth writing this monograph for career purposes? In some fields, writing a monograph (or other type of research-based book) is not especially important; articles published in refereed journals bring more prestige. However, colleagues in other fields, including the social sciences (especially when recruiting candidates for faculty or when they themselves are considered for promotion), know that monographs often weigh more heavily than published articles in the evaluation.

After considering each of these questions, as well as sometimes being impeded or confused by the counsel of faculty advisers, friends, sponsors, or other intimates, the investigator still is confronted with the additional question of how to translate a thesis into a monograph. In fact, trying to answer this question is very likely to affect the decision of whether or not to write a monograph because it includes weighing the time and effort involved. The actual conversion of the dissertation can be carefully guided by considerations touched on heretofore. The writer must think carefully about the targeted audiences and equally carefully about the topics, concepts, or theoretical formulations that are likely to be of greatest interest or value to each audience. Those considerations lead to the issue of style. What format should be used? Should theoretical formulations be the major focus of the monograph and descriptive materials subordinated, or should these be kept in balance? Should the main thesis be argued forthrightly using existing theoretical formulations, or should the argument be kept low key or even implicit? Stylistic considerations, of course, also entail decisions about the type and level of vocabulary to be used, modes of presenting selections from the data, the overall mood of the monograph, and so on.

As stated earlier, conceptual elaboration must be added to the original presentation in the thesis. One can do this by including theoretical materials already developed in the memos but omitted from the dissertation and by thinking through aspects of theoretical formulations that were left unclear, ambiguous, incomplete, or even inconsistent. Also, in a monograph, the writer probably will want to discuss at greater length certain implications of the research with reference to the theoretical literature as well as implications for future research and perhaps for practitioners or policy decision makers.

Any (or all) of these possibilities requires time and effort as well as considerable rethinking of previous analyses and the written expressions of these. Many researchers have found the experience of rewriting for a monograph tremendously rewarding. Others have translated theses into monographs primarily for career advancement and personal reputation, cashing in (literally) on that investment.

TEAM PUBLICATIONS

When projects involve two or more researchers, then there always is a question of how publications are to be written. The answer depends, understandably, on the relationships among team members, their respective abilities and interests, their responsibilities, and the amount of time available to each. Some publications are written by the principal investigator of the project, with varying amounts of input by other team members. Other publications involve more truly collaborative writing rather than just shared research. The same is true of papers based on the team's research.

WRITING PAPERS FOR PUBLICATION

This fourth class of research-based publications is scarcely a homogeneous one. The great variety of options for types of papers can be suggested graphically by a threefold breakdown of those possibilities.

1. For colleagues, one may write papers with a major focus that is theoretical, substantive, argumentative, and/or methodological.

2. For practitioners, papers may provide theoretical frameworks for understanding clients better, substantive findings, practical suggestions for better procedures, suggestions for reform of existing practices, and/or broad policy suggestions.

3. For lay readers, appropriate papers may include those describing substantive findings, giving suggestions for reform of current practices or policies, providing self-help guidelines or tactics for obtaining better services from practitioners or institutions, and/or providing assurance that others share their own experience (e.g., living through a divorce, adopting a child).

This variety of options for papers points to differences in purposes, emphases, styles, and publication outlets. Nevertheless, research findings provide a firm basis for writing all of these types of papers. Qualitative research studies provide theoretical analyses, substantive content, and self-confidence. By completion of the research, the investigator should have considerable sensitivity to issues, audiences, and the strengths and weaknesses of actors and organizations. The investigator also will draw on this knowledge when making decisions about what to write, for whom, and how. Decisions concerning those issues rest on reasoning and procedures not appreciably different from those discussed throughout this chapter. The few important differences can be stated briefly and are easily understood. Following are some conditions that may directly affect how, as well as for whom and whether, certain papers will be written.

1. As noted earlier, researchers may decide to publish papers even relatively early during the research process. They may do this for different reasons, for instance, to present preliminary findings, to satisfy or impress sponsors, or because they have interesting materials bearing on side issues that can easily be written up now but might not get written at a later, more hectic time.

2. Researchers sometimes write papers either because they feel obligated to publish on a given topic or because they are pressured to do so. Of course, this motivation also will affect what and how researchers write.

3. Researchers also may be invited to contribute papers to special issues of journals or to edited volumes of books because they are known to be researching in given areas. They also may be urged or tempted to convert verbal presentations into papers because listeners have responded well to them.

4. Another condition that can affect the writing of a paper is the existence of a deadline for getting the finished product to an editor. For some researchers, this can act as a stimulus, whereas others are daunted by any deadline.

5. The number of pages allowed by the editor also affects whether a paper will be written, at least for a particular publication, and, if so, then what will be written and how.

6. Unless invited by an editor, there is the important decision to be made about which particular journal should be selected as a potential outlet for a given paper. Journals and papers have to be matched; otherwise, the paper might be rejected and the time invested in writing it wasted. Or worse yet, the paper may be accepted but for an

inappropriate or insufficiently appreciative audience. Selecting an appropriate journal may be an easy task if the researcher knows the journal well; otherwise, past issues of the journal should be scrutinized carefully. It helps to also get the counsel of people who are knowledgeable about specific journals. This is especially true when addressing audiences outside of one's own field, as when a social scientist writes for a social work or medical journal.

Having noted these conditions, which sometimes are constraining but at other times are stimulating, we now can discuss what else may be different about writing papers. The most important considerations are the interrelated ones of purpose and audience. Given the variety of purposes and audiences listed here, one can see that this is the central issue facing any researcher who writes a paper. (This is true even when invited to write one.) What should one say to an audience? Topics for some papers seem to emerge rather naturally during the research process. For instance, in our study of the chronically ill and their spouses, we were struck by the stylistically different approaches to management among couples. These ranged from highly collaborative to very conflictual. So, we wrote a paper on this topic relatively early in the research (Corbin & Strauss, 1984). Some papers may be conceived of early or mid-project but do not get written until later, or the ideas become incorporated into the monograph.

Some ideas for papers take much longer to formulate than do others, perhaps because they require deeper understanding of the phenomena or more theoretical sophistication for the researchers to feel comfortable in writing about them. Writing papers that suggest reforms might be delayed because researchers are unable to commit themselves to a reform role until they become sufficiently disturbed at what they are observing or perhaps because the directions in which reform alternatives can be specified are not yet clear to them. After the theoretical formulations are worked out clearly, there is the temptation to present the entire framework in one long paper. As we already have stated, this is a very difficult task because the framework will be very complex and dense with conceptualization. Our advice is not to attempt this task in a paper. If the writer chooses to do so, then it is preferable to provide a frankly stripped-down version, referring readers to the forthcoming monograph. For example, one of us (Strauss) and his colleagues, taking off from a study on medical work in hospitals, wrote about patients and related their work to a couple of other types of staff work such as "safety work" and "comfort work" (Strauss et al., 1985). Then, in another paper by Strauss and his research team, another one of the major concepts to evolve from the study became the focus of the study. This one had to do with "safety work," especially as it pertains to working with potentially hazardous medical equipment and with fragile premature infants (Wiener, Fagerhaugh, Strauss, & Suczek, 1979). Other papers can be written around methodological issues or policy issues. Then, the theoretical materials or the actual research findings will provide the framework or background for the discussion on policy or methodology. A methodological focus might need both substantive and theoretical illustration to make sense to readers. Policy arguments not only can be buttressed by data but can be explicitly or implicitly underpinned by a theoretical framework. For instance, we gave an argument and suggestions for reform of the American health care system (Strauss & Corbin, 1988). These were based on criticism of the dominant acute care orientation of health professionals and institutions despite the current prevalence of chronic illness, a type of illness that has multiple phases, each of which requires a different type of care.

To return to our suggestion that a theoretically oriented article be restricted in the number of categories or ideas discussed, the question, as usual, is how that discussion is to be developed. The same general answer can be given as when writing chapters of a monograph but modified for purposes of writing a paper. First, one decides on a focus. What is the theoretical story that the writer wishes to tell? This decision may arise during the course of the research, or it may actually be prompted by thinking about the most recent integrative diagram or through sorting of memos. The details of conceptual relationships also must be elucidated. Then, it is time to construct an outline of the paper. Just as with an outline for a monograph, the writer might wish to get some distance by waiting some days or weeks before returning to scrutinize the original ideas. As one writes the subsections, reviewing and sorting memos will help jog the writer's memory and allow him or her to fill in additional details.

One danger, however, is permitting too much detail to flood one's thinking. If this occurs, then attempts to crowd too much into the short space of a paper may discourage or at least impede the clarity of one's exposition. The working guideline here for what goes into a paper and what can be omitted, reluctantly or ruthlessly suppressed, can be expressed in the form of a dual question: Do I need this detail to maximize the clarity of the analytic discussion and/or to achieve maximum substantive understanding? The first part of the question pertains to the analysis itself. The second pertains mainly to inclusion of data in the form of quotations and case materials.

As with monographs and theses, the drafts can be given a trial by sharing them with friends, colleagues, and even accommodating practitioners or laypersons if the materials pertain to them. Again, one might wish to have drafts scrutinized by a writing group or a student research group if one is so fortunate as to belong to one. The writer also must incorporate relevant literature. If it is a theoretical paper, then the author might wish to think through its implications to make recommendations for changes in policies or practices.

Then, when the paper finally is finished, and even more when it finally is published, one already should be on his or her way to thinking about, outlining, and beginning to write the next publication.

SUMMARY

Making oral presentations and publishing written reports about findings of research introduces still another challenge for the re-searcher. With so much complex material available, how does one make choices about what to present, to whom, and how? Generally, in a verbal presentation or an article, it is preferable to present only one concept (category) in any depth with perhaps one or two others woven in as related features. In a monograph, one has a wider range of possibilities, but even here, the writer should carefully think through the logical order of the material before doing a detailed outline. A thesis presents problems of its own because a standard format must be followed. Again, the writer must carefully think through how much detail to include and how to present the most relevant facets of the conceptual scheme while still retaining flow and continuity.

16 Criteria for Evaluation

Once the researcher has completed the investigation, how does he or she and others judge the merit of that work? This is a question that has sparked much debate among qualitative researchers. First, there is the question of whether or not one should build theory. Second, there is the question of scientific merit, regardless of whether or not the research is directed at theory building. We recognize that there are divergent opinions about both of these issues and do not intend to take up the argument here.

In this book, we take the stance that theory, although not the only purpose of doing research, has an important role to play in science (Strauss, 1995). Our purpose is to develop valid and grounded theory that speaks to the issues and concerns of those we study. Because there is a considerable body of literature that discusses various methods for, and issues in, evaluating qualitative research in general (e.g., Altheide & Johnson, 1994; Ambert et al., 1995; Bradley, 1993; Elder & Miller, 1995; Ferguson & Halle, 1995; Fitch, 1994), in this chapter we concern ourselves solely with discussing criteria for judging the merits of theory-building research and, more specifically, with *supplementing* published literature with a few additional criteria that we believe are important. These criteria are meant to address the adequacy of the research process and the grounding of its findings.

SCIENTIFIC CANONS AND QUALITATIVE RESEARCH

Some qualitative researchers maintain that the canons or standards by which quantitative studies are judged are quite inappropriate for judging the merit of qualitative studies (Agar, 1986; Guba, 1981; Kirk & Miller, 1986; Merriam, 1995). Most qualitative researchers probably believe that these particular canons must at least be modified to fit qualitative research. We share the conviction that the usual canons of good science have value but require redefinition to fit the realities of qualitative research and the complexities of the social phenomena that we seek to understand. The usual scientific canons include significance, theory-observation compatibility, generalizability, consistency, reproducibility, precision, and verification. (There is a succinct overview of these canons in Gortner & Schultz, 1988.) These canons are so taken for granted by physical and biological scientists that even philosophers of science do not explicitly discuss most of them except for verification. However, other canons such as precision, consistency, and relevance are implicitly assumed (Popper, 1959).

The dangers derived from adherence to the more positivistic interpretations of these canons must be guarded against by qualitative researchers. Every mode of discovery develops its own standards and procedures for achieving them. (For a good discussion, see Diesing, 1971.) What is important is that the criteria used to judge the merit of qualitative (or quantitative) work are made explicit.

For instance, take the canon of reproducibility. Ordinarily, this means that a study can be replicated through the use of either the same or alternative research processes. The ability to reproduce findings gives the original findings credibility. However, reproducing social phenomena can be difficult because it is nearly impossible to replicate the original conditions under which data were collected or to control all the variables that might possibly affect findings. That is the difference between doing research in a laboratory, where one can to some degree "control" variables, and conducting it out in the "real" world, where events and happenings follow a natural course.

However, there are ways of rethinking reproducibility to extend its meaning. Here is another way of looking at it. Given the same theoretical perspective of the original researcher, following the same general rules for data gathering and analysis, and assuming a similar set of conditions, other researchers should be able to come up with either the same or a very similar theoretical explanation about the phenomenon under investigation. The same problems and issues should arise regardless of whether they are conceptualized and integrated a little differently. Whatever discrepancies arise usually can be explained through reexamination of the data and identification of the alternative conditions that may be operating in each case. In fact, we find it very reaffirming when we read the research reports of other qualitative researchers who have studied chronic illness. From a larger conceptual perspective, their findings are very consistent with our own, although they might offer alternative conceptualizations and explanations or place emphases on specific aspects of chronic illness management such as social support or symptom management.

To continue with our illustrations of how the usual canons for judging the merit of good science might be redefined to fit qualitative research designs, consider the canon of generalizability. The purpose of using a theory-building methodology is to build theory. Thus, we are talking more the language of explanatory power rather than that of generalizability. Explanatory power means "predictive ability," that is, the ability to explain what might happen in given situations such as stigma, chronic illness, or closed awareness. Therefore, in writing the theoretical formulations that evolved from our study, we specify the conditions that give rise to certain phenomena—problems, issues, and the use of strategies or actions/interactions to manage these problems or issues—and explain what consequences occur as a result of those actions/interactions. We are not suggesting that a substantive theory (one developed from the study of one small area of investigation and from one specific population) has the explanatory power of a larger, more general theory. It cannot because it does not build in the variation or include the broad propositions of a more general theory. However, the real merit of a substantive theory lies in its ability to speak specifically for the populations from which it was derived and to apply back to them. Naturally, the more systematic and widespread the theoretical sampling, the more conditions and variations will be discovered and built into the theory and, therefore, the greater its explanatory power (and precision). If the original theory fails to account for variation uncovered through additional research, then these new specificities can be added as amendments to the original formulation.

Here, we have touched on only two of the canons (reproducibility and generalizability) because elsewhere we have discussed in detail other important ones in connection with qualitative research methods (Corbin & Strauss, 1990). Instead of pursuing this topic, we would rather discuss what we consider are the essential elements of theory-building research and what we look for in our own work as well as the works of our students, colleagues, and other theory-building researchers.

CRITERIA FOR EVALUATION

The first question to ask when evaluating a study is what one is making judgments about. There are different options, and the evaluator uses different criteria, depending on the specific aspect of the research that is being judged. In reading and evaluating publications in which authors claim to generate, elaborate, or test a theory, one should distinguish clearly among the following issues. First, judgments are made about the validity, reliability, and credibility of the data (Guba, 1981; Kidder, 1981; Kirk & Miller, 1986; LeCompte & Goetz, 1982; Miles & Huberman, 1984; Sandelowski, 1988). Gliner (1994), for example, suggested that methods such as triangulation, negative case analysis, and testing for rival hypotheses are means for judging fairness and rigor of a research project. Second, judgments are made about the theory itself (Glaser & Strauss, 1967; Strauss, 1987). Third, decisions are made regarding the adequacy of the research process through which the theory is generated, elaborated, or tested. Fourth, conclusions are made about the empirical grounding of the research. Our concern here is with the latter two, the adequacy of a study's research process and the grounding of the findings, because the other two areas have been adequately addressed.

THE RESEARCH PROCESS

In judging the quality of research designed to build theory, the reviewer should be able to make judgments about some of the components of the research process. However, even in a monograph, which consists primarily of theoretical formulations and analyzed data, there might be no way in which readers can accurately judge how the analysis was carried out. Readers are not actually present during the actual analytic sessions, and the monograph does not necessarily help them imagine these sessions or their sequence. To remedy this, it would be useful for readers to be given certain types of information bearing on the criteria to follow. The detail need not be great even in a monograph, but it must be sufficient to give some reasonable grounds for judging the adequacy of the research process as such. The types of information needed are presented here in question form, with their answers indicating how they might serve as evaluative criteria.

Criterion 1: How was the original sample selected? On what grounds?

Criterion 2: What major categories emerged?

Criterion 3: What were some of the events, incidents, or actions (indicators) that pointed to some of these major categories?

Criterion 4: On the basis of what categories did theoretical sampling proceed? That is, how did theoretical formulations guide some of the data collection? After the theoretical sampling was done, how representative of the data did the categories prove to be?

Criterion 5: What were some of the hypotheses pertaining to conceptual relations (i.e., among categories), and on what grounds were they formulated and validated?

Criterion 6: Were there instances in which hypotheses did not explain what was happening in the data? How were these discrepancies accounted for? Were hypotheses modified?

Criterion 7: How and why was the core category selected? Was this collection sudden or gradual, and was it difficult or easy? On what grounds were the final analytic decisions made?

We realize that certain of these criteria would be regarded as unconventional (e.g., theoretical sampling rather than types of statistical sampling, the injunction to be explicit about accounting for discrepancies) by most quantitative and even many qualitative researchers. Yet, these are essential to evaluating the analytic logic used by the researcher. If the researcher provides this information, then readers can follow the logic of the researcher's complex coding procedures. Details given in this way would be supplemented with cues that could, at least in longer publications, be read as pointing to extremely careful and thorough tracking of indicators, of conscientious and imaginative theoretical sampling, and so on. Next, we provide a series of questions that are equivalent to criteria for evaluating the empirical grounding of a study.

EMPIRICAL GROUNDING OF A STUDY

Criterion 1: Are Concepts Generated?

Because the building blocks of any theory (indeed, any scientific theory) are a set of concepts grounded in the data, the first questions to be asked of any publication are the following. Does it generate (via coding) or at least use concepts, and what is (are) their source(s)? If concepts are drawn from common usage (e.g., uncertainty), does the author show how they pertain or could have evolved from this research? In any monograph that purports to present theoretical interpretations of data, one can make a quick, albeit very crude, assessment of its concepts merely by checking the index. How many concepts are there, and were they generated from the study itself? For a fuller sense of what concepts were derived and how they were used, one must at least scan the monograph.

Criterion 2: Are the Concepts Systematically Related?

The name of the scientific game is systematic conceptualization and linkages. So, the question to ask here of a research publication is whether linkages have been made between concepts. As in other qualitative writing, the linkages are unlikely to be presented as a listing of hypotheses or propositions. Rather, they will be woven throughout the text of the publication.

Criterion 3: Are There Many Conceptual Linkages, and Are the Categories Well Developed? Do Categories Have Conceptual Density?

Categories should be tightly linked. This pertains both to individual categories and their subcategories as well as to individual categories and the larger core category. Categories should be theoretically dense, that is, have many properties that are dimensionalized. It is the tight linkages and density of the categories (many properties and dimensional variations) that give a theory its specificity and explanatory power.

Criterion 4: Is Variation Built Into the Theory?

Variation is important because it signifies that a concept has been examined under a series of different conditions and developed across its range of dimensions. Some qualitative studies report only a single phenomenon and establish only a few conditions under which it appears; in addition, they specify only a few actions/interactions that characterize it and a limited number or range of consequences. By contrast, by using this methodology, there should be considerable variation built into the theory. In a published article, the range of variations touched on might be more limited, but the author should at least suggest that other writings will include their specification.

Criterion 5: Are the Conditions Under Which Variation Can Be Found Built Into the Study and Explained?

Any explanation of a phenomenon should include the conditions under which it can be found—the broad or more macro conditions as well as the micro conditions or those having more immediate bearing on the phenomenon. Broader conditions should not be listed merely as background information in a separate chapter; rather, they should be woven into the actual analysis with explanations of how they affect the events and actions in the data (see Chapter 12; see also Corbin & Strauss, 1996). These include, but are not limited to, economic factors, organizational policies, rules and regulations, social movements, trends, culture, societal values, language, and professional values and standards.

Criterion 6: Has Process Been Taken Into Account?

Identifying process in research is important because it enables theory users to explain action under changing conditions. Recall from Chapter 11 that process may be described as stages or phases and also as fluidity or movement of action/interaction over the passage of time in response to prevailing conditions. The conceptual scheme used to explain process is less important than attempts to bring it into the analysis.

Criterion 7: Do the Theoretical Findings Seem Significant, and to What Extent?

It is entirely possible to complete a theory-generating study, or any research investigation, yet not produce findings that are significant. If a researcher simply goes through the motions of doing research without drawing on creativity or developing insight into what the data are reflecting, then he or she risks the possibility of arriving at findings that are less than significant. By this, we mean that the research fails to deliver new information or to produce guidelines for action. Remember that there is an interplay between the researcher and the data, and no method can ensure that the interplay will be creative. This depends on three characteristics of the researcher: analytic ability, theoretical sensitivity, and sufficient writing ability to convey the findings. Of course, a creative interplay also depends on the other pole of the researcher-data equation—the quality of data collected or used. An unimaginative analysis might be adequately grounded in the data in a technical sense but be limited for theoretical purposes. This is because the researcher either does not draw on the fuller resources of data or fails to push data collection far enough.

Criterion 8: Does the Theory Stand the Test of Time and Become Part of the Discussions and Ideas Exchanged Among Relevant Social and Professional Groups?

Although theories, in a larger sense, often are time and place specific, major concepts and hypotheses should be able to stand up to continued testing through discourse, research, and application. Take concepts such as stigma, division of labor, uncertainty, stress, and negotiations. These concepts are meaningful to laypersons and professionals alike and are used to explain phenomena, to direct research, and to guide action programs.

A FINAL NOTE

Our readers should keep in mind three additional comments about evaluative criteria. First, these criteria should not be read as hard-and-fast evaluative rules, either for the researcher or for readers who are judging the research publications of others. The criteria are meant as guidelines. Certain investigations might require that the research procedures and evaluative criteria be modified to fit the circumstances of the research. Imaginative researchers who are wrestling with unusual or creative use of materials will, at times, depart somewhat from what can be considered authoritative guidelines for judging their own products or the products of others. In such unusual cases, the researcher should know precisely how and why he or she departed from the procedures, should say so in the writing, and should leave it up to readers to judge the credibility of the findings.

Second, we suggest that researchers who proceeded according to their own procedural operations briefly indicate what these were, especially in longer publications. This would help readers to judge the analytic logic and overall adequacy of the research process. It also would make readers more aware of how a particular research investigation differs from those using other modes of qualitative research. In specifying this information, readers are apprised precisely about what operations were used and their possible inadequacies. In other words, the researcher should identify and convey the strengths and inevitable limitations of the study.

Finally, it might be useful, in certain publications, for the researcher to include a short explanation of his or her own research perspectives and responses to the research process. This enables readers to judge how personal reactions might have influenced the investigation and interpretations placed on data. Maintaining an audit trail through documentation of the research process in memos is one way of ensuring that the researcher will be able to do this at the end of the study (Rodgers & Cowles, 1993).

SUMMARY

Every research study, whether qualitative or quantitative, must be evaluated in terms of the canons and procedures of the method used to generate the research findings. In this chapter, we provided criteria for evaluating both the research process and the empirical grounding of findings. Other areas, such as the validity, reliability, and credibility of the data as well as the value of the theory, already have been amply covered in the literature. The criteria that we presented supplement these and can be useful guides to researchers when writing the methodological sections for theses and publications as well as for committee and faculty members who are placed in positions of evaluating their students' or colleagues' works. The criteria also should be helpful to persons who sit on editorial boards and funding agencies and who are in need of further guidelines for making judgments about the value of theory-generating studies.

17 Student Questions and Answers to These

We have found that students often raise questions in class, during consultations, and following presentations. The questions arise from various concerns. Sometimes, students are puzzled because certain procedures or techniques seem unclear, are ambiguous, or run counter to those of more conventional research methods. Other times, they want to know how to respond to criticism from mentors, thesis committee members, and friends. When students come to us, they want to know, "How can we answer those external voices and also quiet our own internal ones?" The issues they raise are endemic, many doubtlessly raised wherever qualitative research is taught or discussed. Following are some of the most frequently asked questions along with our responses. We have placed this chapter at the end of the book, rather than at the beginning, because it summarizes many of the major points made throughout the book.

1. "I've heard that there are some very good computer programs available that can help with analysis. Do you know anything about these and how they are used?"

   Answer. Many students use Ethnograph and others useful computer programs (Lafaille, 1995; Shapiro et al., 1993) to assist them with their qualitative research. The two programs with which we are most familiar are NUDIST and ATLAS. These tend to be more complex and more geared toward theory building than some other programs. Because neither of us is an expert on the use of computers in research, we asked Heiner Legeiwe, one of the codevelopers of ATLAS, to explain how this program might be used to facilitate analysis. We reproduce his memo here.

How to Use Computers in Qualitative Analysis

Memo by Heiner Legeiwe
Institut für Sozialwissenschaften—Technische Universität Berlin

In the age of text processing, it is difficult to find qualitative analysts who are not using computers in their research work. The following memo, however, addresses the use of more sophisticated software systems, those especially developed to aid with qualitative research of the theory-building type.

To begin with my own experience, I should mention that it was because of our interdisciplinary research project at TU [Technische Universität] Berlin on computer-aided text interpretation and theory building that I first met Anselm Strauss in 1990. I met with him to discuss the potentials of a tailor-made software system for qualitative analysis. Anselm loved the idea, gave us a lot of hints and helpful criticisms, and later on was pleased to test the usefulness of our research product, the prototype of ATLAS.

Most important to understanding the philosophy of computer-aided text interpretation is the fact that computers are absolutely incapable of comprehending the meaning of words or sentences. Their strength comes from being able to help with all kinds of ordering, structuring, retrieving and visualizing tasks. This means it is hopeless to expect a computer to do even the simplest analytical work. But a computer program can be extremely helpful in creating order out of a mass of field notes, interviews, codes, concepts, and memos; in visualizing the network of concepts and relationships in the emerging theory; and in keeping systematic track of the developing theory beginning with the very first data and their preliminary coding, documenting all intermediary steps and ending with the final research report.

Now, [I provide] a short description of the typical steps in computer-aided theory-generating analysis which follows the features of the system I use for my own analyses (ATLAS for Windows).

Before starting your analysis, you have to store your data in the computer memory, for example, transcribed field notes and interviews or scanned data like manuscripts and graphic pictures—even sound tracks and motion pictures. (The common transcription of interviews by text processing results in electronically stored data anyhow.) The first step of your analysis corresponds to preparing a special desk in your office for one study: You open a *hermeneutic unit*—an electronic container which will collect and organize all your data, codes, memos, and diagrams belonging to your analysis under one and the same label—and collect into it all text files you want to analyze. You will start your analysis on the *textual level* (working mainly with texts/documents). In *open coding*, you display and scroll each document on-screen, mark relevant text passages, and assign *codes* and *memos* to them. Codes should be accompanied by explaining commentaries of their use, which is especially important for teamwork analyses. (If you look for key words or word combinations in the text, you may even use a procedure for automatic coding.) The system organizes lists of your codes and memos in special windows. Later on, mouse-clicking an item in the code or memo list will retrieve all text passages indexed of that code or memo within their respective contexts, facilitating *constant comparisons* of all indicators of a given code or concept. Text passages which are indexed by patterns of codes can be retrieved by a Boolean query tool, allowing [you] to test complex hypotheses. Furthermore, the code and memo lists allow different *sorting*, for example, according to *groundedness* (number of text passages of a code or memo) or *conceptual density* (number of other codes connected with a code).

On the *conceptual level* (working mainly with concepts), the steps of *axial and selective coding* are supported by different functions. One step would be to join codes and memos to *families* like the family of all conditions or consequences. For *theory building*, you have to define *concepts* consisting in codes of higher order, which are no more connected to text passages but [rather] to other codes. The most powerful support on this level is achieved by *graphic representations* of text segments, codes, and memos. These objects are easily presented and manipulated on the screen, and relations between them are defined and named according to standard logic relations (e.g., *A* <is part of> *B*) or according to definition of the analyst (e.g., *A* <shows symptom> *B*). By these graphic tools, the analyst is easily able to construct his or her own semantic networks, that is, to *build theories out of text segments, codes, and memos.* Computer-aided theories show two advantages in comparison to ordinary paper-and-pencil sketches of theories. First, their formal properties may be checked, and they may be formally described, in a logical language (e.g., PROLOG). Second, by a few mouse clicks, even the most abstract concept of a theory can be easily connected with all its indicators within the data, thus *testing its groundedness.*

To prevent unrealistic expectations, I should add two warnings. First, a software system for computer-aided theory-generating analysis is at least as complex as a text-processing program like Word. Such a program will be useful only after some routine work with its application. If you use it only occasionally or for one small range study, maybe it is not worthwhile to take the time to learn how to hande the program correctly. Second, computer-aided theory-generating analysis, like every new technology, has the potential to change the quality of the theory. Paper, pencil, scissors, paste, bundles of index cards, and postered walls by colored flip charts may give you a different touch and feeling of your research work than "desktop" computer screens—sized as airplane desks—and may be more important to inspire your creativity than even the nicest computer diagrams.

In the near future, I see different trends of computer-aided theory development:

• *New areas of application:* Computer software will certainly promote theory development application in completely new areas, for example, theory building on the basis of quantitative data in natural sciences, in systems analysis, and in operations research. Even more important are nonresearch applications of computer-aided theory generation as a method for on-line modeling of complex social processes in areas like project management, total quality management, implementation of social and technological innovations, and social conflict mediation (alternate dispute resolution).

• *Teaching:* A software system may help the student to structure and make explicit his or her step-by-step work in theory-generating analysis. Scholarly done analyses may be repeated and used as models for the beginner.

• *Communication:* A hermeneutic unit of a grounded theory study contains all data, and analytic work based on them in a single *hypertext* that may easily be browsed through. Passing from Gutenberg to Turing media, it may become more convenient to publish a

hermeneutic unit (e.g., via the Internet) than a research report. (I am waiting for the first doctoral thesis published this way.)
• *Research:* A hermeneutic unit may be considered a frozen portrait of the whole step-by-step theory-generating analysis to study creative processes of building theories out of data—including cooperation and team research.

A last word on selecting the most suitable software system for your work. As I am strongly biased to the system in whose development I participated, ATLAS, I am not able to provide a completely objective recommendation, but there is an excellent evaluation of the available systems in the following:

Weitzman, E., & Miles, M. B. (1995). *Computer programs for qualitative data analysis.* Thousand Oaks, CA: Sage.

P.S.: The best and quickest way to more information is via the Internet, for example, the home page of Thomas Muhr, author of ATLAS: http://www.atlasti.de. There, you will find not only "all about ATLAS" but even links to competing software systems like NUDIST, a bibliography, and subscription addresses of qualitative research newsgroups.

---

2. Stephan, an anthropologist, who is surrounded at work by psychologists, stated, "They are continually asking, 'Where are the numbers?' " This also is a frequent question asked by thesis committee members and more quantitative researchers.

   Answer. Although some qualitative researchers do quantify their data, as a rule, qualitative researchers are not so much concerned with distribution within populations as they are with process and social mechanisms. Qualitative researchers seek to identify significant concepts and to explore their relationships. (See Chapter 4 for a discussion of the relationship between quantitative and qualitative methods in theory development.) If committee members insist on numbers, then students often include one or two relevant instruments in their studies. These satisfy committee members and often provide additional findings of interest.

---

3. "What is the focus of analysis, if not numbers?"

Answer. This question is a variant of "Where are your numbers?" The skeptic is assuming that the researcher cannot arrive at conclusions unless he or she uses statistical modes of sampling and analysis. For us, the unit of analysis is the concept. As explained in Chapter 13, our sampling procedures are designed to look at how concepts vary along dimensional ranges (how their properties vary), not to measure the distribution of persons along some dimension of a concept. The researcher samples places and persons where he or she expects that differences in the properties of a concept will be maximized. This form of sampling is very important in theory building because it enables the researcher to build variation into his or her theory, thereby increasing its explanatory power. Later, if the researcher wants to quantitatively test the theory by doing cluster analysis, correlational, or other types of quantitative studies using highly sophisticated forms of statistical analysis, then he or she may do so. Remember that our primary purpose is discovery. We do not know which variables are important, what their properties are, or how these vary dimensionally. Therefore, sampling is guided by the developing theory.

---

4. "Can we use data that already have been collected? Must we code all our data? Should we sample randomly? Are there other ways of sampling?" These questions are raised often because students (and other researchers) already have collected their data before coming to the seminar or before they begin their analyses. Sometimes, their concern is "Do I have to start data collection all over so as not to violate the principle of theory building?" which states that data collection and analysis are interwoven procedures. Other times, their concern is "How do I manage so much material, especially because I don't have unlimited time?"

Answer. Our response to the first question is as follows. Essentially, working with already collected data is no different from doing secondary analysis on one's own data or on someone else's data— perhaps long since collected. Also, the problems associated with already collected data are very similar to those confronted by anyone who discovers a large cache of archival materials and wishes to analyze them. The major difference, perhaps, is that with personally collected materials, the researcher has some familiarity with the materials.

Researchers should approach already collected data and secondary or archival materials exactly as they would their own data. To handle these types of data, researchers characteristically begin as usual, examining the earliest interviews, field notes, and documents for significant happenings or events. At first, they might scan the data, find a passage that interests them, and then begin careful open coding and initial axial coding. Likewise, because sampling is done on the basis of concepts, a researcher theoretically can sample, sorting through interviews, observations, or videos to find variations of situations and analyze these. Analytic problems do sometimes occur with already collected or secondary data when researchers attempt to saturate categories or to find variations and then discover, to their dismay, that there are insufficient data. When this situation arises, they must either return to the field to collect additional or updated materials or live with gaps in the theory.

In response to the second question, the answer is as follows: No, not every single bit of data has to be analyzed "microscopically." However, as we said earlier in this book, close inspection of data during the early phases of the research process is necessary to build dense and tightly integrated theory. Usually, microscopic coding of 10 good interviews or observations can provide the skeleton of a theoretical structure. This skeleton must be filled in, extended, and validated through more data gathering and analysis, although coding can be more selective. There is no substitute or shortcuts for open and axial coding, especially during the early phases of the research.

Random sampling is more appropriate for quantitative studies than for qualitative ones for all the reasons listed in Chapter 13. As stated, researchers are not trying to control variables; rather, they are trying to discover them. They are not looking for representativeness or distribution of populations; rather, they are looking for how concepts vary dimensionally along their properties. So, although random sampling is possible, it might be detrimental because it could prevent analysts from discovering the variations that they are looking for.

As for other types of sampling, in almost any qualitative research, the initial data are gathered through a variety of procedures—cashing in on lucky observations, using "snowball sampling," networking, and so on. The lucky researchers are those who have unlimited access to sites and who know where and at what times they might find comparative cases. Most of the time, researchers do not know which persons or places to visit to find examples of how concepts vary. Instead, they sample by "sensible logic" or by convenience, that is, from department to department or from person to person, talking and observing whoever and whatever is available, hoping that variations will occur naturally. Variations almost invariably exist because no two departments, situations, or happenings are quite the same. Each situation that is studied has the potential to present different features of the phenomenon or phenomena. The more interviews or observations researchers conduct, the more likely it is that conceptual variations will emerge naturally. If not, then the inability to sample to the point of saturation becomes a limitation of their studies.

---

5. Valerie and Stephen, a psychologist and an anthropologist, observed, "Psychologists are taught to think up 'mini-theories' out of their heads to see if they work. That is just the opposite of your way of doing research."

Answer. These "mini-theories" are essentially hypotheses, perhaps grounded a bit in a psychological researcher's experience and reading. However, these hypotheses are not derived through systematic analyses of data or validated during the research process. From a practical standpoint, the mini-theories have merit, especially for practitioners who need knowledge to handle problematic situations on-the-spot. Much depends, of course, on how those mini-theories were derived. If they are not grounded, then they can be misleading.

---

6. "What about 'descriptive theory or theories'?"

Answer. The student who asked this question was a doctoral candidate in nursing. The instructor (Strauss) did not know what the student-nurse meant by the term, which apparently is used by some nurse researchers. To him, the terms seemed contradictory; if it is description, then it is not theory. In the clinical research area of nursing, there seems to be a large proportion of "theories" that are normative, that is, that embody prescriptions and proscriptions or "dos and don'ts." What nurses term "descriptive theory" probably constitutes a form of "description" (provides knowledge and understanding about a phenomenon but does not allow for prediction and prescription because concepts are not necessarily ordered or integrated) or "conceptual ordering" (loosely ordered and organized concepts that are not necessarily integrated into a larger theoretical framework) rather than actual theory as we defined it in Chapter 3. In nursing, as in many other disciplines, there are specific disciplinary theories. These are systematic, well-developed, and integrated theories that guide practice. However, for the most part, they are based on borrowed and experientially derived concepts rather than being grounded in research.

7. "Do qualitative researchers do much describing or descriptive quoting from interviews and their field notes?" This question often is asked by beginning qualitative research students or researchers.

Answer. This depends entirely on the researcher's purpose when publishing and on the audience that he or she is attempting to reach. For instance, if it is anticipated that the substantive area is entirely unfamiliar to most readers, then it is likely that the inclusion of many quotations will enable readers to fill out the descriptive blanks in their heads. Also, if the final theoretical formulation is likely to be viewed skeptically by readers, then the researcher is likely to punch home his or her argument with many quotations that function essentially as convincing items (e.g., "See, this is what they say and think"). Strauss et al. (1964, pp. 228-261) presented materials bearing on the beliefs of psychiatric aides working in a psychiatric hospital. One of their points was that the aides, uneducated in psychiatric principles, still considered themselves as "doing good" for the patients. Not only did the aides not recognize the special language and professional work of the nurses and physicians, but sometimes they thought that they themselves did more good for specific patients than did the professionals with all their psychiatric ideologies. To convince potentially skeptical readers, long quotations from interviews with the aides were given. Although individual qualitative researchers handle the matter of quotations differently, we tend to avoid quoting large chunks of interview or field note materials.

In our monographs, we attempt to analyze data closely . . . so as to construct an integrated [conceptually] dense theory. So, the interview and field note quotations tend to be brief, and often [they] are woven in with the analysis within the same or closely related sentences. Longer quotes (especially from field notes) are used for case illustrations . . . or when the events and actions described in the field notes might help readers [to] better visualize the analytical points being made, especially when the analytic points might otherwise be difficult to grasp. . . . In general, however, we think twice about loading a theoretically oriented monograph with too many chunks of descriptive material and are fairly deliberate about those that are included. Understandably, in this style of presentation—where the basic analysis shapes the organization of both the monograph and its descriptive elements—the predominant forms of quotation are the short quote and the precise quote. (Strauss et al., 1964, pp. 295-296)

---

8. Krystof, a visiting sociologist from Poland, noted, "I did an organizational study of one factory in Japan. A colleague asked, 'How can you generalize from studying just this one factory to all other Japanese factories?' "

Answer. The answer to this question is quite complicated. True, one cannot generalize from one case, especially in the quantitative sense of the word. However, one can learn a lot from the study of one factory or organization. Remember that we are studying concepts and their relationships. Manifestations of our concepts might emerge 100 or more times in this one case. We also are specifying the conditions under which events, happenings, or actions/interactions are likely to occur, the forms that they take, and the consequences that occur. In addition, we are looking for dimensional variations and explanations for these. If our concepts are abstract enough, then they are likely to occur in similar or variant forms in other organizations. For example, in our studies of work, the concept of "work flow" is relevant whether it occurs at home, in a hospital, or in a production plant. There is much we can learn about work flow through the study of one organization. However, we will not learn everything there is to know about work flow from one case (person, family, factory, organization, community, or nation). Our theory will be somewhat limited in explanatory power and will require expansion, modification, and extension through other studies of work in similar and different types of organizations. By specifying our contexts (set of conditions in which specific phenomena or concepts are located), we are saying that this is what seems to keep the work flowing here. If similar conditions exist in one's organization, then perhaps much of what we learned about work flow in our study may help one to understand what is going on in his or her organization as well. If they are different, then it is important to note how this changes the work flow.

Abstract concepts such as negotiation, social worlds, arenas, trajectory (a course of action involving multiple actors), and work flow (the flow of work over time) came out of studies we have done and have had widespread application and appeal. However, although some of our concepts are more fully developed than others, it can hardly be said that knowledge about them is saturated.

So, if one asks a researcher, "Is this one case representative of all cases?" then the answer probably is "no" and further study will show why and how. But if one asks, "Is there something we can learn from this case that will give us insight and understanding about a phenomenon as does the concept of 'work flow,' " then the answer is "yes." We can study concepts as negotiation in hospitals, governments, factories, and schools, and what we learn from the study of one of these places will increase our understanding of the concepts and provide a starting point for further research.

---

9. "Should I translate my interviews to code them, or should I code them in the original language (provided, of course, that I speak that language)?" Translating takes **so much** time. This question often is asked by doctoral students from overseas, usually pressed by their thesis committees to translate their interviews into English.

   Answer. There are several reasons, we believe, for doing only **minimal** translating. A main reason for *some* translating is so that English-speaking readers can get at least some degree of feeling about, or insight into, what the interviewee is saying and thinking as well as a sense of what the coding looks like.

   On the other hand, the difficulties of accurate, let alone nuanced, translation are legion. Few of us are specially trained or natively skilled at overcoming those difficulties, especially for extended passages. Our foreign students (mostly Asian) have reported additional difficulties in trying to code in English; often, there is no equivalent English word capable of capturing the subtle nuances in meaning of the original language. To quote Hoffman (1989), meanings become "lost in translation." For presentation or publication in a country other than the one in which the data were collected (if the language is different), key passages and their codes can be translated, approximating the original as closely as possible. However, as a general rule, we would say that too much valuable time and meaning can be lost in trying to translate all of one's materials. Also, many of the original subtleties of meaning are lost in translation.

In our research seminars, when students are presenting materials, we do ask them to translate some passages; otherwise, other students cannot work on these data. However, each presenting student is asked whether a given translated word or phrase really approximates what the interviewee intended. For instance, an African mother spoke of the care of her mentally ill son as "difficult." When queried, the native researcher agreed that the native word for "difficult," as used in this situation, actually was quite equivalent to the English term. However, on other occasions, there were nuances and differences that were not quite picked up by English translations of the native words. When this happened, the student did her best to give words and descriptions that conveyed the original native meanings. In other words, in seminar or teamwork sessions, there are additional opportunities to explore the parameters of translated meanings and to avoid imposing outsider interpretations on the data.

---

10. "Are there special problems with doing qualitative studies in nonindustrialized societies or with doing them in industrialized non-European cultures? After all, so much emphasis is placed on this methodology in close linguistic analysis."

Answer. This question raises a thorny issue that surely deserves serious consideration. In a general sense, qualitative analysts face precisely the same difficulties when trying to comprehend the meanings of acts, events, or objects when these are profoundly "cultural" in nature. It is all too easy for people living in Western countries to misinterpret foreigners or persons who are only partly assimilated when comparing their acts and words to American ones. As the anthropologists have taught us, to avoid such misinterpretations, researchers must spend a fair amount (some say a great deal) of time at the foreign sites and must engage in a lot of observations and conversations (informal interviews). Also, they must understand at least some of the foreign languages in addition to examining their own often culture-based assumptions. Even with this counsel, anthropologists cannot guarantee that misinterpretations (sometimes gross ones) have not occurred.

However, if a foreign student is studying here but wishes to collect data in his or her own country, then most certainly he or she can use this method or other qualitative methods. It is important that other countries not borrow theories but instead develop their own, ones that reflect their societies' or citizens' cultures and behaviors. Alas, a mistake frequently made is that theories developed in industrialized nations are superimposed on nonindustrialized ones or on other industrialized nations that have different populations and cultures. The imposed theories just do not fit, either in whole or in part, and thus can be very misguiding.

As for the use of procedures, there is no reason why the procedures described in this book cannot be of service when studying cultures other than one's own or when studying non-North American cultures. After all, the procedures work when studying ethnic Americans and other "subcultural" groups such as "punks" and "junkies," whose cultural meanings and behaviors often differ from the usual ones. As an illustration: one of our American students studied conceptions of health among the Sioux Indians, living among them on a reservation and having previously worked there as a public health worker for several years. She concluded that anthropologists who had studied these people did not accurately grasp how Sioux philosophy of the world affected their conceptions of health and medicine—ideas very different from the usual Western ones.

---

11. Krystof had a mass of data already collected. He asked, "How do I winnow my many paragraphs [about 5,000 in 40 interviews] to the specific ones so that I can code? How do I choose these by theoretical sampling?"

Answer. The answer to this question is similar to the response already given about previously collected data. Suppose that a student is studying a business organization that is flourishing despite a bad recession and that he or she wants to know how the organization has managed this feat, that is, the basis for the decisions the organization has made, the visions that guide its executives' actions, the incentives it provides, and so on. The data might consist of organizational documents only, but masses of them. To begin, the analyst would choose some documents and familiarize himself or herself with their contents, just as if they were interviews. Then, once the student had a sense of the types of information they contain, he or she could begin intensive coding. Then, the analyst could turn to successive documents, analyzing each as if it was incoming data in a developing study.

When doing *secondary analysis* on previously collected data of any form, it might not be possible to return to the original source to gather more data. In that case, although the researcher still would sample theoretically (based on concepts), sampling would have to be confined to the documents themselves. However, there should be ample variation within cases to enable the researcher to compare concepts for similarities and differences and to determine major properties of a category and their dimensions. Some categories might be less dense than if the researcher had access to the original respondents; nevertheless, the researcher should be able to come up with a competent and coherent theoretical formulation about a topic, even from previously collected data.

---

12. "Can the analytic process be speeded up or shortened given that many practitioners and professionals do not have the time required for full-scale theory development?"

Answer. If the researcher's intent is to develop dense and tightly integrated theory, then the answer to this question is "no." The process cannot be shortened. However, not all persons who use the procedures described in this book have as their aim the development of dense and tightly integrated theory or, indeed, any theory at all. Their aim might be description, conceptual ordering, or discovery of categories to build measurement scales. Although in many publications there is reference to having used this method, what persons sometimes actually mean is that they use some of the procedures, such as making constant comparisons, rather than adopting the method in its entirety. Sometimes, they use particular procedures in conjunction with other qualitative methods or philosophical orientations.

This gives an additional basis for answering this question. The researcher can use some, but not all, of the procedures to satisfy his or her research purposes. Say, for example, that the researcher does some theoretical coding (i.e., identifies categories or themes) but does not want to take the time to develop the categories elaborately in terms of their properties, dimensions, variations, or relationships. To identify categories, the researcher may systematically make use of comparative analysis and theoretical sampling. He or she may look for in vivo words and phrases that suggest patterns of actors' concerns and problems. The researcher surely will attempt to capture viewpoints of the seemingly most relevant actors. Using the procedures described in this book should make the researcher more sensitive to his or her own assumptions. If the researcher chooses to write memos and do diagrams, then these may be less elaborate than more theoretical models because there is less analysis with which to fill them in. Through the steps we just described, very important descriptive knowledge can be ascertained. (Findings do not necessarily constitute "theory" unless concepts are integrated to form a larger theoretical framework.)

We make two further points here. First, if the researcher records his or her procedures, then the researcher will be more able to explain specifically to audiences how interpretations were reached. Second, the researcher will feel that his or her interpretations are more firmly grounded than if concepts were preselected from disciplinary or professional literature or only from experience. Third, experienced qualitative analysts work more rapidly than do beginners. This is true whether experienced researchers are developing theory or doing brief exploratory studies. They work faster because they have internalized this mode of thinking and can go about it less self-consciously.

---

13. "Can you say something about the work involved in doing qualitative analysis—the amount, types, and so on?"

Answer. This again is a very complicated question. Before commenting on it briefly, we quote a few relevant remarks from Strauss (1987):

[This type of] research should be understood and analyzed as work. Essentially, we are advocating a highly self-conscious approach to the work of research: to how it is and can be actually carried out under a variety of circumstances, during its various phases, by researchers who stand in different relationships to the work of getting and examining and interpreting the information that becomes their data. . . . Research work consists of more than sets of tasks. . . . It involves the organization of work—the articulation of tasks (itself a type of work) including the management of physical, social, and personal resources necessary for getting the research work done, whether working alone, with someone else, or in a team. (p. 9)

"But how *much* work?" the readers want to know. That is an impossible question to answer definitively because so many different issues may be involved. Let us reverse the question because the answer will vary accordingly. Is the researcher talking about a study in which there is unlimited access or one in which access is limited or difficult to obtain? Is the researcher somewhat knowledgeable about the area that he or she is studying? Is he or she an experienced researcher whose analytic skills are finely honed?

Relevant to the *psychology* of the amount of work is who does the work. If the researcher is doing the transcription of interviews in addition to doing the interviewing and data analysis, then he or she has a sizable job to do. If the transcription can be done by someone else, then perhaps the workload can be reduced somewhat. If the researcher encounters difficulties in data collection or in analysis, then understandably, there is more work—both actually and psychologically.

Unquestionably, the most important issue bearing on the amount and types of work is the ultimate aim of the researcher. If the aim is for densely conceptualized theory, then there will be more analytic work than for studies aiming at conceptual ordering. Yet, the process of doing conceptual ordering can be quite complicated, so unfortunately for this question, there is no definitive answer.

Another issue is what types of work are involved. If this book has been read carefully, then the researcher is aware of the many forms of work involved in data collection and analysis. There is the work of data collection (with all the potential difficulties), the work of recording and perhaps transcribing (even translating), and the different types of coding. Then, when this work finally is finished, there still is the work of writing papers or books and making presentations. Before the study begins, there is the work of grant writing, of obtaining human subjects committee consent, and so on. In short, the only major difference between doing theory-building research and doing other forms of qualitative analysis or even other forms of research is the work that goes into the coding process. A computer can help with the work, but it still requires effort on the part of the analyst.

There also is the issue of what types of resources are needed for this type of work in addition to requisite skills. Really nothing is needed in addition to notepads, a telephone, a tape recorder and tapes, a computer or typewriter, and the usual paraphernalia of qualitative research. Money sometimes is necessary for travel and occasionally is needed for paying interviewees and the like. A good research library also can be very helpful or even a necessity, as can consultants and/or helpful friends. Included in the investigator's resource pool, if he or she is lucky, is an indispensable supportive spouse or significant other. In addition, perhaps one is fortunate enough to have an efficient and committed secretary.

---

14. "What is the relationship of everyday life explanations to our theoretical explanations?"

    Answer. The former are grist for our analytic mill. As we said earlier, one must listen very carefully to what the various actors are saying. Their words and expressions may provide in vivo concepts. Also, they usually are revealing of the actors' perceptions, ideologies, and unwitting assumptions. So, we note these and are respectful of them, not because we necessarily believe these lay explanations but rather because we need to incorporate these into our analyses. Our aim must be to integrate (not just accept) actors' explanations into our own interpretations. If we accept them without questioning, then, as the anthropologists would say, we have "gone native."

---

15. "If you had been trained in psychoanalytic theory, then how would you integrate this into qualitative analysis?"

    Answer. The techniques and procedures for qualitative analysis explained in this book can be used by people trained in different disciplines and with their respective theoretical approaches. In fact, the methodology and its procedures have been used successfully by diversely trained researchers. For the most part, disciplinary theory tends to focus users on certain problems and provides them with a perspective for interpretion. For example, a person coming from a Freudian perpective might be more concerned with hidden motives and deep psychological meanings than would an organizational sociologist, who is more interested in social organizational process and structure. The important thing is to be aware that a perspective can block discovery; that is, placing one's perspectives on data (e.g., interpreting all data from a Freudian perspective) rather than letting the data speak for themselves (letting meaning evolve) limits discovery. Certainly, if it is the analyst's choice, then the analytic procedures we offer in this text can help any analyst discover deep and hidden meanings, develop new interpretations, or open up "black boxes" (ambiguous concepts) in his or her favorite theories. Again, it is the difference between interpreting everything in terms of a theory (laying preassumed meanings and relationships on data) and beginning with data and then seeing where they lead.

More specifically, there is a basic tenet of the methodology that is relevant to the question. *All* assumptions of preexisting theories are subject to potential skepticism and, therefore, must be scrutinized in light of one's own data. The latter allow the researcher to question and qualify as well as to give assent to his or her received theories. Concepts must "earn their way" into a study rather than be blindly accepted and imposed on data. ("Received" theories might work brilliantly for some data but not so well on other data.) To summarize, psychoanalytic theory, or any other theory, must pass the empirical test.

---

16. "How many interviews or observations are enough? When do I stop gathering data?"

Answer. These are perennial research questions asked of all researchers using qualitative methods. For most theory-building researchers, data collection continues "until theoretical saturation takes place." This simply means (within the limits of available time and money) that the researcher finds that no new data are being unearthed. Any new data would only add, in a minor way, to the many variations of major patterns.

However, we realize that there always are constraints of time, energy, availability of participants, and other conditions that affect data collection. These can impose limits on how much and what types of data are collected. The researcher must keep in mind, however, that if he or she stops gathering data before theoretical saturation, then the researcher's theory might not be fully developed in terms of density and variation. Sometimes, the researcher has no choice and must settle for a theoretical scheme that is less developed than desired.

---

17. "How is this methodology similar to, and different from, case analysis?

    Answer. This is another one of those complicated questions because, in some part, the answer depends on what is meant by a "case" and its analysis. The book *What Is a Case?* (Ragin & Becker, 1992) reflected on this problem. Two sociological authors asked a number of respected colleagues to discuss how they used cases in their research. There was a wide disparity, both on the nature of these cases and on how they were analyzed. Frequently, when one speaks of cases, persons interpret them as interviews of individual persons or groups. Often, these take the form of narrative life stories, careers, or the handling of personal crises. But a moment's reflection tells us that a case also can be a study of one business organization, an African village, the Vietnam war, or a public celebration. Whether one is analyzing a single organization or several organizations, the process of analysis remains the same when using this methodology. One still would want to theoretically sample and to continue sampling until categories are saturated.

---

18. "Is using a 'basic social-psychological process' the only way in which to integrate a study? I notice that some researchers seem to assume this."

    Answer. Usually, when persons say this, they mean that the findings are integrated around a concept and explained in terms of how the concept evolves in steps or phases. No, it is not the *only* way in which to integrate. This assumption (certainly not made in Glaser's [1978] discussion of basic social processes) represents a grave underestimation of the complexity of the phenomena that are likely to be encountered in any given study. It also hampers the potential flexibility of this methodology, restricting the strategies for integrating analyses. In every study, one finds process, but process should not be limited to steps and phases, as stated in Chapter 11. Nor should it be restricted to basic social or psychological processes unless the term "social process" also includes family, organizational, arena, political, educational, and community processes as well as whatever other processes might be relevant to a study. To summarize, one can usefully code for *a* basic social or psychological process, but to organize every study around the idea of steps, phases, or social-psychological processes limits creativity.

---

19. "You emphasize that your method is both inductive and deductive, yet I often see it referred to in the literature as wholly or primarily inductive. Sometimes the reference is appreciative, and sometimes it is critical. Can you comment?"

    Answer. Again, this is a misunderstanding. In some part, it stems from a misreading of *The Discovery of Grounded Theory* (Glaser & Strauss, 1967). There, as noted early in Chapters 1 and 2 of Glaser and Strauss's book, those authors emphasized induction because of their attack on ungrounded speculative theories. The desire was to focus readers' attention on the inestimable value of grounding theories in systematic analyses of data. However, that book also emphasized the interplay of data and researcher, that is, of data themselves and the researcher's interpretation of meaning. Because no researcher enters into the process with a completely blank and empty mind, interpretations are the researcher's abstractions of what is in the data. These interpretations, which take the form of concepts and relationships, are continuously validated through comparisons with incoming data. These are then validated through comparisons with incoming data.

---

20. "I am absolutely flooded with interviews. Unfortunately, I have not been able to prevent the flood. I never dreamed I would get caught up in this situation and not be able to stop the stream of interviews. I am so sated with the interviewing and information that I cannot even think of asking new interview questions. Worse yet, I have not followed the rules and done analysis while interviewing. What should I do?" (This researcher is an ex-student who decided to interview black grandmothers who are raising their grandchildren because their daughters [the children's mothers] were severely addicted to drugs or alcohol. Initially anticipating that access to the grandmothers by herself [a white woman] would be difficult, she first approached a black minister. The latter spoke to his congregation and found grandmothers eager to be interviewed immediately.)

Answer. Your plight puts you in exactly the same position as most interviewers who put off analyzing data until most of the data are collected. This situation is precisely what we discourage because further data collection should be guided by analysis. Therefore, the best thing to do at this point is stop interviewing and start analyzing. Get telephone numbers and make later dates with respondents. You will need these people later to fill in categories and validate the evolving theory.

SUMMARY

This concludes our chapter on questions and answers. There are, no doubt, a great many more that could be asked. We advise students not to worry needlessly about every little facet of analysis. Sometimes, one has to use common sense and not get caught up in worrying about what is the right or wrong way. The important thing is to trust oneself and the process. Students should stay within the general guidelines outlined in this book and use the procedures and techniques flexibly according to their abilities and the realities of their studies.

References

Adler, P. A., & Adler, P. (1987). *Membership roles in field research.* Newbury Park, CA: Sage.

Agar, M. (1986). *Speaking of ethnography.* Beverly Hills, CA: Sage.

Altheide, D. L., & Johnson, J. (1994). Criteria for assessing interpretive validity in qualitative research. In N. Denzin & Y. Lincoln (Eds.), *Handbook of qualitative research* (pp. 485-499). Thousand Oaks, CA: Sage.

Alvermann, D. E., et al. (1996). On writing qualitative research. *Reading Research Quarterly, 31*(1), 114-120.

Ambert, A. M., et al. (1995). Understanding and evaluating qualitative research. *Journal of Marriage and the Family, 57,* 879-893.

Becker, H. (1970). *Sociological work: Method and substance.* New Brunswick, NJ: Transaction.

Becker, H. (1986). *Writing for social scientists.* Chicago: University of Chicago Press.

Begley, C. M. (1996). Triangulation of communication skills in qualitative research instruments. *Journal of Advanced Nursing, 24,* 688-693.

Biernacki, P. (1986). *Pathways from heroin addiction.* Philadelphia: Temple University Press.

Blumer, H. (1969). *Symbolic interactionism.* Englewood Cliffs, NJ: Prentice Hall.

Bradley, J. (1993). Methodological issues and practices in qualitative research. *Library Quarterly, 63,* 411-430.

Breitmayer, B. J., Ayers, L., & Knafl, K. A. (1993). Triangulation in qualitative research: Evaluation of completeness and confirmation purposes. *Image, 25,* 237-243.

Bresler, L. (1995). Ethical issues in qualitative research methodology. *Bulletin of the Council for Research in Music Education, 126,* 29-41.

Broadhead, R. (1983). *Private lives and professional identity of medical students.* New Brunswick, NJ: Transaction.

Cassell, C., & Symon, G. (Eds.). (1994). *Qualitative methods in organizational research.* Thousand Oaks, CA: Sage.

Cauhape, E. (1983). *Fresh starts: Men and women after divorce.* New York: Basic Books.

Charmaz, K. (1983). The grounded theory method: An explication and interpretation. In R. Emerson (Ed.), *Contemporary field research* (pp. 109-126). Boston: Little, Brown.

Charmaz, K. (1991). *Good days, bad days: The self in chronic illness and time.* New Brunswick, NJ: Rutgers University Press.

Charmaz, K. (1995). Grounded theory. In J. Smith, R. Hane, & L. Longenhore (Eds.), *Rethinking methods in psychology* (pp. 27-49). London: Sage.

Cheek, J. (1996). Taking a view: Qualitative research as representation. *Qualitative Health Research, 6,* 492-505.

Chick, N., Crisp, J., Rodgers, J., & Smith, T. (1996). Publishing workshops number 3—Preparing a manuscript: Reporting qualitative research findings. *Nursing Praxis New Zealand, 11*(3), 19-26.

Clarke, A. (1990). A social worlds research adventure. In S. Cozzens & T. Gieryn (Eds.), *Theories of science in society* (pp. 15-35). Bloomington: Indiana University Press.

Corbin, J., & Strauss, A. (1984). Collaboration: Couples working together to manage chronic illness. *Image, 16,* 109-115.

Corbin, J., & Strauss, A. (1988). *Unending work and care: Managing chronic illness at home.* San Francisco: Jossey-Bass.

Corbin, J., & Strauss, A. (1990). Grounded theory method: Procedures, canons, and evaluative procedures. *Qualitative Sociology, 13,* 13-21.

Corbin, J., & Strauss, A. (1996). Analytic ordering for theoretical purposes. *Qualitative Inquiry, 2,* 139-150.

Creswell, J. W. (1994). *Research design: Qualitative and quantitative approaches.* Thousand Oaks, CA: Sage.

Cuevas, N. M., Dinero, T. E., & Feit, M. D. (1996). Reading qualitative research from a methodological point of view. *Journal of Health and Social Policy, 8,* 73-90.

Dalton, M. (1954). *Men who manage.* New York: John Wiley.

Daly, K. (1997). Replacing theory in ethnography: A postmodern view. *Qualitative Inquiry, 3*(3).

Davis, F. (1963). *Passage through crisis.* Indianapolis, IN: Bobbs-Merrill.

Denzin, N. (1970). *The research act: A theoretical introduction to sociological methods.* New York: McGraw-Hill.

Denzin, N. (1987). *The alcoholic self.* Newbury Park, CA: Sage.

Denzin, N., & Lincoln, Y. (Eds.). (1994). *Handbook of qualitative research.* Thousand Oaks, CA: Sage.

Dewey, J. (1922). *Human nature and conduct.* New York: Holt.

Dewey, J. (1934). *Art as experience.* New York: Minton, Blach.

Dewey, J. (1938). *Logic: The theory of inquiry.* New York: Holt, Rinehart & Winston.

Dey, I. (1993). *Qualitative data analysis.* Thousand Oaks, CA: Sage.

Diesing, P. ((1971). *Patterns of discovery in the social sciences.* Chicago: Aldine.

Drake, S. (1957). *Discoveries and opinions of Galileo.* Garden City, NY: Doubleday Anchor Books.

Dzurec, L. C., & Abraham, I. L. (1993). The nature of inquiry: Linking quantitative and qualitative research. *Advances in Nursing Science, 16,* 73-79.

Elder, N. C., & Miller, W. L. (1995). Reading and evaluating qualitative research studies. *Journal of Family Practice, 41,* 279-285.

Fagerhaugh, S., & Strauss, A. (1977). *The politics of pain management.* Menlo Park, CA: Addison-Wesley.

Feldman, M. S. (1995). *Strategies for interpreting qualitative data.* Thousand Oaks, CA: Sage.

Ferguson, D. L., & Halle, J. W. (1995). Consideration for readers of qualitative research. *Journal of the Association for Persons With Severe Handicaps, 20*(1), 1-2.

Fielding, N., & Fielding, J. (1984). *Linking data.* Beverly Hills, CA: Sage.

Fielding, N., & Lee, R. (Eds.). (1991). *Using computers in qualitative research.* London: Sage.

Fitch, K. L. (1994). Criteria for evidence in qualitative resarch. *Western Journal of Communication, 58*(1), 32-38.

Fujimura, J. H. (1988). The molecular biological bandwagon in cancer research. *Social Problems, 35,* 261-283.

Gephart, R. P., Jr. (1988). *Ethnostatistics: Qualitative foundations for quantitative research.* Newbury Park, CA: Sage.

Gilgun, J. F., Daly, K., & Handel, G. (Eds.). (1992). *Qualitative methods in family research.* Thousand Oaks, CA: Sage.

Glaser, B. (1978). *Theoretical sensitivity.* Mill Valley, CA: Sociology Press.

Glaser, B. (1992). *Basics of grounded theory analysis: Emergence versus forcing.* Mill Valley, CA: Sociology Press.

Glaser, B., & Strauss, A. (1965). *Awareness of dying.* Chicago: Aldine.

Glaser, B., & Strauss, A. (1967). *Discovery of grounded theory.* Chicago: Aldine.

Glaser, B., & Strauss, A. (1968). *Time for dying.* Chicago: Aldine.

Glaser, B., & Strauss, A. (1975). *Chronic illness and the quality of life.* St. Louis, MO: C. V. Mosby.

Gliner, J. A. (1994). Reviewing qualitative research: Proposed criteria for fairness and rigor. *Occupational Therapy Journal of Research, 14*(2), 78-90.

Gortner, S., & Schultz, P. (1988). Approaches to nursing science methods. *Image, 20,* 22-23.

Greene, J. C., Caracelli, V. J., & Graham, W. F. (1989). Toward a conceptual framework for mixed-method evaluation designs. *Educational Evaluation and Policy Analysis, 11,* 255-274.

Guba, E. (1981). Criteria for judging the trustworthiness of naturalistic inquiries. *ETCJ, 19,* 75-91.

Gubrium, J. F., & Sankar, A. (Eds.). (1994). *Qualitative methods in aging research.* Thousand Oaks, CA: Sage.

Guesing, J. C. (1995). *Fragile alliances: Negotiating global teaming in a turbulent environment* (Microform 9613463). Unpublished dissertation, University of Michigan.

Hage, J. (1972). *Techniques and problems of theory construction in sociology.* New York: John Wiley.

Hammersley, M. (1995). Theory and evidence in qualitative research. *Quality and Quantity, 29*(1), 55-66.

Hammersley, M., & Atkinson, P. (1983). *Ethnography: Principles in practice.* New York: Tavistock.

Hathaway, R. S. (1995). Assumptions underlying quantitative and qualitative research: Implications for institutional research. *Research in Higher Education, 36,* 535-562.

Hoffman, E. (1989). *Lost in translation: Life in a new language.* New York: Penguin.

Hughes, E. C. (1971). *The sociological eye: Selected papers.* Chicago: Aldine.

Johnson, J. (1975). *Doing field research.* New York: Free Press.

Kaplan, R. D. (1996). *The ends of the earth.* New York: Random House.

Kelle, U. (Ed.). (1995). *Computer aided qualitative data analysis: Theory, methods and practice.* London: Sage.

Khurana, B. (1995). *The older spouse caregiver: Paradox and pain of Alzheimer's disease.* Unpublished dissertation, Center for Psychological Studies, Albany, CA.

Kidder, L. (1981). Qualitative research and quasi-experimental frameworks. In M. Brewer & B. Collings (Eds.), *Scientific inquiry and the social sciences*. San Francisco: Jossey-Bass.

Kirk, J., & Miller, M. (1986). *Reliability, validity and qualitative research*. Beverly Hills, CA: Sage.

Kvale, S. (1994). Ten standard objections to qualitative research interviews—Special issue: Qualitative research. *Journal of Phenomenological Psychology, 25*(2), 147-173.

Lafaille, R. (1995). Computer programs for qualitative research. *Historical Social Research, 20*(1), 91-97.

Lakoff, G., & Johnson, M. (1981). *Metaphors we live by*. Chicago: University of Chicago Press.

Lamont, A. (1994). *Some instructions on writing and life*. New York: Anchor Doubleday.

Lazersfeld, P. F., & Wagner, T., Jr. (1958). *Academic mind*. New York: Free Press.

LeCompte, N., & Goetz, J. (1982). Problems of reliability and validity in ethnographic research. *Review of Education Research, 52*, 31-60.

Lofland, J. (1971). *Analyzing social settings*. Belmont, CA: Wadsworth.

Lofland, J. (1974). Styles of reporting in qualitative field research. *The American Sociologist, 9*, 101-111.

Lonkilla, M. (1995). Grounded theory and computer assisted qualitative data analysis. In U. Kelle (Ed.), *Computers and qualitative methododology*. London: Sage.

Maines, D. R. (1991). Reflection, framing, and appreciations. In D. R. Maines (Ed.), *Social organization and social process* (pp. 3-9). New York: Aldine de Gruyter.

McKeganney, N. (1995). Quantitative and qualitative research in the additions: An unhelpful divide. *Addiction, 90*, 749-751.

Mead, G. H. (1934). *Mind, self and society*. Chicago: University of Chicago Press.

Merriam, S. B. (1995). What can you tell from an N of 1? Issues of validity and reliability in qualitative research. *PAACE: Journal of Lifelong Learning, 4*, 54-60. (Pennsylvania Association for Adult and Continuing Education)

Merriam-Webster. (1984). *Webster's ninth new college dictionary*. Springfield, MA: Author.

Miles, M., & Huberman, A. (1994). *Qualitative data analysis*. Thousand Oaks, CA: Sage.

Morse, J. M. (1991). Approaches to qualitative-quantitative methodological triangulation. *Nursing Research, 40*, 120-123.

Morse, J. M., & Field, P. A. (1995). *Qualitative research methods for health professionals* (2nd ed.). Thousand Oaks, CA: Sage.

Murdaugh, C. L. (1987). Nursing research: Theory generating through methodological flexibility. *Journal of Cardiovascular Nursing, 1*(4), 81-84.

Park, R. E. (1967). *On social control and collective behavior* (R. Turner, Ed.). Chicago: University of Chicago Press.

Parsons, T. (1937). *The structure of social action*. New York: McGraw-Hill.

Parsons, T. (1951). *The social system*. New York: Free Press.

Patton, M. Q. (1990). *Qualitative evaluation and research methods*. Newbury Park, CA: Sage.

Peshkin, A. (1993). The goodness of qualitative research. *Educational Research, 22*(2), 23-29.

Pfaffenberger, B. (1988). *Microcomputer applications in qualitative research*. Newbury Park, CA: Sage.

Pierce, B. N. (1995). The theory of methodology in qualitative research. *TESOL Quarterly, 29*, 569-576.

Popper, K. (1959). *The logic of scientific inquiry*. New York: Basic Books.

Porter, E. J. (1989). The qualitative-quantitative dualism. *Image, 21,* 98-102.

Power, R. (1996). "Quantitative and qualitative research in the addictions: An unhelpful divide": Comment. *Addiction, 91,* 146-147.

Punch, M. (1986). *The politics and ethics of fieldwork.* Beverly Hills, CA: Sage.

Ragin, C., & Becker, H. (Eds.). (1992). *What is a case? Exploring the foundations of social inquiry.* Cambridge, UK: Cambridge University Press.

Rew, L., Bechtel, D., & Sapp, A. (1993). Self as an instrument in qualitative research. *Nursing Research, 16,* 300-301.

Richards, T., & Richards, L. (1994). Using computers in qualitative analysis. In N. Denzin & Y. Lincoln (Eds.), *Handbook of qualitative research* (pp. 445-462). Thousand Oaks, CA: Sage.

Rodgers, B. L., & Cowles, K. V. (1993). The qualitative research audit trail: A complex collection documentation. *Research in Nursing and Health, 16,* 219-226.

Rosenbaum, M. (1981). *Women on heroin.* New Brunswick, NJ: Rutgers University Press.

Sandelowski, M. (1988). The problem of rigor in qualitative research. *Advances in Nursing Science, 8,* 27-37.

Sandelowski, M. (1993). Theory unmasked: The uses and guises of theory in qualitative research. *Research in Nursing and Health, 16,* 213-218.

Sandelowski, M. (1995a). Aesthetics of qualitative research. *Image, 27,* 205-209.

Sandelowski, M. (1995b). Sample size in qualitative research. *Research in Nursing and Health, 18,* 179-183.

Sandelowski, M. (1996). Triangles and crystals: On the geometry of qualitative research. *Research in Nursing and Health, 18,* 569-574.

Schatzman, L. (1991). Dimensional analysis: Notes on an alternative approach to the grounding of theory in qualitative research. In D. Maines (Ed.), *Social organization and social process* (pp. 303-314). New York: Aldine de Gruyter.

Schatzman L., & Strauss, A. (1973). *Field research.* Englewood Cliffs, NJ: Prentice Hall.

Schneider, J., & Conrad, P. (1983). *Having epilepsy: The experience and control of the illness.* Philadelphia: Temple University Press.

Selye, H. (1956). *The stress of life.* New York: McGraw-Hill.

Shapiro, W. L., et al. (1993). Metamorph: Computer support for qualitative research. *Midwestern Educational Researcher, 6*(2), 30-34.

Shibutani, T. (1966). *Improvised news: A sociological study of rumor.* Indianapolis, IN: Bobbs-Merrill.

Silverman, D. (1993). *Interpreting qualitative data.* Newbury Park, CA: Sage.

Star, S. L. (1989). *Regions of the mind: Brain research and the quest for scientific certainty.* Stanford, CA: Stanford University Press.

Star, S. L., & Ruhleder, K. (1996). Steps toward an ecology of infrastructure: Problems of design and access in large-scale information systems. *Information Systems Research, 7,* 27-57.

Stern, P. N. (1980). Grounded theory methodology: Its uses and processes. *Image, 12,* 20-23.

Stewart, G. R. (1941). *Storm.* New York: Random House.

Strauss, A. (1969). *Mirrors and masks.* Mill Valley, CA: Sociology Press. (Republished in 1997 [New Brunswick, NJ: Transaction])

Strauss, A. (1970). Discovering new theory from previous theory. In T. Shibutani (Ed.), *Human nature and collective behavior: Papers in honor of Herbert Blumer* (pp. 46-53). Englewood Cliffs, NJ: Prentice Hall.

Strauss, A. (1978). *Negotiations: Varieties, contexts, processes, and social order.* San Francisco: Jossey-Bass.

Strauss, A. (1987). *Qualitative analysis for social scientists.* Cambridge, UK: University of Cambridge Press.

Strauss, A. (1995). Notes on the nature and development of general theories. *Qualitative Inquiry, 1,* 7-18.

Strauss, A., & Corbin, J. (1988). *Shaping a new health care system.* San Francisco: Jossey-Bass.

Strauss, A., & Corbin, J. (1990). *Basics of qualitative research* (1st ed.). Thousand Oaks, CA: Sage.

Strauss, A., & Corbin, J. (Eds.). (1997). *Grounded theory in practice.* Thousand Oaks, CA: Sage.

Strauss, A., Fagerhaugh, S., Suczek, B., & Wiener, C. (1981). Patients' work in the technologized hospital. *Nursing Outlook, 29,* 404-412.

Strauss, A., Fagerhaugh, S., Suczek, B., & Wiener, C. (1982). The work of hospitalized patients. *Social Science and Medicine, 16,* 977-986.

Strauss, A., Fagerhaugh, S., Suczek, B., & Wiener, C. (1985). *Social organization of medical work.* Chicago: University of Chicago Press. (Republished in 1997 [New Brunswick, NJ: Transaction])

Strauss, A., Schatzman, L., Bucher, R., Ehrlich, D., & Sabshin, M. (1964). *Psychiatric ideologies and institutions.* New York: Free Press.

Street, A. (1996). Writing qualitative research for publication [editorial]. *Contemporary Nurse, 5*(1), 6-11.

Stringer, E. (1996). *Action research: A handbook for practitioners.* Thousand Oaks, CA: Sage.

Tesch, R. (1990). *Qualitative research: Analysis types and software tools.* New York: Falmer.

Thomas, W. I. (1966). *On social organization and social personality* (M. Janowitz, Ed.). Chicago: University of Chicago Press.

Weber, M. (1958). *The Protestant ethic and the spirit of capitalism.* New York: Scribner.

Weitzman, E. A., & Miles, M. B. (1995). *Computer programs for qualitative data analysis.* Thousand Oaks, CA: Sage.

Westbrook, L. (1994). Qualitative research methods: A review of major stages, data analysis techniques, and quality controls. *Library and Information Science Research, 16,* 241-245.

Whyte, W. (1955). *Street corner society.* Chicago: University of Chicago Press.

Wiener, C. (1983). *The politics of alcoholism: Building an arena around a social problem.* New Brunswick, NJ: Transaction.

Wiener, C., Fagerhaugh, S., Strauss, A., & Suczek, B. (1979). Trajectories, biographies and the evolving medical scene: Labor and delivery and the intensive care nursery. *Sociology of Health and Illness, 1,* 261-283.

Wolcott, H. F. (1990). *Writing up qualitative research.* Newbury Park, CA: Sage.

Wolcott, H. F. (1994). *Transforming qualitative data.* Thousand Oaks, CA: Sage.

Wolcott, H. F. (1995). *The art of fieldwork.* Thousand Oaks, CA: Sage.

Index

About the Authors

Juliet Corbin (M.S. in nursing, D.N.Sc. in nursing, family nurse practitioner) is a clinical instructor in community health nursing in the School of Nursing at San Jose State University. She is coauthor (with Anselm Strauss) of the first edition of *Basics of Qualitative Research* (1990), *Unending Work and Care* (1988), and *Shaping a New Health Care System* (1988) and is coeditor (with Strauss) of *Grounded Theory in Practice* (1997). Her research interests, teaching, presentations, and publications are in the areas of qualitative methodology, chronic illness, and the sociology of work and the professions.

Anselm Strauss, born December 18, 1916 and died September 5, 1996. He was, at the time of his death, Professor Emeritus, Department of Social and Behavioral Sciences, University of California, San Francisco. His main research and teaching activities were in the sociology of health and illness and of work and professions. His approach to doing research was qualitative with the aim of theory building, and with Barney Glaser is co-founder of the method that has come to be known as Grounded Theory. Over the years, he was asked to be a visiting professor to the universities of Cambridge, Paris, Manchester, Constance, Hagen, and Adelaide. During his lifetime he wrote numerous papers and books, many of which have been translated into foreign languages. Among his books, written with various co-workers are *Awareness of Dying* (1965), *Mirrors and Masks* (1969), *Professions, Work and Careers* (1971), *Negotiations* (1978), *The Social Organization of Medical Work* (1985), *Unending Work and Care* (1988), and *Continual Permutations of Action* (1993). Though formally retired, he was still actively engaged in writing and research at the time of his death, on topics including work in hospitals and a sociological perspective on body.